# Inerrancy and Hermeneutic

# Inerrancy and Hermeneutic

## A Tradition, A Challenge, A Debate

*Edited by*

**Harvie M. Conn**

**BAKER BOOK HOUSE**
Grand Rapids, Michigan 49516

Printed in the United States of America

**Library of Congress Cataloging-in-Publication Data**

Inerrancy and hermeneutic : a tradition, a challenge, a debate /
edited by Harvie M. Conn.
 p. cm.
 Includes bibliographical references and indexes.
 ISBN 0-8010-2533-8
 1. Bible—Inspiration. 2. Bible—Hermeneutics. 3. Bible—
Criticism, interpretation, etc.—History—20th century.
4. Reformed Church—Doctrines. 5. Evangelicalism—United States—
History—20th century. I. Westminster Theological Seminary
(Philadelphia, Pa.) II. Conn, Harvie M.
BS480.I4234 1988
220.1'3—dc19                                           88-39477
                                                             CIP

Chapter 7, "Oral Tradition," by Bruce K. Waltke, originally appeared in *A Tribute to
Gleason Archer,* edited by Walter C. Kaiser, Jr., and Ronald F. Youngblood (Chicago:
Moody, 1986). Chapter 11, "Normativity, Relevance, and Relativism," by Harvie M. Conn,
was first published in *TSF Bulletin* 10, no. 3 (January–February 1987). Both are
reprinted by permission.

To the memory of

**Cornelius Van Til,** 1895–1987:

colleague, brother, guide

# Contents

# Preface

Twice before, the faculty of Westminster Theological Seminary has published symposia by its members on topics directly related to the written Word of God. And in each instance the work was motivated by questions posed within the church. The last to appear was *Scripture and Confession* (1973), occasioned by the adoption of the Confession of 1967 in the United Presbyterian Church in the USA.

Now, fifteen years later, we turn to the troublesome topic of Scripture and hermeneutics. The necessity of study in this area should be apparent as the reader looks at the opening chapter of this anthology. There the developments and changes of the last forty years are surveyed, along with a sketch of the institution's interaction with the problems created for the evangelical by these academic shifts.

In this volume we address ourselves primarily to the Reformed and evangelical pastor whose allotted time and finances do not always provide the opportunity to keep up as one should. A pastor's knowledge of questions of this kind often either stops with graduation from the theological training school or remains several years behind the current discussions in academic circles.

This volume is an effort to provide some sort of "continuing education" for that pastor. Because of this intention, the essays, though introducing technical, academic issues, attempt to do so in a more popular style. We hope that this volume will also be of some help to that ubiquitous individual known as the intelligent layperson. But our primary interest is in helping the pastor understand what has been going on in the last couple of decades and how these developments can be analyzed and, to a degree, appropriated by someone with a continuing commitment to the inerrancy of the Bible. Our goals, then, are not only defensive but also creative and affirming.

This dual goal remains important within our community. The last decade has witnessed the growth of a fluid situation within evangelical circles, in particular over past attitudes to Scripture. In the growing resurgence of scholarship, boundary limits are not as clear as they were in the 1940s and 1950s. Evangelicals are finding they disagree more and more among themselves. In the language of Mark Noll:

> Evangelicals in the 1980s are being forced to face squarely an issue which at an earlier stage of the scholarly resurgence received only sporadic attention. This question is whether a believing criticism, a scholarship that embodies more than marginal insights from the academic world as well as more than formal allegiance to evangelical views of the Bible, is in fact possible.[1]

Older pastors, trained in the years surrounding the 1940s, may have the greatest amount of difficulty in understanding the question as posed by Noll. It may sound on the surface like a door to the compromised concessions made about Scripture in the past by the church.

In some instances, those instinctive fears may have real justification. Within the traditional evangelical camp in the last two decades, the term *inerrancy* has become sometimes more a point of debate than an affirmation of faith. Robert K. Johnston has called it *"the issue* among evangelicals."[2] In reexaminations of biblical data on women, some known for their evangelical commitments have proposed the presence in the New Testament of "two Pauls"—Paul the Christian and Paul the rabbi. Others use even stronger language, attempting to reconcile what they perceive as contradictions on such matters with traditional affirmations of infallibility. In the name of evangelical harmonization, others debate in new form what earlier was called limited inspiration. And still others explore the alleged use of the literary conventions of Jewish Midrash and Haggadah by Gospel writers like Matthew. Using the tool of modern redaction criticism, they admit nonhistorical elements in the text but attempt to fit such admissions into the framework of biblical inerrancy. The reader may ask with some legitimacy, Which dominos will fall next?

At the same time, some of the difficulty in understanding the current state of affairs may come from the very problem that has partly motivated the gathering of these essays. We speak of the learning gap related

---

1. Mark Noll, *Between Faith and Criticism: Evangelicals, Scholarship, and the Bible in America* (San Francisco: Harper and Row, 1986), p. 163.
2. Robert K. Johnston, *Evangelicals at an Impasse* (Atlanta: John Knox, 1979), p. 15.

to the time lapse between our potential readers' initial studies and the current situation.

Noll argues, we think fairly, that evangelical scholarship in the 1930s and 1940s was marked not so much by new positions as by more learned, more reasonable defenses of the old. Even into the early 1970s, that defensive mentality persisted. Legitimate concerns over what some have called liberal extravaganzas of speculation sometimes became fixations that inhibited freedom of action in creative theological work. Evangelical academic interaction took on more the form of journalistic reaction.

With the 1970s have come new creative directions and more hermeneutical sophistication on the part of the evangelical. Will the pastor, trained in the earlier decades and armed with the remnants of learning from a defensive past, comprehend adequately this more recent shift toward theological creativity in the community? The dangers of mistaken suspicion become very great.

This book seeks to warn against both superficial or reactionary orthodoxy and unguarded academic speculation. Critical scholarship will judge our arguments as too conservative. Defenders of the evangelical status quo may fear we yield too much ground. The latter judgment is our deepest concern in this volume.

Out of concern for such possible misunderstanding, three of the four opening essays review Westminster's traditional commitment to the integrity and trustworthiness of Scripture. In an analysis of our past and in the face of current issues, we reaffirm our continued confidence in that high Protestant doctrine of the Bible.

New questions demand our attention; new perspectives add nuances to our arguments. But, with the earlier faculty, whose voices introduce each of our chapters, we remain intransigent on this matter. As the faculty affirmed in 1946, we affirm again,

> the fundamental issue is not that of the knowledge or even of the interpretation of details. It is rather the issue whether the total view of the world and of life which the Bible presents is true. To approach the Bible in terms of an antibiblical philosophy of reality is to transform the Bible into something quite at variance with what it purports to be. To approach it, however, in the perspective provided by its own Christian theistic philosophy is to acknowledge it at its face value. Unless this fundamental matter is recognized at all times in the modern debate, confusion and distortion must result.[3]

We have taken more pains to be careful than may be usual in a book of

---

3. N. B. Stonehouse and Paul Woolley, eds., *The Infallible Word* (Philadelphia: Presbyterian Guardian, 1946), pp. vi–vii.

this sort. All of the essays have been circulated among full members of the Philadelphia faculty for mutual corrections and suggestions. In addition, we have appreciated the cooperation and editorial insights of six others outside the present Philadelphia teaching faculty: Viola Braun, Edmund P. Clowney, John Frame, Allen Harris, Jack Peterson, and Michael Smith have given freely of their time and wisdom to examine the manuscripts in their entirety and offer many valuable comments to the writers.

This should not be understood as implying any or all of us are in total, detailed agreement. Or that all of our suggestions have always been followed. As editor, I have been impressed with the remarkable degree of unanimity we have achieved. But differences of interpretation and formulation undoubtedly remain. After all, this volume is not an official seminary production.

Not all the faculty members have contributed essays to it. Time limitations and other writing projects have not made that possible. It does not benefit from participation by members of our California campus. Early in the planning process it was the editor's judgment that such participation would make editorial work ungainly because of distance and might unduly lengthen the volume.

Many people must be thanked. Mr. John Muether, our librarian, in addition to his preparation of the bibliographical essay that concludes the anthology, volunteered to draw up the extensive indexes. He walked still a third mile and joined the editor in final proofreading. The secretarial staff of the seminary—Dorothy Krieke, Patty Comber, and Elizabeth O'Neill—prepared the typescripts for several of the chapters. To everyone who has given freely of their talents, I express my deep appreciation.

—Harvie M. Conn

# Contributors

All contributors are members of the faculty of Westminster Theological Seminary.

David Clowney. Assistant professor of apologetics. Ph.D., Temple University.

Harvie M. Conn. Professor of missions. Th.M., Westminster Theological Seminary.

D. Clair Davis. Professor of church history. D.Theol., Georg-August University, Göttingen.

Raymond B. Dillard. Professor of Old Testament language and literature. Ph.D., Dropsie University.

Sinclair B. Ferguson. Associate professor of systematic theology. Ph.D., University of Aberdeen.

George C. Fuller. Associate professor of practical theology and president. Th.D., Westminster Theological Seminary.

Richard B. Gaffin, Jr. Professor of systematic theology. Th.D., Westminster Theological Seminary.

Samuel T. Logan, Jr. Professor of church history and academic dean. Ph.D., Emory University.

Tremper Longman III. Associate professor of Old Testament. Ph.D., Yale University.

Dan G. McCartney. Instructor in New Testament. Ph.D. candidate, Westminster Theological Seminary.

John R. Muether. Assistant professor of theological bibliography and librarian. M.A.R., Westminster Theological Seminary; M.S.L.S., Simmons College.

Vern Sheridan Poythress. Associate professor of New Testament. Ph.D., Harvard University; D.Th., University of Stellenbosch.

Moisés Silva. Professor of New Testament. Ph.D., University of Manchester.

Bruce K. Waltke. Professor of Old Testament. Th.D., Dallas Theological Seminary; Ph.D., Harvard University.

# 1

# A Historical Prologue
## *Inerrancy, Hermeneutic, and Westminster*

### Harvie M. Conn

*For what does Westminster Seminary stand? It stands for
the whole counsel of God, for unswerving fidelity to that
permanent and unchanging deposit of truth embodied in
the Scriptures of the Old and New Testaments and for the
consistent application of that truth to the whole of life.*
                                                    —John Murray, 1944

A little over forty years ago, the faculty of Westminster Theological
Seminary published their first symposium, *The Infallible Word* (1946).
For many reasons, it was not an easy time nor an easy task. Only six students graduated from the institution that year. And there were only
seven full-time faculty members, all of whom wrote for the anthology.

The focus of the book was a clarification of the position of orthodox
Christianity with respect to the Bible. For some time, that position had
been questioned in academic and church circles. Was it still possible, in
the face of such doubt, to reaffirm belief in Scripture as "the Word of God,
the only infallible rule of faith and practice"? Had scholarship proved
that such a point of view was hopelessly outmoded, obscurantist?

The decades immediately before the appearance of the anthology

15

found school after school and church after church questioning the wisdom of such confidence in the integrity of the Bible. Theological pluralism had been accepted as a standard means of operation in wide circles, many of which intersected Westminster's orbit of interest. Christian scholarship in the English-speaking world was listening more and more to voices like that of Karl Barth on revelation. And few seemed deeply sensitive to the seriousness of his polemic against the classic formulations of Holy Scripture.

The significance of Westminster's academic stance on this issue and its role in the church up till 1946 was, according to some, crucial. Writes one recent observer:

> It is an exaggeration to say that conservative evangelical Bible scholarship during the 1930s was confined to the faculty common room of Westminster Theological Seminary. But not by much. A few other academically certified and intellectually responsible evangelicals, especially in the confessional European denominations, were still at work. And a good bit of competent popularization appeared in various evangelical forums. But beyond the remnant from Old Princeton now at Westminster . . . very few evangelicals were engaged in the serious wrestling with ancient texts, the comparison of historical interpretations, and the weighing of contemporary research that constitutes scholarship on Scripture.[1]

In the years that followed 1946, other theological schools joined Westminster in its scholarly reaffirmations of Scripture. Some went through transitions and conflict over this issue. Still other organizations joined their voices to defend the classical posture.

The Evangelical Theological Society was formed in 1949 with a simple but profound doctrinal basis: "The Bible alone, and the Bible in its entirety, is the Word of God written, and is therefore inerrant in the autographs." In 1977, the International Council on Biblical Inerrancy was formed to "take a united stand in elucidating, vindicating and applying the truth of Biblical inerrancy as an integral element in the authority of Scripture."

In short, Westminster's strong emphasis on the infallibility of Scripture in the 1946 symposium was not the last hurrah of a soon-to-die theological dinosaur; it was, rather, one of the first guns fired in what might have been perceived then as a skirmish but is now seen as a growing, wide-scale conflict. That discussion is not an isolated one. It is carried on by many institutions over a sophisticated agenda, matched

---

1. Mark A. Noll, *Between Faith and Criticism: Evangelicals, Scholarship, and the Bible in America* (San Francisco: Harper and Row, 1986), p. 93.

by increasingly sophisticated evangelical and Reformed scholarship. Westminster did not abandon or minimize its interests in these areas, even with participation of these new allies. Edward J. Young, a member of the faculty since 1936, published in 1957 a lengthy volume on the biblical doctrine of inspiration. Not intended as "a technical theological treatise," it was to be simply "a popular book" aimed for "the intelligent layman."[2] From the pen of Cornelius Van Til came *The Protestant Doctrine of Scripture* (Philadelphia: den Dulk Christian Foundation, 1967).

In the late 1960s and early 1970s another threat to the Bible's view of itself became the occasion for faculty attention. The adoption by the (then) United Presbyterian Church in the USA of the Confession of 1967 was seen as an attempt, along with other shifts, to replace the Westminster Confession's doctrine of Scripture. Edmund P. Clowney, serving as acting president of the institution, published the booklet *Another Confession* (Philadelphia: Presbyterian and Reformed, 1965). In it he attacked the Barthian doctrine of Scripture in the new confession. This booklet was followed in 1967 by a larger study from the pen of Van Til, *The Confession of 1967: Its Theological Background and Ecumenical Significance* (Philadelphia: Presbyterian and Reformed, 1967).

In 1973, the faculty continued the debate with the appearance of *Scripture and Confession* (Philadelphia: Presbyterian and Reformed). The second symposium to be issued by the faculty, the work reechoed the school's continued commitment to the full infallibility of Scripture against what it saw to be the changed direction apparent in the Confession of 1967.

In 1974 Van Til's *The New Hermeneutic* appeared (Nutley, N.J.: Presbyterian and Reformed). The title represented something of a crossroads in the seminary's involvement in these discussions. Reflective of the shift in discussions of Scripture, the agenda had begun to move to questions of hermeneutic, questions which have, in fact, prompted the appearance of this book.

And yet the major thesis of Van Til remained defensive. The issues on the deepest level were the same as before, though the battles were now to be fought along different skirmish lines. The same Kantian philosophical and theological presuppositions Van Til had found earlier in Barth's work he identified again in the "post-Bultmannian school," around which the New Hermeneutic debate raged.

The results, then and now, were described by him as "the destruction of an intelligible basis for human predication. What is needed is a really Reformational philosophy and theology. Only if we have this can the

2. Edward J. Young, *Thy Word Is Truth* (Grand Rapids: Eerdmans, 1957), p. 5.

depth of the contrast between the self-attesting Christ of the Scripture and the Christ-Event of neo-orthodoxy be seen for what it is."[3]

The year 1974 might also have significance for another reason. For almost forty-five years, with a few exceptions, virtually the entire original faculty had continued to teach. By 1974, only four remained, now on emeritus status (although three of the four continued to teach). In addition to them, fifteen men held faculty status. There was, as it were, a new Westminster by the beginning of the 1970s.

## Westminster and Infallibility in the 1970s

How would this "new Westminster" see the issue of Scripture? Has the last decade shown any breaking of step with the academic and theological traditions of the institution?

No full-length books have yet appeared from the present faculty on these issues. But that fact indicates very little. Young's 1957 title was the first full monograph on the topic by a member of the early faculty. And it did not appear until Young had passed his twentieth year of teaching. On the other hand, a considerable number of essays have appeared over the last decade from a wide faculty representation.

In line with the seminary's past, the literature of the 1970s continued a vigorous defense of the infallible character of Scripture. John Frame, with the school since 1968 (and now teaching at its California campus), contributed two chapters on the topic to a 1974 symposium. The first was an extensive analysis of what he called "one of the most persuasive and frequent contemporary objections to the orthodox view of biblical authority . . . : the Bible cannot be the words of God because *no* human language can be the word of God."[4]

In dialogue with logical positivism and language philosophy, the essay was one of the first appearing from a Reformed pen to deal with the arguments of Antony Flew and Ludwig Wittgenstein. Nor did it neglect Karl Barth. In a tightly argued chapter, Frame found all forms of the original objection unsound. He concluded, in affirmation, that "human language *may* convey the infallible word of God, because God is *lord*— even of human language!"[5]

In the second essay, "Scripture Speaks for Itself," Frame expounded

3. C. Van Til, *The New Hermeneutic* (Nutley, N.J.: Presbyterian and Reformed, 1974), p. vii.

4. John M. Frame, "God and Biblical Language: Transcendence and Immanence," in *God's Inerrant Word,* ed. John Warwick Montgomery (Minneapolis: Bethany Fellowship, 1974), p. 159.

5. Ibid., p. 175.

the alleged circularity of the self-witness of Scripture. In keeping with the presuppositional approach of Van Til, the first half of the essay provides a full summary of biblical materials underlining the pervasiveness of that self-witness. The focus is on the role of verbal revelation in the biblical understanding of salvation. The second half examines the most common theological objections to this line of thinking. Barth and Brunner are given particular attention.[6]

Analyses of historical perspectives related to the issues have also appeared. Richard B. Gaffin, Jr., associated with the institution since 1965 and now professor of systematic theology, has responded to recent reevaluations of the views of Abraham Kuyper and Herman Bavinck. Two lengthy essays by Gaffin argue that both theologians were concerned to maintain that Scripture is without error, though he recognizes that their position is not without its difficulties and unresolved questions. His primary concern is historical, pleading for an accurate representation of their views.[7]

A similar apologetic interest characterizes the 1984 essay of W. Robert Godfrey, on staff since 1974 and now professor of church history at the California campus. Godfrey defends inerrancy as the teaching of the major Reformers in the sixteenth century and sees no appreciable break in that historical stance in the period immediately following.[8]

D. Clair Davis studied the history of classic liberalism of nineteenth- and early twentieth-century thought, showing the development of attacks on inerrancy. Davis's essay, however, unlike those of Gaffin already mentioned, signals another dimension of Westminster's interests in these years. After a careful study of the movement in Europe and the United States, Davis closes with a proposed agenda of concerns that are prompted by our interaction with liberalism. And among the list is our calling to rethink hermeneutics.[9] Says the church historian, "Surely the hermeneutical questions are the most pressing of all before the evangelical world. A doctrine of inerrancy with no perceptible use, which in practice makes no difference, is hardly worth exerting the energies of the church for."[10]

---

6. John M. Frame, "Scripture Speaks for Itself," in *God's Inerrant Word*, pp. 178–200.

7. Richard B. Gaffin, Jr., "Old Amsterdam and Inerrancy?" *Westminster Theological Journal* 44, no. 2 (Fall 1982): 250–89; 45, no. 2 (Fall 1983): 219–72.

8. W. Robert Godfrey, "Biblical Authority in the Sixteenth and Seventeenth Centuries: A Question of Transition," in *Scripture and Truth*, ed. D. A. Carson and John D. Woodbridge (Grand Rapids: Zondervan, 1983), pp. 225–43.

9. D. Clair Davis, "Liberalism: The Challenge of Progress," in *Challenges to Inerrancy: A Theological Response*, ed. Gordon Lewis and Bruce Demarest (Chicago: Moody, 1984), pp. 84–86.

10. Ibid., p. 88.

## Westminster and the Emerging Debate over Hermeneutics

This area of hermeneutic and its correlation with questions of scriptural authority have increasingly occupied faculty attention. Even before 1974 and Van Til's book-length study, questions had begun to be raised.

Gaffin initiated the discussion in a 1968 address entitled "Contemporary Hermeneutics and the Study of the New Testament." He reviewed the movement called the New Hermeneutic, at the initial stages of its entrance into the English-speaking theological world.

Gaffin underscored, as Van Til also was to do, the roots of the new approach in the Enlightenment outlook and its relativizing of history. For him, the relationship between the questioning of the integrity of Scripture and the rise of the New Hermeneutic was integral.

> Despite the complex and shaded idiom of much of current absorption with the question of hermeneutics, the motive which drives it is not too difficult to understand. . . . I would underscore that the intensity of this preoccupation reflects just how pressing has become the dilemma created by the rejection of the divine origin and authority of the Bible. A crisis in understanding is the price paid for autonomy, for making man the interpreter constitutive for meaning and revelation.[11]

Out of this integral relationship, Gaffin saw a threefold responsibility of the theologian: (1) a continued and unabated opposition to the presuppositions of the Enlightenment, with a continued, metahermeneutical confidence in the Bible as God's Word; (2) an affirmation of the hermeneutical consequences that flow from such a conviction—the unity of Scripture as text, and God's interpretation as the ground for our interpretation; and (3) the use of a hermeneutical methodology that will stress the continuity between our interpretation and God's, one that will maintain the link between the history of revelation and the history of redemption.[12]

At the end of the 1970s, the issues raised by the New Hermeneutic began to enlarge in scope. Literary tools began to appear, expanding some of the original concerns, modifying others, assuming still others.

> When these literary tools were first introduced, they did not make their appearance as hermeneutical principles but as ways of getting behind the

---

11. Richard B. Gaffin, Jr., "Contemporary Hermeneutics and the Study of the New Testament," in *Studying the New Testament Today,* ed. John H. Skilton (Nutley, N.J.: Presbyterian and Reformed, 1974), p. 9.

12. Ibid., pp. 11–18.

Gospels as we have them in order to illumine the "tunnel" period and perhaps learn something more about the historical Jesus. To use these tools at that stage usually meant buying into a large conceptual framework concerning the descent of the tradition—a framework with which evangelicals (and many others, for that matter) were bound to differ.[13]

The literary reactions to Gaffin in 1968 and Van Til in 1974 were directed to this stage of the discussion.

Out of this ferment, hermeneutics as a category underwent a semantic shift, calling for studies on a new level. Scholarly attention turned away from a search for grammatical and historical rules in our understanding of the text. Hermeneutics became "the discipline by which we examine how a thought or event in one cultural and religious context becomes understandable in another cultural and religious context."[14] The classical tradition had asked, What does *the text* mean? The new question became, What do we mean by *meaning*?

In responding to this new direction, it is no longer sufficient to ask simply, What does an infallible Bible teach us? Now the question becomes, How do we decide what an infallible Bible teaches us? How will we understand the process by which God speaks through Paul in the first century so that we still hear him speak through Paul in the twentieth? The question of authority in hermeneutics becomes also the question of the responsibility of hermeneutics. Searching the text is said to yield only its *meaning;* the text must also search us as we yield to its *significance.* How do we cross that line between meaning and significance in hermeneutics?

## Hermeneutic and the New Tools

Obviously there are links between the earlier discussions of the infallibility and authority of Scripture and the contemporary discussion of hermeneutics. As J. I. Packer has said, "The truth is that ever since Karl Barth linked his version of Reformation teaching on biblical authority with a method of interpretation that at key points led away from Reformation beliefs, hermeneutics has been the real heart of the debate about Scripture."[15]

Yet, at the same time, the complications created by new academic tools call for more than a reiteration of past arguments. The problem, suggests Mark Noll, calls for two tasks:

13. D. A. Carson, "Hermeneutics: A Brief Assessment of Some Recent Trends," *Themelios* 5, no. 2 (January 1980): 13–14.
14. Ibid., 15.
15. J. I. Packer, "Infallible Scripture and the Role of Hermeneutics," in *Scripture and Truth,* p. 325.

The first is a crash program to study the important twentieth-century theoreticians of interpretation, from Max Weber to Paul Riceour. The second requires a careful exercise in discrimination to extract from this modern hermeneutical theory the elements that genuinely enhance the self-understanding of interpretation, while at the same time counteracting those which undermine Christian convictions.[16]

Westminster's direction in the 1980s has moved closely along the two tracks suggested by Noll. In 1981, the institution initiated a program of doctoral studies in the area of hermeneutics. Seeking to use its limited faculty resources to the best advantage and recognizing the importance of the field, it departed from traditional patterns of concentration in such areas as Old Testament or New Testament studies.

In faculty writings, the school participates in an exploration of the emerging disciplines of research that are linked to hermeneutical theory. Its concerns over issues relating to the full trustworthiness of Scripture have not diminished; it has just taken them into new avenues of research. The tone of the study is more positive. But the old issues continue to be reflected on, in the light of the new.

Structuralism, as an emerging theological discipline, furnishes one example of this kind of participation. Difficult to define, structuralism on its simplest level "does little more than examine literary structures (e.g. chiasm, repetition, various kinds of narrative interchange), often in terms of set roles, schematized plots, and binary oppositions in order the better to understand a biblical passage. As such, it becomes another hermeneutical tool, nothing more."[17] Vern Poythress, teaching New Testament since 1976, has made use of these tools in a number of essays.[18]

At the same time, while commending in a controlled way this new approach for the help it can provide the exegete, Poythress has also warned us that it is a total package, a holistic method of approaching Scripture. And even in its less radical forms, its strategies have minus factors as well as plus ones for the study of Scripture. In a 1978 essay Poythress identifies three fundamental principles of structuralism. In connection with each, he elaborates its advantages and its dangers. For example, he notes the commitment of structuralists to search behind the text and its relationships of words and themes for those codes which are said to reflect the "deep structures" of the human brain. "Below" the surface of empirical manifestation, it is said, one will find the fundamental structures.

16. Noll, *Between Faith and Criticism,* p. 180.
17. Carson, "Hermeneutics," p. 17.
18. Vern Poythress, "Analysing a Biblical Text: Some Important Linguisitic Distinctions," *Scottish Journal of Theology* 32 (1979): 113–37; idem, "Analysing a Biblical Text: What Are We After?" ibid., pp. 319–31.

What are the advantages of this principle for the Bible scholar? First, it offers the potential for uncovering a greater fulness and depth of meaning in Scripture; it may help us sometimes to see two texts in closer relation to one another by pointing out a common "deep" structure. And then, it may uncover in this search further evidence for the unity and integrity of biblical texts that have been split into pieces by source critics.

The disadvantage, however, is that

> the general theoretical framework that a structuralist develops can allow him to "read in" the deep structures before reading them out. A certain arbitrariness is thus possible, as well as a reductionism that finds information only at one particular predetermined layer of meaning. The structuralist search for universals can, moreover, be turned into a flight from the particulars of Biblical revelation. Universals can play the role of a kind of ultimate metaphysics regarded as giving more basic answers than the Bible itself gives.[19]

Sensitive to Van Til's call for presuppositional criticism, Poythress goes even deeper. He sees the common link between the historical-critical method of previous decades and structuralism in a naturalism born of post-Kantian developments.[20] The end result of the structural approach, then, "need not imply the disappearance of the historico-critical approach but may involve a mutual reinforcement of the naturalism so frequently involved in both."[21]

Still other hermeneutical disciplines, such as form criticism and redaction criticism, have begun to capture Westminster's critical interest. In one sense, form criticism is not new to the academic scene. In Old Testament research, Hermann Gunkel's turn-of-the-century studies of literary forms or types in Genesis and the psalms inaugurated these interests. They found a New Testament home in the years following the publication of Martin Dibelius's *Die Formgeschichte des Evangeliums* (1919). By the early 1960s, redaction criticism had appeared as a fully developed reaction to form criticism.

Throughout these developments Westminster was interacting with the movements. Edward J. Young and Ned B. Stonehouse published warnings of their dangers.[22] Of concern to Young especially was the dam-

19. Vern Poythress, "Structuralism and Biblical Studies," *Journal of the Evangelical Theological Society* 21 (1978): 234.
20. Vern Poythress, "Philosophical Roots of Phenomenological and Structuralist Literary Criticism," *Westminster Theological Journal* 41, no. 1 (Fall 1978): 165–71.
21. Poythress, "Structuralism and Biblical Studies," p. 236.
22. For example: Edward J. Young, *The Study of Old Testament Theology Today* (Westwood, N.J.: Revell, 1959); idem, *My Servants the Prophets* (Grand Rapids: Eerdmans,

age done to the historicity of the biblical record by the form-critical affirmation of genres and life settings for those genres. Yet, even with a desire to underline the historical truth of the message, Stonehouse in particular paid more attention to the uniqueness of the Gospel genres than was customary for the biographically oriented evangelical scholars of his time.

Stonehouse saw the Gospel writers like Luke as "least concerned with the chronological and topographical settings of the incidents and teachings which he reports."[23] He affirmed that Matthew used a genuine "measure of freedom" in his literary composition of the narrative."[24] Moisés Silva, who eventually followed Stonehouse in the seminary's New Testament department (from 1981), has drawn many parallels between his predecessor's creative analysis of the Gospel genre and redaction criticism, which was beginning its domination of New Testament studies at the time of Stonehouse's death in 1962.[25]

In 1963, Meredith Kline (at Westminster, 1950–1965, 1982–  ) used one form of genre studies to critique an area of form-critical studies in the Old Testament. Employing research that explored the relationships between Hittite suzerainty treaty codes and the genre elements of covenant formularies found in Scripture, he applied the data not to isolated text fragments but to the entire Book of Deuteronomy. In the covenant-treaty genre, he argued that the modern biblical critic had a tiger by the tail. The analysis of the covenant formulary was seen as an apologetic weapon in the defense of a dating in the Mosaic period for the Pentateuchal book.

> Now that the form critical data compel the recognition of the antiquity not merely of this or that element within Deuteronomy but of the Deuteronomic treaty in its integrity, any persistent insistence on a final edition of the book around the seventh century B.C. can be nothing more than a vestigial hypothesis, no longer performing a significant function in Old Testament criticism. Is it too much to hope that modern higher criticism's notorious traditionalism will no longer prove inertial enough to prevent the Deuteronomic bark from setting sail once more for its native port?[26]

---

1952), pp. 154–58; Ned B. Stonehouse, *Paul Before the Areopagus* (Grand Rapids: Eerdmans, 1957), pp. 109–85.

23. Ned B. Stonehouse, *The Witness of Luke to Christ* (Grand Rapids: Eerdmans, 1951), p. 145.

24. Quoted in Moisés Silva, "Ned B. Stonehouse and Redaction Criticism," *Westminster Theological Journal* 40, no. 2 (Spring 1978): 284.

25. Moisés Silva, "Ned B. Stonehouse and Redaction Criticism," *Westminster Theological Journal* 40, no. 1 (Fall 1977): 77–88.

26. Meredith G. Kline, *Treaty of the Great King* (Grand Rapids: Eerdmans, 1963), p. 44.

In the last decade especially, the seminary has pursued these early interests of Stonehouse and Kline in creative directions. This has been possible partly because of significant changes in critical studies. Influenced by new studies in rhetorical and literary criticism and by growing research in tradition history and oral tradition, even liberal critics are becoming especially wary of the rigid genres identified by the early pioneers. And within the evangelical camp there has developed a cautious but more explicit appreciation and use of the discipline's skills.

Tremper Longman III, a 1980 addition to the Philadelphia faculty, sees this constructive move toward form criticism in its role of hermeneutical tool as a proper one—with the proviso that the discipline be "shorn of the negative presuppositions of the method as applied by critics."[27]

Using the insights of modern literary theory, he questions two basic assumptions of Gunkel's genre theory: (1) the assumption that genres were pure and fixed, discrete entities, without fluidity or capability of intermixing; (2) the subsequent rigidity of methods used in classifying texts into genres. With these corrections, he contends, the evangelical may benefit in at least four ways from the application of genre analysis to exegesis.

Since the meaning of a text is genre-bound, there is more at stake in the search for genres than simply classification. The reader arrives at a correct understanding of a text only through a correct genre analysis. Genre study becomes a guide to textual meaning. Second, genres may help us recover the original setting of a text. And, unlike Gunkel's argument, there may be multiple settings—social, historical, and intellectual.

Third, the purpose of analysis by genres is not so much to classify as to clarify. Examining a collection of generically related texts can help to illuminate each individual text. So, suggests Longman, it is more fruitful to study Psalm 30 in the context of other thanksgiving hymns rather than in comparison with Psalms 29 and 31. Finally, the study of genres opens more easily the beneficial route of comparative studies with materials from other cultures and their literatures. Kline's exciting research into the parallels between Old Testament covenant texts and Hittite treaties illustrates this value.[28]

A creative example of this use of genre study is provided by Raymond B. Dillard, a member of the Old Testament department since 1971. Con-

27. Tremper Longman III, "Form Criticism, Recent Developments in Genre Theory and the Evangelical," *Westminster Theological Journal* 47, no. 1 (Spring 1985): 47–48.
28. Ibid., pp. 60–67. A sample of Longman's use of genre criticism can be found in his "Comparative Methods in Old Testament Studies: Ecclesiastes Reconsidered," *TSF Bulletin* 7, no. 4 (1984): 5–9.

centrating his written research in the 1980s on Chronicles, Dillard has found it necessary to explore in depth what might be called the Synoptic Problem of the Old Testament. Here he has found reduplicated those issues long explored in connection with New Testament research—the problems of redaction and textual history, the author's audience and theology, dates and principles of composition, historical reliability. But, he adds, in the environment of Old Testament research, they are "exaggerated to a new intensity."[29]

It should be noted that the issues involved in the study of Chronicles have long suffered benign neglect by researchers of every theological hue. Past evangelical scholarship on these questions has sought a resolution of differences often through harmonization methods.

Dillard, as chapter 9 will illustrate, sees many positive values to harmonization. And, in fact, he makes use of it repeatedly, for example, in his study of the chronology of the divided monarchy.[30] But at the same time, it would appear that the Chronicler's distinctive treatment of the larger history and theology of his narrative creates an agenda almost too large to be handled by a methodology better suited for comparisons of more limited texts.

What shall we make of the author's distinctive handling of David and Solomon? Notes Dillard:

> Any fault or transgression which might tarnish the image of David and Solomon has been removed. Instead the Chronicler portrays glorious, obedient, all-conquering figures who enjoy not only divine blessing but the total support of the people as well; he presents us not only the David and Solomon of history, but also the David and Solomon of his messianic expectation.[31]

Solomon, under the Chronicler's hand, appears as a second David. The succession of Moses and Joshua becomes a paradigm for that of David and Solomon. Numerous parallels are drawn between the building of the tabernacle and the building of the temple; Solomon and Huram-Abi are the new Bezalel and Oholiab.

Given confidence in the inerrancy of Scripture, and confidence also in Chronicles as "through and through a theological essay," how shall we seek resolution? One response, acceptable to Dillard, is what he calls the

29. Raymond Dillard, "The Reign of Asa (2 Chronicles 14–16): An Example of the Chronicler's Theological Method," *Journal of the Evangelical Theological Society* 23 (1980): 208.

30. Ibid., pp. 214–17.

31. Raymond Dillard, "The Chronicler's Solomon," *Westminster Theological Journal* 43, no. 2 (Spring 1981): 290–91.

theological approach. "The numerous points at which he [the Chronicler] assumes the reader's familiarity with the account in Samuel/Kings shows that he is using the Deuteronomic history as a 'control' to an audience well familiar with that account."[32] Much of Chronicles is unclear without a prior knowledge on the part of the intended audience of the material in Samuel-Kings.

Dillard also warns against too easy a reference to this proposed method of resolution. "A cavalier invoking of this solution can be as arbitrary as any other special pleading through appeal to *ad hoc* harmonization devices."[33]

Like Stonehouse before him, Dillard is raising questions about a long evangelical tradition that had regarded the sayings of the biblical historians as simply reports of facts that are unrelated to the author's theological intentions. Also like Stonehouse, his final purpose is anything but liberal or radical. It is to explore the uniqueness of the Chronicler's literary purposes.

At the same time, harmonization of another sort is not totally missing. Another exegetical instrument Dillard uses allows him to search for what we might call harmonizations on a macro scale. With it he can speak of Moses and Joshua as paradigms, of parallels between Solomon and Bezalel and Paul, the Bezalel of the new covenant (1 Cor. 3:5–17).

Such harmonization is the discipline of biblical theology, long a trademark of the Reformed community and Westminster's work. In the history of special revelation, the Chronicler's theme of immediate and deferred judgment points us, he maintains, to the deferred eschatological day of reward and punishment and to those individuals who bear the consequences of their actions in the present day (Acts 5:1–10; 1 Cor. 11:30; 1 Tim. 5:24).[34]

## Hermeneutic and the Emerging Evangelical Agenda

At least two things can be affirmed about Westminster's movement over the last forty years—its continued commitment to the foundational character of the inerrancy of Scripture in theological construction and its creative effort to address new theological questions and hermeneutical constructions as they arise.

Westminster has never been content simply to repeat. Nor has it been

32. Dillard, "Reign of Asa," p. 214.
33. Ibid.
34. Raymond Dillard, "Reward and Punishment in Chronicles: The Theology of Immediate Retribution," *Westminster Theological Journal* 46, no. 1 (Spring 1984): 164–72.

afraid to reaffirm. And as should be apparent already, neither position is very easy to take in the troubled setting of the last decade of studies. Many evangelicals today, concerned about the treatment of Scripture within even their own traditional orbit, find it easier to oppose modern constructions rather than to reexamine them and creatively respond. Such a pattern is linked to our recent history of largely apologetic defense of Scripture.

On the other side, scholars like James D. G. Dunn remain critical of any proponents of biblical inerrancy as a form of "revived fundamentalism." For Dunn, such insistence on the inerrancy of Scripture, employed in the study of current hermeneutical issues, "is in fact a flight from the relativities of the historical documents which make up the Bible. Such a position can be maintained only at the cost of abstracting the documents from their original life-settings in order to give them an absoluteness which is to all intents and purposes timeless—though the programme is never quite carried through with complete consistency."[35]

Responding to each of these extremes and to the mediating views in between has never been easy, and never more difficult than now. But respond we must. The pastoral (and theological) dimensions required of that response are addressed by George Fuller, the institution's president, and Samuel Logan, the academic dean in chapter 13 in this volume. What do we say to the right and to the left from our position on the theological spectrum? What demands does Christian courtesy make on Christian certitudes? How can we preserve the demand of Paul to "be on your guard; stand firm in the faith," along with his insistence to "do everything in love" (1 Cor. 16:13–14)? To borrow a favorite classroom motto of Cornelius Van Til, our calling is to be *suaviter in modo* and, at the same time, *fortiter in re*. What basis will we draw upon for this kind of pastoral response? Is there a minimal agenda that flows from these commitments and from the new interests of a reconstructing hermeneutic?

We are compelled, first of all, to take another look at the self-testimony of Scripture. In the same way that we are driven from the authority of the Bible to hermeneutic, we are also driven back again from hermeneutic to biblical authority. In the language of contemporary studies, the hermeneutical search for contemporary *significance* becomes inevitably the hermeneutical search for the biblical text's *meaning*.

The slippery confusion of new issues that have modified and transformed hermeneutics into hermeneutic makes this step even more important. Alien ideologies can easily be imposed onto the biblical frame-

---

35. James D. G. Dunn, *Testing the Foundations: Current Trends in New Testament Study* (Durham: University of Durham, 1984), p. 24.

work. Hermeneutics, warns Stanley Gundry, "can also become a guise to evacuate the inerrancy concept of any real meaning."[36]

Sinclair Ferguson, teaching systematic theology at Westminster since 1982, draws that foundational picture of the Scripture's own witness to itself in this volume. His chapter may appear deceptively simple to some readers. But behind it are serious questions which he addresses with the still-rich answers of the past. Can we still legitimately speak of Scripture's view of itself? Is there really one view or several (and at odds with one another)? Are we limited only to affirmations $Y$, spoken by $X$ about $Z$? What about "the human dimension of the Bible"? Does it distort, as some argue, the entire trustworthiness of Scripture? Shall we sweep the supposed difficulties under the inerrancy rug?

Just how flexible may our view of inerrancy be in our interaction with hermeneutical issues and still call itself inerrancy with integrity? Some on the left fear a dogmatically controlled exegesis with too little awareness of the genuineness of the struggles of hermeneutic with the "phenomena" of Scripture. Harold Lindsell's call to arms, *Battle for the Bible* (1977), is seen as typical both of this dogmatic mentality and of those who would defend inerrancy.

Paralleling these concerns are those on the right who fear a dogmatically controlled exegesis of another sort. The danger seen in this dogmatic mentality is that the experts in hermeneutic will sharpen their tools and their questions at the expense of serious commitment to the believability of Scripture as norm. Will the concerns of our new hermeneutical agenda leave us with a Bible that critiques us as well as our critiquing it?

The chapter by Moisés Silva begins to answer some of these questions with a reinvestigation of our Reformed and evangelical past and the exegetical work of B. B. Warfield and his theological successors. How much hermeneutical flexibility did this tradition allow in its commitment to inerrancy? How much force was applied to achieve hermeneutical unanimity? Did they neglect the biblical phenomena that today are often called error? Was there any place given to a legitimate form of higher criticism?

Contemporary studies place great emphasis on authorial intention. The interpreter recognizes the distance between his or her own cultural horizon and that of the text. One then seeks to reduce that gap through a "fusion" of the interpreter's contemporary horizon with that of the text's author by means of a hermeneutical dialogue. In this "circle," the role of the text's original author becomes one of the crucial elements. Writes

36. Stanley Gundry, "Evangelical Theology: Where *Should* We Be Going?" in *Evangelicals and Inerrancy*, ed. Ronald Youngblood (Nashville: Nelson, 1984), p. 243.

James D. G. Dunn, "The integrity of the text is primarily the integrity given to it by the person who formulated it."[37]

Evangelical scholarship is more conscious of what might be called the dual authorship of the text—divine as well as human (2 Peter 1:21). That feature adds a new complication to these current issues. To adapt the language of Dunn, is the integrity of any biblical text solely dependent on the integrity of its human author? What is the relation between God and the human authors of Scripture?

The chapter by Vern Poythress turns to this question and to the various solutions offered by evangelicals. Does God's intention always coincide with the intention of the human author? Were the human authors aware of those divine intentions? How shall we relate our commitment to progressive revelation to these issues? The intentions of a human author are limited by contexts of space and time. The intentions of the divine author are part of a long history of God's communications. Do they always converge and how? What really can one find "in" a text?

Closely related to the issue of authorial intention is what has sometimes been called the question of *sensus plenior*, the "fuller meaning" of Scripture. Most frequently, discussions of this issue revolve around the Old Testament. Can one legitimately find there an even deeper meaning than that which the human writers understood or intended? Does the New Testament aid us in our grammatical-historical search of the Old Testament for a full disclosure of its truth? Does authorial intention necessarily exhaust the full meaning of Scripture? Is there only one single meaning to a text?

Dan McCartney, a 1987 addition to the New Testament staff, addresses some of these issues in his chapter on the New Testament's use of the Old Testament. In the Bible's use of itself, he argues, we will find the Bible's own self-hermeneutic. Here we see hermeneutical method subservient to hermeneutical goal, not allegory but eschatology, and eschatology always with its focus on Jesus.

The method called "tradition history" in Old Testament studies today has placed new emphasis on the transmission of literature in the ancient world. It builds on the long-standing interest of earlier form criticism and its successors in the oral traditions which were said to be reshaped and modified by Old Testament literature. But in comparison with form criticism, which placed its emphasis on a form analysis of differing types of literature such as songs, fables, and sagas, tradition history has underlined the other interest of form criticism—the priority of oral tradition in the composition of Old Testament literature. The formation of the writ-

---

37. Dunn, *Testing the Foundations*, p. 23.

ten canon is said to be really the last stage in the history of the transmission of the Old Testament.

In the passage of oral tradition to written tradition, modifications of a radical sort in narrative history and theological perspective were suggested. Editorial redactors of the traditions make their own contributions, adding and subtracting as they rebuilt, through long periods of oral transmission.

Bruce Waltke, on the Philadelphia faculty since 1985, offers a critical assessment of this methodology. Exactly how fluid and complicated was the prehistory of Israel's written heritage? How large a role did oral tradition play in the transmission of the text? His chapter surveys the oral traditions and their histories in the literary genres of several cultures of the ancient Near East and outside it. He asks two questions. Do the traditions recorded in Genesis come from an oral base? What is the relation of our findings to our confidence in the historicity of the biblical record as revelation from God?

Interest in literary criticism as a tool in analyzing the hermeneutical procedure has continued to grow. We have already commented on renewed research in literary genres. Can we use the same procedures of interpretation in speaking of a text for whose author divine authority is claimed (2 Peter 3:16–17)?

Evangelical scholarship has long recognized in the Bible

> different types of composition both on the scale of whole writings and on the scale of brief units within them. It makes a difference to our understanding of a book to know whether it is history or fiction, a letter or an apocalypse; and similarly it makes a difference whether a particular passage is prose or poetry, straight teaching or parable, a command or an example of a type of behaviour.[38]

Tremper Longman's chapter presses this commitment on to harder questions. The popular mind divides fiction from nonfiction, placing fiction over against the truth. How, then, will we understand literary artifice in biblical narrative? In a passage, for example, like the Genesis flood narrative, must we assume the modern thesis of a gap between the literary and the historical? Traditional historical-critical scholarship has always accepted this assumption and, on that basis, questioned whether the Book of Acts conveys true information. Can the evangelical link together literary artifice and historical narrative in a way that does not diminish the veracity of the Scripture?

38. I. Howard Marshall, "How Do We Interpret the Bible Today?" *Themelios* 5, no. 2 (January 1980): 7.

Closely linked to questions of literary criticism and authorial intention, is the issue of harmonization. On the broadest level, the topic returns us to the old issues of the unity and diversity of the biblical narratives. But the recent answers proposed have raised evangelical stakes in the game. Even among those critical writers more willing to affirm a fundamental unity, the diversity becomes a good deal wider than many of us are willing to concede. And in corresponding fashion the area of unity becomes narrower.

On the level of theological a priori, liberals possess no commitment to textual inerrancy that might slow them down. Harmonization, then, as an effort at exegetical resolution of textual difficulties, has held little attraction for them except for some limited usefulness in searching for sources or commonality of genre forms.

For the evangelical, however, harmonization has long held strong appeal as an apologetic tool of exegesis. We are concerned, after all, with seeking to understand and, if legitimate propriety allows, to eliminate apparent discrepancies in Scripture.

In his chapter, Raymond Dillard proposes the need for a review of this harmonization method. Does this approach run the risk of domesticating the difficult and homogenizing it too easily with the familiar? Does harmonization become too quick an answer for that one obstinate fact that will not go away? How do we balance its assets and its liabilities? Is harmonization an exegetical style that accompanies, of necessity, a biblical view of inerrancy? Will modifications of the harmonization appeal leave us with a modified Bible as well?

Out of the new directions in hermeneutic has come a renewed interest in the nature of the Scriptures as canon, and a new discipline, canon criticism, to accommodate the discussion. In the past, critical academic discussions of canon revolved generally around the history of when and by what process the church came to accept the books it did as Holy Scripture. Evangelical studies demanded to know on what basis the church made such decisions. Essays by Edward J. Young and Ned Stonehouse in the 1946 faculty symposium, *The Infallible Word,* were oriented to these sets of questions.

Canonical hermeneutics today builds both on the earlier attention to the ecclesiastical history of canonical reception and its minimization of the grounds for canonization in its divine source. These are merged with the current interest in the hermeneutical process. And canonical studies concentrate on "the means whereby early authoritative traditions were utilized by Israel (in the Old Testament) and the Church (in the New Testament) to span the gaps of time and culture to be reformed according to the needs of the new community. The process itself is as canonical as the traditions found in the canon."[39]

Again, as in the older tradition of critical studies, normativity does not lie in the text itself. That text is still seen as cluttered with historical inaccuracies, mutual contradictions, and parts unworthy of the canonical label. What becomes normative are the changes in tradition, the process in which the traditions are transformed from generation to generation.

Richard Gaffin's chapter attempts to return the discussion to what he sees as the crucial question: Where is the dividing line between canonical and noncanonical? And how does the Bible itself draw that line? Is the criterion to be found in the process of the church's reception of Scripture, in inspiration, or where? Can we, in the face of the contemporary search for canon in process, still speak of canon as closed?

Recent developments in hermeneutic have accented a long-term interest in the historical particularity of the text. Scholars seem more sensitive to the cultural, social, and historical distance between the cultural world of the Bible and ours. The gap is widened further by a growing awareness of the difficulty in "objectively" moving through twenty centuries or more of experience to reexperience that ancient world. The shared humanity of text and interpreter is said to make connections with an ancient canon more difficult.

Attempts are made to bridge the gap with the model of a "hermeneutical circle." In this circle the interpreter recognizes the distance between his or her world and the world of the text and searches, in dialogue with the text, for some common horizon.

My chapter examines the propriety of this circle model. Does an evangelical recognition of the historical, cultural particularity of divine revelation lead us always to historical, cultural relativity? Can we recognize the impossibility of human objectivity in understanding Scripture and still recognize the cultural universality of the Bible as norm? How do we find those norms, given the reality of the gap that separates the biblical horizon from ours? Are there guidelines to help us in this search?

In the area of ethics, issues of inerrancy and hermeneutics often create tension. What guidelines aid us in our search for both hermeneutical and ethical responsibility? What does an infallible Bible provide us with regarding contemporary instructions on male-female relationships or on modern matters of justice and mercy that seem remote from first-century society? May we legitimately stretch situationally appropriate principles of the first century to cover abolitionism in the nineteenth century and polygyny in the twentieth? Once again, we are confronted

39. Carson, "Hermeneutics," p. 16.

with the implications of the two horizons. And now the issue becomes contemporary obedience to an ancient word from God.

These are the questions posed by David Clowney, a member of the apologetics department of the Philadelphia campus from 1980 to 1988. How, he asks, can a better grasp of hermeneutics aid us in our disagreements about how the Bible should guide our lives? In the face of current thinking, can we still speak of the Scriptures as law, as norm? Do modern times really call for more modern rules?

## The Tip of the Iceberg

A plethora of other questions, some much more technical, await analysis and response. Many of them have already been addressed elsewhere by the writers in this collection.

How do we understand the nature of language in interpretation? How does the language of the text function to bring us closer to the goal of hermeneutics, the encounter in which the "meaning" of the text is seen?[40]

What clues are provided for our investigation of the hermeneutical approach of the New Testament to the Old Testament? Will our search through the New Testament uncover rabbinical models of hermeneutics that will aid in our understanding?[41] What effect will such study have on the historical reconstruction of first-century Christianity? What does all of this do to past evangelical commitments to historical objectivity?[42]

The list could continue. But our intention has been only to illustrate the scope of study we must continue to explore. The chapters in this volume are, as stated in the preface, only bridge building in intention. They attempt to sketch the agenda changes over four decades. They are catch-up exercises for the evangelical, concerned with affirming the reliability of our fundamental commitment to the inerrant Word of God in the face of new questions. The problems shift and move; the Word of our God abides forever.

40. Vern Poythress, "Adequacy of Language and Accommodation," in *Hermeneutics, Inerrancy, and the Bible,* ed. Earl D. Radmacher and Robert D. Preuss (Grand Rapids: Zondervan, 1984), pp. 351–76.

41. Moisés Silva, *Biblical Words and Their Meanings: An Introduction to Lexical Statements* (Grand Rapids: Zondervan, 1983); idem, "The New Testament Use of the Old Testament: Text Form and Authority," in *Scripture and Truth,* pp. 147–65.

42. Moisés Silva, "The Place of Historical Reconstruction in New Testament Criticism," in *Hermeneutics, Authority, and Canon,* ed. D. A. Carson and John D. Woodbridge (Grand Rapids: Zondervan, 1986), pp. 109–33.

# 2

# Inerrancy and Westminster Calvinism

## D. Clair Davis

*Standing on the shoulders of Warfield and Kuyper we honor*
*them best if we build on the main thrust of their thought*
*rather than if we insist on carrying on what is inconsistent*
*with their basic position. Then we are most faithful to*
*Calvin and to St. Paul.*

—C. Van Til, 1955

When considering the perspective of the Westminster faculty on inerrancy, we should first determine how its Calvinistic orientation has influenced its attitude toward Scripture. We must look at the place of Westminster's theology first within the broader evangelical context and then within the setting of the larger Reformed world.

## Calvinism and Evangelicalism on Scripture

Is a Calvinistic understanding of the Bible at all distinctive? Evangelicals have long believed that all conservative Protestants defend the absolute authority of the Bible and the corollary doctrine of its inerrancy. That is what a fundamental of the faith is—a doctrine which by definition all evangelicals accept. Though there were dif-

35

ferences concerning the *interpretation* of Scripture, it could be taken for granted that there was agreement that the reliability of the Bible was the starting point for all evangelical theologians, that which united them against modernistic unbelief. *Sola Scriptura*, the formal principle of the Reformation, was seen as the firm foundation common to all Bible believers.

Fundamentalists were careful to avoid including divisive doctrines in their statements of faith. No mention was made of the sacraments or even of the precise nature of Christ's atonement. But they believed a common commitment to inerrancy transcended traditionally divisive issues. For the great post–World War II evangelical movement, this was even more the case than it had been for fundamentalists. When issues concerning the large liberal denominations threatened to divide evangelicals, then those issues were also suppressed. The 1949 creed of the Evangelical Theological Society affirmed nothing except the inerrancy of the Bible. Inerrancy came to be the most ecumenical doctrine of all evangelical theology.

But does this prove that it is correct to regard inerrancy as a theologically neutral matter? Reformation Protestants were not always united on this point, at least not in its application. Reformed and Lutheran scholars were convinced that Anabaptist emphasis on the continuing work of the Holy Spirit tended to obscure the objective character of biblical revelation. High Lutherans thought the Reformed refusal to accept consubstantiation (seen by Lutherans as the plain teaching of the Bible) revealed an intrinsically rationalist approach to Scripture. Some asserted that the Roman Catholic attitude to Scripture was preferable to the Calvinistic. Within the Reformed context, Puritans suspected that Anglican delay in implementing biblical church government and worship was due to unwillingness to subordinate tradition to Scripture. It was not easy for theologians with widely differing interpretations of Scripture to recognize that they all held the same view of its nature as God's infallible Word. The line between theologies concerning Scripture and hermeneutical differences concerning its interpretation has never been easy to draw.

But Protestants continued to be firmly committed to the doctrine of the perspicuity, or clarity, of Scripture, and its corollary of the priesthood of all believers. That commitment implied the necessity of continued endeavor toward a unified understanding of scriptural teaching. Though previous attempts to discover theological consensus between Reformed and Lutherans had failed, there remained the conviction that the attempt must be continued. If Reformed Puritans and Lutheran Pietists alike accepted the heart of the Reformation gospel—justification by faith—then it was reasonable to assume that their inability to formulate a common theology was due not to differing understandings of the gospel itself but rather to a faulty theological methodology that worked against discovering that consensus. The new "biblical" theology was designed to create a theological climate where agreements rather than disagreements among believers could be more easily seen. This approach arranged theological topics not from logical or metaphysical perspectives but, instead, as corresponding with the order of God's dealings in history with his people.

It can be debated whether that goal was achieved. But Calvinists believed that, since others had adopted a more biblical orientation to the theological enterprise, inevitably they would come to more biblical (i.e., Calvinistic) answers to theological questions. Probably that development actually happened, with European and American evangelical thought taking on a distinctively, if not admittedly, Calvinistic character. The Calvinistic approach to Scripture became in practice the Protestant or evangelical one.

That conclusion requires amplification. What does it mean to follow a Calvinistic approach to the Christian faith? Calvinists believe that there is something partial and incomplete in both the Lutheran orientation (salvation is primarily the forgiveness of sins) but also in the Anabaptist orientation (salvation is primarily obedience). Calvinists believe that true Christianity must be considered from the perspective of both justification and sanctification, both seen as aspects of the believer's union with Christ. Calvinism refuses to oversimplify, preferring the search for all of God's truth over pedagogical neatness.

For the doctrine of Scripture, that orientation means that God's Word and the believer's obedience to it must be considered together. An alleged science of Christian theology that does not at the same time reflect the art of living unto God is a meaningless abstraction. It is valueless to consider the faithfulness of God in his revelation without a commitment to faithful response.

Calvinists are thus convinced they can most usefully consider the doctrine of Scripture from the perspective of God's sovereign providential care of his people. To understand how God deals with all his people is the key to understanding the way he deals with human authors. A classical statement of this position is found in B. B. Warfield's masterpiece, *The Inspiration and Authority of the Bible.* Warfield considers the question of whether God's Word is inevitably distorted by its passage through the personality of its human author:

What if this personality has itself been formed by God into precisely the personality it is, for the express purpose of communicating to the word given through it just the colors which it gives it? What if the colors of the stained-glass window have been designed by the architect for the express purpose of giving to the light that floods the cathedral precisely the tone and quality which it receives from them? What if the word of God that comes to His people is framed by God into the word of God that it is, precisely by means of the qualities of the men formed by Him for the purpose, through which it is given? When we think of God the Lord giving by His Spirit a body of authoritative Scriptures to His people, we must remember that He is the God of providence and grace as well as of revelation and inspiration, and that He holds all the lines of preparation as fully under His direction as He does the specific operation which we call technically, in the narrow sense, by the name of "inspiration."[1]

Furthermore Calvinists understand God's providence to mean that human responsibility does not compete with, much less subtract from, divine sovereignty. No matter how comprehensively human one understands the Bible to be, that quality never threatens its divine character. To take seriously humanity and its history does not take away from God's direction of the course of history. The reality of human thoughts, emotions, and decisions is never antithetical to the reality of God's power and love in his communication with his people. Calvinism believes that sin itself is not outside God's direction, so it can hardly have difficulty in understanding how God reveals himself through weak sinners. The fact that God chooses to make use of a culture whose language structure has been molded by pagan influences (whose has not?) does not undermine his ability to speak faithfully and accurately through that culture.

Such an understanding does not in itself determine how God has chosen to speak, or whether the Bible is his Word. But the Calvinistic doctrine of providence ensures that there is no human factor which limits how God may speak, or interferes with identifying the Bible with the Word of God. When God does reveal the nature of his revelation, that what "the Bible says" is what "he says," then God's word about his Word can be taken at face value immediately.

The Calvinist doctrine of providence may not seem to be sufficient. God teaches believers much more about himself than just his orderliness and regularity. Christian thought about God's direction and control of history and culture is diametrically different from a deist or humanist principle of regularity. Not a principle, but a loving heavenly Father is the object of a believer's thought—and worship. To think of God's providence in his revelation is much more than to observe how God solves the puzzle of infinity's communicating with finitude. Rather, it is to marvel

1. B. B. Warfield, *The Inspiration and Authority of the Bible* (Nutley, N.J.: Presbyterian and Reformed, 1948), pp. 155–56.

at the love and grace of God, who continues to pour out his heart to those who are stubborn and slow to hear him.

But because of the superficial way providence is so frequently understood, as merely a pious way of talking about order and purpose in the universe, it seems necessary to make Warfield's point more clearly. To be sure, the doctrine of providence is further subdivided to make clear that God deals in a special way with his people, and in an even more special way in his supernatural dealings with them. But even those clarifications may not seem to express adequately the fact that God's care for his sinful people is loving and merciful. As we think of revelation, surely the fact of God's loving care is primary, and the method of its outworking derivative. So there is no good reason to restrict Christian thinking about the Bible to just the doctrine of providence. That is the reason for seeking to make greater use of the doctrine of Christ's incarnation as a key to the proper understanding of revelation.

But that approach is not always followed in a helpful way. Writing directly in opposition to Warfield, but more so in opposition to Van Til's interpretation of Warfield, T. F. Torrance has vigorously advocated an incarnational approach to biblical revelation to rule out the old evangelical view:

> There is no question about the fact that a proper doctrine of Scripture must be grounded analogically upon the birth, life, death, and resurrection of Jesus Christ; but in the Incarnation with the hypostatic union of God and man which it involves, and in Holy Scripture with its derived relation between the Word of God and the word of man, we must take seriously the fact that the Word has assumed our fallen humanity, and was made in the likeness of sinful flesh. . . . In itself the Word of God is perfect, but even in Holy Scripture we see through a glass darkly, not yet face to face, for the perfection of our union with Christ awaits the *Parousia* and the resurrection of the dead.[2]

This is an especially clear and helpful statement of the modern neo-orthodox position. Certainly evangelicals consider the reasoning faulty. They have long pointed out that, while Christ in his incarnation did not possess all knowledge, what he did know was correct, and was true as far as it went. No doubt Christ lived by faith in that he did not know the implications of all that was to befall him, but still he trusted in the sure promises of his Father.

Still, more should be done theologically with seeing revelation as in-

---

2. T. F. Torrance, review of *The Inspiration and Authority of the Bible,* by B. B. Warfield, *Scottish Journal of Theology* 7 (1954): 106.

carnational. Perhaps orthodox Calvinism has not done as much as it should. But that is not the only way in which theological thought can be carried ahead, so that revelation and inspiration can be seen from a perspective broader than that of providence. It may also be done by comprehensive use of the biblical-theological method, the path Westminster has chosen throughout its curriculum.

But now let us digress in order to look more closely at Westminster's place with the broader Calvinistic community. While Calvinism is a generic whole, with the differences among its many species only of secondary importance, still there is something uniquely valuable about Westminster's position within the genus.

## Calvinism and Westminster on Scripture

Westminster's theological parent, old Princeton, from its beginning intended to have an orientation broader than America. It saw itself called to be aware of and to interact with global theological developments. Perceiving that Andover in particular was introducing destructive elements of German theology into U.S. churches, Princeton deliberately set out to see that its own orientation would be gleaned from the broadest possible context, beyond the parameters of American Presbyterianism, in order that its teaching would not be dated or parochial. Charles Hodge studied extensively in Germany at the beginning of his career, interacting substantially with German evangelical leaders such as Friedrich Tholuck and Ernst Hengstenberg. J. A. Alexander based his commentaries on Hengstenberg's. The *Princeton Theological Review* and its predecessors featured reports of the newest developments in European theology. Princeton saw itself called to give the church its foreign missions vision. It is hardly surprising that Westminster continued that tradition. Its own early tempestuous years featured the great debate over the significance of foreign missions within modern culture. And its founding faculty included many from outside the American Presbyterian tradition.

That multifaceted character of its theology may well be the most significant feature about Westminster's orientation. As old Princeton had interacted with New England, southern, and German theological positions, Westminster now considered it important to interact with and to build upon the great Reformed heritage of the Netherlands.

What influence did this broader outlook have on Westminster's understanding of the Bible? That question is especially pertinent today, when so many attempts have been made to play off differing elements of the Calvinistic heritage against each other with the intent of isolating the one considered to be the most objectionably orthodox. Ordinarily this is done by exalting Reformation theology and by deprecating seventeenth-century theology, particularly with respect to the question of the inspiration and inerrancy of the Bible. It is alleged that the former saw the Bible's authority deriving from Jesus Christ, the latter from rationalistic human-exalting philosophies. One specialized application of this thesis tries to drive a wedge between American "rationalistic" commitment to inerrancy and a Continental perspective alleged to be more faithful to the Christ-centered focus of the Reformation.

John Woodbridge has given the definitive evangelical response to the broader thesis in his book *Biblical Authority: A Critique of the Rogers/McKim Proposal* (Grand Rapids: Zondervan, 1982). But more instructive for our purpose is the careful analysis of the narrower thesis by Richard B. Gaffin, Jr. In his "Old Amsterdam and Inerrancy?" he has demonstrated beyond doubt that the position of Amsterdam and Princeton in all essentials is identical.[3] He has found some difference of emphasis in the two schools, but in the end the "organic" understanding of Herman Bavinck resembles very closely the Princeton approach.

But Dutch insights have certainly greatly enriched the Princeton/Westminster understanding of inerrancy, though they are not antithetical to it. This has been especially true of the contribution of the covenantal biblical theology of Geerhardus Vos, pioneer of that discipline in America. We have noted already that the discipline originally was an attempt to overcome the theological impasse between Lutheran and Reformed theology by following the biblical order of revelation in theological structure.

The new approach served to clarify much standard Calvinistic doctrine. Theology structured by the sequence of revelatory epochs made clear that the reality of the return of Christ is the key to understanding the nature of his presence now in the Lord's Supper, long a Calvinistic argument. The reality of the future coming of Christ must include the reality of his absence now. But even more significantly, the covenantal character of biblical theology served to underline the reality of human obedience within God's gracious calling.

This latter element has proved extremely fruitful in amplifying a Calvinistic doctrine of inspiration in our own day. Whatever other agenda modern thought has, foremost in its concerns is emphasizing the historical character of men's and women's relation to God. That includes consideration of the successive, developing nature of that relationship but emphasizes even more its *responsible* character. It is not enough to believe that God communicates with human beings. It is much more to

3. Richard B. Gaffin, Jr., "Old Amsterdam and Inerrancy?" *Westminster Theological Journal* 44, no. 2 (Fall 1982): 250–89; 45, no. 2 (Fall 1983): 219–72.

the point to believe specifically that he calls us to faith and obedience. So while the analogy of the incarnation should not be ignored (revelation in Jesus Christ is, after all, the most fundamental revelation there is), a covenantal and biblical-theological approach may be even better suited to meet the legitimate concerns of our day. To take the most prominent example, the contemporary discipline of hermeneutics involves more than the older questions of the methodology of interpretation but stresses responsibility to the text on the part of both interpreter and audience. To be sure, much of that agenda comes from existentialist philosophy, but it is not surprising that a covenantal, responsibility-oriented approach is equipped to address those concerns with thoroughly biblical answers.

To what extent is the biblical-theological orientation a break with the Princeton heritage? Of course, if one thinks that old Princeton had essentially the right orientation, and also that there is a systematic character to revealed truth, then one anticipates the fact that development in biblical understanding serves to strengthen the validity and timeliness of the insights of the past. But where is the specific continuity between inspiration as providential and as covenantal? What is the connection between God's control and his care? What is the connection between God's direction of our lives and our responsibility to live for him? There is no real discontinuity between the differing perspectives. Practically any theological subject can be discussed with profit from the perspective of any other theological subdivision or locus, and that is certainly the case here.

But perhaps a biblical-theological approach can do justice to human responsibility better than a providential one can. Certainly the older orientation always stressed the reality of secondary causes, which no doubt included the reality and responsibility of the human authorship of Scripture. But the theology of providence had more to say than that. A Reformed discussion of providence always included the proviso that God's control of history in no way undermines human responsibility. So it is plain that a biblical-theological focus does not replace the position of old Princeton or of classical Calvinism but rather brings it into sharper focus.

We are convinced, then, that specifically Calvinist theological emphases have made a decisive difference in Westminster's understanding of Scripture. Can the same be said for Calvinist philosophical or apologetic emphases? While a doctrine of the Bible's inspiration and authority depends primarily upon a proper understanding of the providential relation between God and his fallen creation, the question of the relation between Christianity and its surrounding culture is almost of equal importance. Modern form criticism, for example, has affirmed that it impossible to identify divine revelation anywhere in the Bible, since everywhere that revelation is inevitably expressed in secular or sub-Christian clichés. The question of how the Christian faith may be distinguished from today's civil religion is virtually identical with the question of how it ever could be distinguished from any culture, including that of the first century.

So the question of Christianity and culture, or in the language of the Westminster curriculum, apologetics and missions, is of vital importance in the construction of a valid perspective on biblical authority. It was no accident that for many years at Westminster the concerns of theological prolegomena (where the nature of Scripture is discussed) were virtually identical with those of apologetics—to the extent that students of Van Til were not always certain which class they were attending!

It is well known that the apologetic approach at Westminster has been substantially different from that held at old Princeton. But one must not forget that Van Til considered his task as incorporating the best elements of both Amsterdam and old Princeton. That the apologetics prize at Westminster is named after the great Princeton apologist William Brenton Greene is due to more than sentimentality. So one should expect continuity and development as well as divergence between the apologetic stances of old Princeton and Westminster.

Attention to that development is highly instructive. Underlying the old Princeton apologetic was the philosophy of Scottish common-sense realism as brought to America by John Witherspoon. That movement intended to avoid the skeptical, stalemated philosophy of David Hume. This was done by affirming that people should regard themselves competent to reflect on the way they think, for there must be reality underlying the experience of human perception. Theologically, common sense displayed a similar determination to consider only relevant questions. Note the sharp contrast between Princeton and the development within nineteenth-century New England Calvinism. While the questions raised by Jonathan Edwards concerning the freedom of the will dogged New England theological thinking for more than a hundred years, in Presbyterian territory such preoccupations were noticeably absent. For John Witherspoon's followers it was sufficient to know that men and women were conscious of making decisions, and it was important to make the right ones. Giving attention to the possibility of doing so was patently redundant. We should build upon the knowledge we already have and not avoid the real issues of life by useless speculation concerning what we really know already.

In the same way, Princeton apologetics was convinced that people have an obligation to make use of the knowledge of God that they have. The pattern of argumentation in Charles Hodge's *Systematic Theology* is well known. After almost every biblical proof of doctrine, there follows a supplementary appeal to human experience. While today it may seem naive to look for Calvinistic theology in the common beliefs of humankind, surely even nineteenth-century Calvinism could not have been foolish enough to have meant that uncritically. Is light shed on the puzzle by the affirmation in chapter 1 of Witherspoon's *Form of Government* for the Presbyterian church, that the church's discipline depends upon "enlightened public opinion"? It is hardly likely that anyone could have meant ordinary unbelieving opinion. That could hardly be called enlightened. Surely what Witherspoon intended was that the right living of Presbyterians should be supported by all U.S. evangelicals. And surely what was intended by the common-sense method in general was that emphasis should be placed on the areas of the faith that were especially antithetical to the spirit of the age, giving lesser emphasis to those congenial to the thought of the day.

Relating common sense to questions of the authority and the inerrancy of the Bible, Princeton men clearly were unwilling to be involved in discussing unfruitful questions where biblical data was scant. In that spirit Princeton men could see no great issues involved in some of the great controversial questions of the day, such as the age of human beings or the age of the earth. Considering the Synoptic Problem, Princeton men had no difficulty in affirming that the interests of the Gospel writers were not necessarily chronological. But where there are real difficulties, they were quick to commit their lives in working toward their resolution. Think of the prodigious efforts of Robert Dick Wilson, also one of Westminster's founding faculty, as he worked through the problems of the Book of Daniel.

What difference did the great shift in apologetics brought in by Cornelius Van Til make? Certainly he considered it major, not shrinking at labeling some traditional Princeton argumentation as Arminian. Van Til considered the older methodology superficial at best. He regarded it misleading to work on the surface of a question, considering the probability of one solution over another. Rather, a truly Reformed apologist must constantly remember that probability arguments are not appropriately applied to the Creator and his works. What old Princeton saw fit to take for granted, Van Til now insisted must be understood "self-consciously."

As attacks upon Christianity became more radical and comprehensive, the new apologetic proved especially timely. To a great measure the faculty followed its lead and stressed the unbelieving presuppositions of much modern biblical scholarship. Faculty interest turned from the older detailed defense of a Wilsonian sort. Probably only Meredith Kline has produced a defense of the reliability of the Bible that the old Princeton faculty could have recognized, in his argumentation on the early date of

Deuteronomy because of its treaty form. But that was incidental and serendipitous to his real concern!

But if Van Til's method has led to Westminster's giving less attention to point-by-point refutation of liberal argumentation, at the same time it has provided especially fruitful insights to the faculty concerning the riches of the Bible. The real impact of Van Til has come from his far-ranging methodology, best explained in John Frame's *Van Til the Theologian* (1976). Van Til has shown that no theological model can exhaustively comprehend the revelation of the sovereign Lord. But that view has not at all led to theological apathy. Instead it has given birth to new perceptions of the great variety and wealth within God's Word. Frame has derived from Van Til a threefold way of looking at Christian ethics, convinced that any single approach impoverishes our understanding of God's Law. Vern Poythress has made sweeping use of his multiperspectival method, discovering an emphasis on sanctification in texts ordinarily identified with justification. Raymond Dillard has found something beyond the theology of Kings in Chronicles. Harvie Conn has used his grasp on non-Western, non-middle-class cultures to mine still broader insights from the Bible. Richard Gaffin has combined the insights of the biblical-theological method with the Van Tilian focus to set forth new perspectives in systematic theology. Showing them all the way has been the creative example of the biblical-theological exegete and preacher, Edmund P. Clowney.

Continuity between old Princeton and Westminster's doctrines of Scripture was not hard to see. Is that also true of the apologetics of Scripture? If the above observations are essentially correct—that Princeton concentrated on the detailed refutation of error, while Westminster has concentrated upon uncovering the powerful riches of God's Word, letting God speak for himself in his Word—where is the continuity to be seen?

In a preliminary way, it is worth noting that both chose to focus on the significant issues of their day, setting aside others as capable of being taken for granted. That today's Westminster focuses on the most difficult but important issue of all, biblical hermeneutics, is especially meaningful. Older questions, such as harmonization of biblical passages, have already received about all the answers they ever will. It is highly appropriate that Westminster go on. The motto under Robert Dick Wilson's portrait stands for the goal of the entire faculty: "I have not shirked the difficult questions."

Both Witherspoon and Van Til would approve; the cause of the Bible is not well served by endlessly rehearsing matters that should be received as clear and obvious. No doubt there would be differences between the two lists of what those matters are and of the best way to build on what a Christian knows. But for both, Christian thinking does not take place in thin air but builds on the sure foundation that God has provided. Both old and new varieties of Calvinistic apologetic seek to show the truth of God's Word by showing the reality of God. For both, no doubt more self-consciously for Van Til, the foundational issue for inerrancy is the nature of God himself, the great covenant-keeper.

Inerrancy is, however, not an end in itself, but the foundation for clear, believing, biblical thinking. Inerrancy means that only God and his Word are clear and infallible. That restricts but also liberates the theological enterprise. Old Princeton wanted the Bible itself and the Bible alone to determine its mandate in the study of God's Word. When the fundamentalist world wanted a definitive statement on a young earth, Princeton declined politely. When new light on alcohol was requested, Princeton did the same. Westminster's issues are different. It has considered the question of whether it is legitimate to make use of Hittite covenant forms as a tool for biblical understanding. Then it took up the question of the legitimacy of the sociological insights behind the church-growth movement. Now it is going on to the issues surrounding women in modern society. These are the down-to-earth issues of Christian thought and life. Again, it is not enough to know that unbelievers are in favor of something for us to be against it. We must look once more at the Bible, recognizing God's grace in how the needs of our day force us to look longer and harder at his Word.

That is the beginning of the Princeton/Westminster understanding of the authority and inerrancy of God's Word. The rest is yet to come, as men and women of conviction and humility seek after God's truth as he shows it to them ever more clearly in his Word.

# 3

## How Does the Bible Look at Itself?

### Sinclair B. Ferguson

*If the Bible does not witness to its own infallibility, then we have no right to believe that it is infallible. If it does bear witness to its infallibility then our faith in it must rest upon that witness, however much difficulty may be entertained with this belief. If this position with respect to the ground of faith in Scripture is abandoned, then appeal to the Bible for the ground of faith in any other doctrine must also be abandoned. The doctrine of Scripture must be elicited from the Scripture just as any other doctrine should be. If the doctrine of Scripture is denied its right of appeal to Scripture for support, then what right does any other doctrine have to make this appeal?*

—John Murray, 1946

In the final Latin edition of his *Institutes* (1559), John Calvin wrote that "Scripture exhibits fully as clear evidence of its own truth as white and black things do of their color, or sweet or bitter things do of their taste. . . . Let this point therefore stand: that those whom the Holy Spirit has inwardly taught truly rest upon Scripture, and that Scripture indeed is self authenticated [*autopiston*]."[1] Few things more characterize the view of Scripture espoused by Calvin's evangelical successors than the assumptions implicit in his words: (1) Scripture bears witness to its own character as God's Word; (2) Scripture is the Word of God written; and (3) Scripture as written bears the marks of its human authors; as God-given, it bears the marks of its divine origin, namely, uncompromised reliability.

This view is based on several biblical passages, notably 2 Timothy 3:16 and 2 Peter 1:19–21, and on a host of ancillary statements scattered throughout both Testaments. But it has never been regarded as the last word on Scripture. Indeed, it is simply the first word, providing a solid foundation for the rigorous discipline of biblical exposition. For such a conviction about Scripture does not answer in an a priori fashion many of the questions we might raise about its teaching. As a biblical doctrine it will influence the interpretation of other passages. But any decision about the "meaning" of a given passage must still be decided on the basis of careful exegetical study. Only when we lapse from such sensitivity to the text does the principle of the self-witness of Scripture become confused with an a priori dogmatism about what certain texts must mean.

Implicit in this whole approach to the doctrine of Scripture lies a presupposition which was, in the past, rarely expounded, largely because it was so universally held to be self-evident. It was assumed that we can in fact speak about "Scripture's view of itself." Today that assumption is contested and therefore needs to be established as legitimate. Since Scripture could not be a finalized entity until the last of its books had been written, is it not anachronistic to speak of "Scripture's view of itself"?

The issue is expressed with characteristically pugilistic vigor by James Barr, when he writes:

> According to conservative arguments, it is not only Jesus who made "claims"; the Bible made "claims" about itself. The Book of Daniel "claims" to have been written by a historical Daniel some time in the sixth century B.C.; the Book of Deuteronomy "claims" to have been written by Moses; and more important still, the Bible as a whole "claims" to be divinely inspired. All this is nonsense. There is no "the Bible" that "claims" to be divinely inspired, there is no "it" that has a "view of itself." There is only this or that source, like 2 Timothy or 2 Peter, which makes statements about certain other writings, these rather undefined. There is no such thing as "the Bible's view of itself" from which a fully authoritative answer to these questions can be obtained. This whole side of traditional conserva-

---

1. John Calvin, *Institutes of the Christian Religion,* ed. John T. McNeill, 2 vols. (Philadelphia: Westminster, 1960), 1:76, 80.

tive apologetic, though loudly vociferated, just does not exist; there is no case to answer.[2]

Barr's power of debunking are considerable, and well known. Nor have they been directed exclusively against those he regards as fundamentalists. His critique cannot, therefore, be treated in an off-hand fashion. Indeed, it underlines a hiatus in much conservative writing on the doctrine of Scripture. But is he correct in suggesting that we cannot legitimately speak of "Scripture's view of itself"? If so, he would seem to have destroyed a linchpin in the traditional orthodox view of Scripture and shown that the so-called biblical view is essentially nonbiblical. How can it be claimed that "Scripture teaches $X$ or $Y$ about Scripture" if such reflection does not (and in the very nature of the case, could not) take place in Scripture itself?

This argument has the appearance of devastating power; but in fact it fails to take account of the direction of the evidence Scripture provides. In what follows, our intention is (1) to demonstrate the legitimacy of speaking of "Scripture's view of itself," and (2) to expound briefly what this view entails for the doctrine of Scripture.

## Does the Bible Have "A View of Itself"?

Can we really speak about "the Bible's view of itself," or, with Barr, say only that $X$ (a biblical author) said $Y$ about $Z$ (a section of the Christian canon of Scripture)?

Merely to cite 2 Timothy 3:16 to defend the view that Scripture does indeed have a view of itself is an inadequate response. It begs the question, since (1) Paul here refers apparently to the Old Testament (the "holy Scriptures," v. 15), not to the entire Christian canon; (2) evidence must be offered that 2 Timothy 3:16 is itself Scripture, to show that it gives Scripture's view of Scripture; and (3) evidence must be furnished that 2 Timothy 3:16 has the rest of the New Testament canon in view. Only when these conditions are met can this statement justify the claim that it presents Scripture's view of itself.

Is the traditional conservative view of Scripture then justifiable? In the very nature of the case, such justification must rise above the mere citation of proof texts.

If one objects that any sophisticated reasoning or preunderstanding would bar the ordinary Christian from reaching the conviction that Scripture claims to be the Word of God, the answer is at hand. We are ultimately persuaded of the inspiration and authority of Scripture not on

2. James Barr, *Fundamentalism* (London: SCM, 1977), p. 78.

the basis of coherent arguments in textbooks of doctrine but through "the inward work of the Holy Spirit, bearing witness by and with the Word in our hearts."[3] It is by reading Scripture under the Spirit's influence, rather than by skill in logic, that trust in God's Word is born.

There is no finer illustration of this principle than J. Gresham Machen's experience when exposed in his earlier years to the cream of German liberal theological teaching. It was his reading of the Gospels themselves that strengthened his faith in biblical inspiration and authority.

The function of our discussion here is not to usurp the ministry of the Holy Spirit but to vindicate the inner consistency of the view that Scripture *does* bear witness to its own character. We seek to show that such a conviction is neither incoherent nor irrelevant because of a category mistake.

What, then, are the propositions involved in saying that Scripture bears witness to its own nature? We may note briefly four of them.

First, there is evidence within the Old Testament of a canonical self-consciousness, a recognition that what is written is given by God to rule and direct his people. That is already indicated by the fact that written documentation accompanies the covenant relationship between God and his people and is intended to rule and direct their lives (see Deut. 5:22, 32; 29:9; 30:9–10, 15–16; 31:24–29; Josh. 1:7–8; 8:34). The rest of the books of the Old Testament are written, in various ways, in exposition of this authoritative, canonical, covenant word. The Old Testament grows from this root. Out of this flows, in part, the Chronicler's covenantal, canonical interpretation of history and the confidence of the prophetic "This is what the Sovereign Lord says." New Scripture is written in the confidence that it is "Scripture" only because of its inherent relationship to what God has already given.[4]

Second, there is, in the New Testament, the clear recognition of the divinely given canon we now know as the Old Testament. The New Testament's use of the word *Scripture* and such expressions as "the law and the prophets," "it is written," "God said," and "Scripture says" abundantly illustrate this fact. Both Jesus and the apostles use Scripture in a normative canonical role. In Jesus' life, Scripture must be fulfilled, simply because it is Scripture. For him, as for the apostles, the appeal to the Old Testament settles all matters, because of its canonical status for God's people. It is "the mouth of God," by whose every word people are to live (Matt. 4:4).

To the authors of the New Testament, the Old Testament is God's Word.

3. *Westminster Confession of Faith,* chap. 1, sec. 5.
4. For an extended discussion of a similar argument, see Meredith G. Kline, *The Structure of Biblical Authority* (Grand Rapids: Eerdmans, 1972), esp. pp. 21–68.

But further development of this proposition is required. It must be shown that the New Testament is organically one with the Old, and self-consciously Scripture, to enable us to affirm that this is Scripture's view of Scripture.

Third, there is, in the New Testament, a consciousness among the authors as a whole that the authority of their own writing is on a par with that of the Old Testament and that the content of the revelation given to them is, in some sense, superior to it, not in terms of inspiration, but in the clarity and progress of the revelation recorded (see, e.g., Eph. 3:2–6). This consciousness in the apostolic writings is tantamount to a deliberate addition to the canon in order to bring it to completion in the light of Christ's coming. In this sense, the New Testament as canon is virtually demanded by the coming of Christ. If the older revelation, which was spasmodic and fragmentary (Heb. 1:1), was inscripturated, how much more is inscripturation anticipated of the consummation of revelation?

We find hints of this self-conscious adding to canonical Scripture throughout the New Testament. These are, in the nature of the case, often subtle, but they are almost commonplace. Thus, for example, in keeping with New Testament practice, John's Gospel introduces quotations from the Old Testament with the words, "it is written (6:31; 8:17; 12:14; etc.). It is a phrase which "in the New Testament puts an end to all contradiction."[5] But a similar expression, "these are written," marks the rounding off of John's own work (20:31). In John's Gospel the allusion is unlikely to be accidental. Here, as elsewhere, the verb *graphō* (write) seems to retain its quasi-authoritative sense (cf. Pilate's words: "What I have written, I have written" [19:22]).[6]

Hebrews 2:2–3 argues from the lesser authority of the Law, given through the angels, to the greater authority of the gospel, given through the preaching of the apostles. But if the apostles' spoken word was regarded as the Word of God (as they themselves believed it to be [1 Thess. 2:13]), no less will be their written word. No one knows God's thoughts, except God's Spirit. But God's Spirit teaches the apostles to speak the words he teaches (1 Cor. 2:11–13). Those who posses the Spirit therefore recognize the divine canonicity of the apostolic word. Nor is this simply the conclusion of deductive logic. What Paul writes are the Lord's commands, and a mark of a truly spiritual person is that he or she recognizes them as such (1 Cor. 14:37). Disobedience to the teaching given in his letters can lead to excommunication (2 Thess. 3:14). Here Paul aligns his

5. Herman Ridderbos, *Studies in Scripture and Its Authority* (Grand Rapids: Eerdmans, 1978), p. 21.
6. G. Kittel, ed., *Theological Dictionary of the New Testament*, trans. and ed. G. W. Bromiley, 10 vols. (Grand Rapids: Eerdmans, 1964–76), 1:747.

written teaching with the Law of the old covenant; rejection of it as canon for life involves the repudiation of the covenant of which it is the canonical record and then the coming under the divine curse of expulsion from the covenant community. For this reason, apostolic letters are read not only by the church but alongside the sacred writings of the Old Testament, in and to the church (Col. 4:16).

The same inherent canon-consciousness emerges in the opening and closing sections of the Book of Revelation. It is assumed that the book will be read in public to the church (1:3). Both reader and hearer are promised "blessing"—that is, divine, covenantal benediction. In view of this, a similarly covenant-oriented warning closes the book: "I warn everyone who hears the words of the prophecy of this book: If anyone adds anything to them, God will add to him the plagues described in this book. And if anyone takes words away from this book of prophecy, God will take away from him his share in the tree of life and in the holy city, which are described in this book" (22:18–19).

These words are not a naive piece of personal vindictiveness. Rather, they reflect the apex of canon-consciousness in the New Testament. They deliberately echo the warnings of the Old Testament canonical Scripture: "Do not add to what I command you and do not subtract from it, but keep the commands of the LORD your God that I give you" (Deut. 4:2; see also vv. 5, 14, 40; 12:32). Here, the Book of Revelation "claims" the authority which it assumes for the Old Testament itself. This is nothing less than self-conscious canonicity.

Fourth, in the New Testament we also notice that some sources express a sense not only of their own canonical character but of the existence of a class of literature sharing that status. Admittedly this cross-fertilization does little more than surface in the New Testament documents. But the fact that it does surface is adequate justification for believing that it reflects a wider ecclesiastical consciousness that God was giving a new canon of Scripture for the new age of the gospel.

This sense may be the explanation of the otherwise mysterious citing of words in 1 Timothy 5:18 (from both Deut. 25:4 and Luke 10:7) under the common rubric "for the Scripture says." Another interpretation is possible, namely, that the rubric refers only to the first citation, the second being a "free" logion of Jesus. But there is nothing inherently questionable about the first interpretation, and it is in fact the more natural reading of the text. Moreover, given the emergence of the canon of the New Testament and the citation of New Testament documents by the apostolic fathers, it would seem inevitable that already in the first century—and especially by Paul, to whom Luke was such a faithful companion—the Gospel of Luke would be cited as "Scripture."

More certain yet is the well-known statement of 2 Peter 3:16. Paul's "letters contain some things that are hard to understand, which ignorant and unstable people distort, as they do the other Scriptures *(tas loipas graphas)*, to their own destruction." Here we find confirmation of the fact that Paul's letters are already regarded as Scripture. To refer to his writings in the same category as "the rest of the Scriptures" assumes their canonicity. Paul's letters, therefore, are placed on a par with the Old Testament. It is possible that Peter has in view in the phrase "the rest of the Scriptures" (2 Peter 3:16) other apostolic writings. We have already noted a sufficiently wide-ranging canon-consciousness in the New Testament documents for that to be possible, perhaps even probable. But in strict logic, this statement enables us to affirm only that Peter regarded Paul's letters as canonical Scripture. More, however, may yet be affirmed.

Why does 2 Peter recognize Paul's letters as Scripture? Materially we may here appeal to the testimony of the Spirit. As in the contemporary church, so in the early church the Holy Spirit bore witness to canonical Scripture. He gave the inner persuasion that it was Sacred Writ. But formally, the answer lies in the recognition of Paul's apostolic office and its significance. Apostleship existed in order to give Scripture to the church.

This is the thrust of several statements of Jesus' farewell discourse in John 13–17. An apostle of Christ is his special representative: "I tell you the truth, whoever accepts anyone I send accepts me; and whoever accepts me accepts the one who sent me" (13:20). "The Holy Spirit, whom the Father will send in my name, will teach you all things and will remind you of everything I have said to you" (14:26). "When the Counselor comes . . . the Spirit of truth . . . he will testify about me. And you also must testify, for you have been with me from the beginning" (15:26–27). "But when he, the Spirit of truth, comes, he will guide you into all truth . . . he will tell you what is yet to come" (16:3).

All this is part of the same strand of teaching which begins in such passages as Luke 10:16 and culminates in the Great Commission in Matthew 28:20. The apostles were to testify to and teach everything that Christ had commanded. They were already prepared to bear their unique witness by their relationship to Jesus and the promise of the Spirit. But implicit in the perspective that their labors will last "to the very end of the age" is the prospect—indeed, the necessity—of the development of a new canonical Scripture flowing from the apostolic circle.

The apostles were called precisely for the purpose of being witnesses of Jesus (note, with the above, Paul's affirmation that he was a witness-apostle to the risen Lord Jesus Christ [1 Cor. 9:1]; see also Acts 1:8, 22; 2:32; 3:15; 5:32; 10:39, 41; 13:31; 22:15; 26:16). They were vehicles of new revelation which was written down (see Eph. 3:2–5) and therefore conscious, to a degree, that they were adding to the already-received canon of Scripture. This is not to insist that every book in the New Testament was written directly by an apostle; but we have no reason to believe that any book emerged from outside the general apostolic circle.

Such is the relationship, therefore, between apostleship and Scripture that the connection (in 2 Peter 3:16) between Paul and the "other Scriptures" (and by parity of reasoning, between the apostles and the "other Scriptures") is not at all surprising. In a sense it might even be anticipated by the sensitive reader of the New Testament.

In what way, then, do these considerations justify our speaking of "Scripture's view of itself"? They indicate a consciousness of canonical status within the books of the Old Testament; they emphasize that this canonicity is confirmed by the documents of the New Testament and that they place themselves in the same category as canonical Scripture. The New Testament, then, views the whole of the Old Testament as Scripture, and in the very act of being given to the church by the apostles seals its own canonicity. We may conclude, then, that inherent in the books of our New Testament, as well as the Old, is the self-consciousness of belonging to a divinely given canon.

Clearly there is nothing simple about this reasoning. But it would be a mistake to think that we could or should have a "simple" explanation. The manner in which God has given Scripture to the church—in space and time, through a variety of human authors—precludes such a simple demonstration of Scripture's self-testimony. Nevertheless, that self-testimony does exist with sufficient clarity for us to speak legitimately of "Scripture's view of itself."

## The Bible's View of Itself

Assuming the validity of our earlier considerations, what is "the Bible's view of itself"? Within the scope of this essay, four features of Scripture's self-testimony call for attention: inspiration, authority, reliability, and necessity.

### Inspiration

No element is more central to Scripture's testimony to its own nature than the concept of inspiration. Many passages point in this direction, especially Paul's consciously programmatic statement in 2 Timothy 3:16 that "all Scripture is inspired by God" (NASB).

It has long been realized that the term *inspiration* is problematic and, indeed, an inadequate translation of *theopneustos*. "It is very desirable that we should free ourselves at the outset from influences arising from the current employment of the term 'inspiration.' This term is not a biblical term, and its etymological implications are not perfectly accordant with the biblical conception of the modes of the divine operation in giving the Scripture."[7]

At first glance this may appear an inexplicable statement from one of the greatest of all defenders of the inspiration of Scripture. The words "Warfield denies Bible is inspired" would make a startling headline! But this would of course be to misconstrue Warfield (and Paul) completely. What is in view here is that *theopneustos* refers not to the in-breathing of God (either into the authors or into the text of Scripture) but to the "God-breathed" character of the product of the author's writing. What is stressed is not the manner of Scripture's coming into being but its divine source. Paul's language therefore obviates what many readers of the Bible have found to be a stumbling block: large parts of the Bible do not seem very inspiring, and it is difficult to see how the authors of them were in an "inspired" state of mind when writing them. Paul affirms that the product is God-breathed. But it came into being through a variety of means (careful research and study, ecstatic experience, and even, in the case of some parts, dictation).

Paul's words require future elucidation. Three issues of interpretation arise. First, does the anarthrous *pasa graphē* suggest that Paul means "every Scripture," rather than "all Scripture"? That meaning is possible. But in fact the point is of minimal importance. If every Scripture is God-breathed, it follows that all Scripture will also be God-breathed. Either translation underlines the inspiration of the entire Old Testament.

Second, should *theopneustos* be taken in an attributive sense ("all God-breathed Scripture is useful . . .")? If so, it could be taken to limit the extent of inspiration and to imply that some Scripture may not be God-breathed.

In the very nature of the case we cannot demonstrate that every single verse of Scripture is spoken of seriatim as God-breathed. But the fact that all sections of Scripture are cited almost randomly in the New Testament, with equal force, emphasizes how far removed such a distinction was from the minds of the New Testament writers. So widespread are the New Testament's quotations and allusions from the Old Testament that no distinction surfaces between the "God-breathed" and the "man-made." Such a distinction is alien to the evidence of Scripture itself and cannot therefore have been the apostle's meaning.

Third, should *theopneustos* be taken in an active, rather than a passive, sense (God-breathing, rather than breathed out by God)? While *theopneustos* appears only here in the New Testament, the translation

---

7. B. B. Warfield, *The Inspiration and Authority of the Bible* (Philadelphia: Presbyterian and Reformed, 1951), p. 153.

"all [every] Scripture is God-breathed" is favored by the testimony of the rest of Scripture. The idea of Scripture as the Word of God, that which is carried forth by the breath or speech of God, is commonplace. The notion of Scripture as "breathing out God" (rather than breathed out by God) is foreign to the statements of Scripture concerning its own nature.

Abundant evidence exists to substantiate this view. Jeremiah's experience may be taken as paradigmatic of biblical writers: "Then the LORD reached out his hand and touched my mouth and said to me, 'Now, I have put my words in your mouth'" (Jer. 1:9; cf. Isa. 6:7). Similarly, David's final oracle (the word itself is significant) assumes what is true of all of "the oracles of God," or "the very words of God" (Acts 7:38; Rom. 3:2; Heb. 5:12; 1 Peter 4:11): "The Spirit of the LORD spoke through me; his word was on my tongue" (2 Sam. 23:2). When Jesus quotes Deuteronomy 8:3 with such manifest approval, he speaks of man's living not by bread alone but by "every word that comes from the mouth of God" (Matt. 4:4). Again, the way in which God's speech and the words of Scripture are virtually synonymous terms in biblical usage underlines the equation of Scripture with what has been breathed out by God. (See Rom. 9:17 and Gal. 3:8, where "Scripture" is really equivalent to "God"; and Matt. 19:4–5 [quoting Gen. 2:24], Heb. 3:7 [Ps. 95:7], and Acts 4:24–25 [Ps. 2:1], where "Scripture says" and "God says" are equivalent expressions.) Such evidence, coupled with Warfield's extensive demonstration that the form *theopneustos* is active rather than passive, leaves the issue beyond doubt.[8]

About this inspiration several features should be noted.

*Inspiration is given no final explanation.* No doctrine of the exact nature of inspiration is gained from 2 Timothy 3:16. This passage considers, as we have seen, the product of God's powerful working (his "breath"), not the way in which his Spirit has engaged men's lives and minds in order to create the product of Scripture. The nature of inspiration cannot be determined in an a priori fashion from the simple fact of it. Nor, indeed, does 2 Peter 1:21, which speaks of the Holy Spirit's carrying or bearing the biblical authors, shed much light. The mode of inspiration must be discovered exegetically, not dogmatically, in an a posteriori manner, by the examination of the whole of Scripture, with special attention to its reflection on the mode of the production of its various parts. This exercise will drive us to the conclusion that we can no more fully explain inspiration than we can explain providence.

In fact, Scripture came into being through a variety of modes. Some passages are the fruit of ecstatic experience; others are the product of historical research and thoughtful interpretation—such as Luke's account of Christ, or the Chronicler's account of the history of Israel from a cov-

8. Ibid., pp. 245–96.

enantal perspective. There is poetry, much of which must have been the fruit of hard literary labor (only those who have never written poetry assume it is always the result of immediate "inspiration"); but there is also material which is indeed the immediate fruit of profound experience.

In view of this, two elements characterize the manner of inspiration. The first is God's general providential superintendence of the lives, experiences, and circumstances of the biblical authors. "If God wished to give his people a series of letters like Paul's, he prepared a Paul to write them, and the Paul he brought to the task was a Paul who simultaneously would write just such letters."[9]

But second, Scripture is the result of the activity of divine power, through the Spirit. He works in the lives of the authors specifically in the production of Scripture. He bears them along (2 Peter 1:21) so that the product of their writing is safeguarded as God's own Word. In this sense, God not only governs their lives in equipping them but actually (if mysteriously) teaches them the words they use (see 1 Cor. 2:13).

*Inspiration characterizes all Scripture.* We have argued above that Paul did not intend to limit the inspiration in Scripture. Even if 2 Timothy 3:16 were translated "All God-breathed Scripture is useful . . . ," the connotation that only parts of Scripture are God-breathed is completely absent. Inspiration extends to every section of Scripture.

This point is well illustrated by a glance through the United Bible Societies' edition of the Greek New Testament (which prints citations and allusions from the Old Testament in bold in the text). The index lists some 300 texts from the Old Testament quoted in the New, and more than 1500 allusions from the Old Testament employed in the New. The random, rather than selective, use of Scripture is manifest. If any part is God-breathed, then the whole is God-breathed.

We must not, however, draw unbiblical deductions from this conclusion. For while there are no degrees of inspiration, there are degrees of revelation. Inspiration is not subject to levels of development, but revelation is—it is progressive and cumulative. It develops through the epochs of redemptive history, reaching several high points before coming to its peak in Jesus Christ. Yet, each stage of revelation, when recorded, is enshrined in an equally inspired Scripture. It is to the embarrassment of those who see different levels of inspiration in the Old Testament that the New Testament writers cite with equanimity the imprecatory psalms (e.g., Pss. 69:25 and 109:8 in Acts 1:20), while they do not directly cite Psalm 23!

The universality of inspiration is epitomized in the notion of verbal inspiration, which affirms that the inspiration of Scripture is not limited to its general teaching or to particular doctrines but extends even to the

9. Ibid., p. 155.

words. This fact Paul affirms of apostolic teaching in 1 Corinthians 2:13. But such words do not stand in isolation from one another, nor do they possess their God-intended meaning apart from each other.[10] Because words express meaning, and a particular word may possess different meanings in different contexts, the meaning communicated depends on the significance of all the words used. If Scripture is God-breathed at all, that inspiration must extend to all the words that are employed. For evangelical scholars this teaching is clearly one of the great motives for the pursuit of so-called textual criticism. If inspiration reaches to the words, the identification of what was originally written is a sacred task to be pursued with joy and zeal.

*Inspiration does not render redundant the necessity of interpretation.* No passage of Scripture discloses its meaning to us apart from actual exegesis. Conviction about the fact of inspiration does not guarantee that we understand even 2 Timothy 3:16 aright or the precise nature of inspiration. Correspondingly, differences of interpretation do not necessarily involve differences in conviction about inspiration.

But if this is so, why is it so important to emphasize Scripture's inspiration? Because our doctrine of inspiration affects our understanding of and response to biblical authority.

### Authority

If Scripture made no claim to divine inspiration, it could still possess authority—as the unique (and, to that extent, authoritative) witness of the people of God to the acts of God in history and as the source book of all original Christian tradition. It could even be regarded as possessing supreme authority for the faith and life of the church.

The doctrine of plenary divine inspiration implies that Scripture comes to us as an expression of divine authority. It is the "mouth of God" (Matt. 4:4). What Scripture says, God says. It speaks with his authority. Hence Calvin's famous formulation: "The Scriptures obtain full authority among believers only when men regard them as having sprung from heaven, as if there the living words of God were heard."[11] This authority is already evident within the pages of Scripture itself.

*The fact of biblical authority.* Nothing is more characteristic of the New Testament's appeal to the Old Testament as Scripture, and therefore characteristic of Scripture as a class, than the expression "it is written." The appeal is not the naive one of "if it is in a book, it must be true." Rather, the phrase means: It is written in the document of divine author-

---

10. See John Murray, "The Attestation of Scripture," in *The Infallible Word,* 3d ed., ed. Paul Woolley and Ned B. Stonehouse (Philadelphia: Presbyterian and Reformed, 1967), p. 23 n.9.

11. Calvin, *Institutes* 1:74.

ity, in the canon of the community of God's people. Since what is written there is divinely inspired, appeal to it settles all discussion.

Such an appeal to Scripture's authority is, it should be stressed, an appeal to Scripture rightly interpreted. Scripture erroneously interpreted is no longer God's Word—as Jesus' confrontation with Satan in the wilderness underlines (Matt. 4:1ff.; John 10:34).[12]

Interestingly, precisely in such contexts Jesus gives expression to the final authority of Scripture in his own life. But perhaps even more striking is his use of Scripture immediately before his arrest and immediately after his resurrection. On both occasions, the one under intense duress, the other as Son of God in the power of the new and resurrected humanity (Rom. 1:4), Jesus appeals to the authority of Scripture (see Matt. 26:24, 31; Luke 24:44, 46). If there was any point in his ministry at which it would have been instinctive or appropriate to refer to his own authority instead of the authority of Scripture, these would have been occasions. But precisely in these circumstances he places enormous stress on Scripture's authority.

This use of Scripture and recognition of its authority by Jesus give special significance to his mandate to the apostles to teach whatever he has commanded them to all the world and to every age (Matt. 28:18–20). At the back of the apostles' incessant appeals to Scripture as divinely authoritative lies what they first learned from Jesus himself. The authority of the Old Testament was given the imprimatur of Jesus the Son of God; the authority of the New Testament is anticipated in the words of the Great Commission. On his authority the apostles are to teach throughout the ages what he has taught them. Enshrined in these words is the concept that such teaching must be preserved in Scripture for the church to come.

*The extent of Scripture's authority.* Already the complexity of this issue is apparent. Simply put, "The Bible says" ends all questioning—except the great question, "What does the Bible say?"

Scripture is given in the context of ongoing redemptive history, and the authority of its several parts is related to this phenomenon. There is teaching in Scripture which is either further developed or even superseded before the last book of the Bible is written. Thus, to take an obvious example, the dietary laws of the Mosaic legislation and epoch do not carry the final authority for the New Testament Christian that they did

---

12. The fact that Christians sometimes make right decisions on the basis of wrong interpretations of Scripture in no way negates this principle. In such circumstances account must be taken of (1) the providential overruling by God of his people's lives (Rom. 8:28), and (2) the fact that such actions may be consistent with Scripture's teaching generally, even when based on a misunderstanding of one part of Scripture. Such a misunderstanding is not necessarily the same as the repudiation of the teaching of Scripture as a whole.

for the Old Testament believer (Mark 7:19; Rom. 14:14). All Scripture is authoritative, but its authority is intimately related to its context in the flow of redemptive history.

The authority of God in Scripture is also expressed in an accommodated, phenomenological form, and with specific focus. Not only do the Scriptures actually make us "wise for salvation through faith in Christ Jesus" (2 Tim. 3:15); that is also their specific intention. They may do other things incidentally; they do this task intentionally. Thus Calvin, commenting on the biblical account of creation writes: "He who would learn astronomy [astrologia], and other recondite arts, let him go elsewhere."[13] The Bible is not intended to be an authoritative textbook on physics, chemistry, mathematics, or human biology. The word *heart* in Scripture rarely means the organ in the body! Scripture's focus lies elsewhere: it has been given "for teaching, rebuking, correcting and training in righteousness, so that the man of God may be thoroughly equipped for every good work" (2 Tim. 3:16–17).

Is, then, the authority of Scripture limited? The use of the word *limited* here may be misleading, because it masks a false dichotomy. If we say that Scripture's authority is limited, we are in danger of denying its plenary authority as God's Word; if we say that it is not limited, without further explanation of what we mean, we may be in danger of misreading its intentions.

If the Scriptures are God-breathed, they carry God's authority. All they say, on every subject on which they speak, will be authoritative. But they speak on every subject from a particular perspective, not in the intentionally exhaustive fashion of a textbook. That fact does not diminish their authority, nor the universality of their applicability, but provides both with the focus in which it is to be understood and applied.

The Scriptures are like a stone thrown into the water, creating a whole series of concentric circles around the point of entry. Scripture's authority dominates the whole of life, but it does so in different ways through its entry into the human situation. In some areas its authority is immediate and direct, in others it is indirect and mediated. The computer programmer who is a member of God's church sees Scripture as his or her final authority. But that authority functions in different ways. It is not diminished in any sphere. It is one's authority in the fellowship of the church; but one's whole approach to programming will also be dominated and influenced by what God's Word says. But we do not read the Scriptures to learn computer programming, because we realize God has not given them in the form of a textbook for such a purpose. Biblical authority is not compromised one iota by recognizing this principle.

13. John Calvin, *Commentary on Genesis,* trans. and ed. John King, 2 vols. (Grand Rapids: Eerdmans, 1948), 1:79.

*Authority and Sufficiency.* Scripture's authority is intimately related to its sufficiency as our guide to the way of salvation (2 Tim. 3:15). This is the meaning of the Reformation watchword *sola Scriptura,* Scripture alone.

*Sola Scriptura* did not emerge as an issue only with the Reformation.[14] But at the Reformation it stood over against any principle which either added to or usurped the prerogative of God to speak adequately through his Word. In particular, the teaching office of the Roman church was in view. In this context it remains necessary to insist on *sola Scriptura.*

Today it is also necessary to recognize that *sola Scriptura* contrasts with much current evangelical teaching. In many of the debates over the question of spiritual gifts, it has not always been realized how central this question is. Involved in the view that such gifts as prophecy and tongues have ceased is the fact that the New Testament regards certain gifts as signs of the apostle and evidence of the apostolic nature of the church (2 Cor. 12:12; Heb. 2:3b–4). But also implied is the conviction that, *as revelatory,* these gifts were exercised prior to the coming into being and universal recognition of the entire New Testament canon. Insofar as prophecy and tongues plus interpretation were regarded as divine revelation, they served an interim function prior to the inscripturating of the apostolic message.

Any contemporary declaration which adds to information given in Scripture and is prefaced by the words "this is what the Lord says," formally implies more than merely illumination. It is a claim to be new divine revelation. This dynamic is not always recognized. In principle, is there any difference between a Protestant claim to give (immediate) revelation in prophecy and interpreted tongues and a Roman Catholic claim to give (carefully thought out) revelation through the teaching office of the church? Rapprochement between Protestant and Roman Catholic "charismatic Christians" suggests that this mindset is often shared quite unconsciously. Debates over the continuation or cessation of certain spiritual gifts will never make headway until it is realized that, to Christians in the Reformed tradition of Calvin, Owen, and Warfield, reservations of the exercise of such gifts are deeply rooted in *sola Scriptura.* To them it is not merely a traditional conviction about the cessation of gifts that is at stake, but 2 Timothy 3:16 itself.

### Reliability

The Scriptures, said Jesus almost incidentally, "cannot be broken" (John 10:35). These words appear in the context of a wider ad hominem argument. But this part of his statement is not itself ad hominem in na-

14. Heiko Oberman, *The Harvest of Medieval Theology* (Cambridge: Harvard University Press, 1963), pp. 201, 361ff., 389.

ture. Jesus is not merely accepting his opponents' point of view for the sake of argument, basing his position on a presupposition shared equally by them—the authority and reliability of the Old Testament. Its authority in this respect, as even Bultmann recognizes, "stands just as fast for him as for the scribes, and he feels himself in opposition to them only in the way he understands and applies the Old Testament."[15]

But what is claimed when Scripture's reliability (inability to be "broken") is thus affirmed? It is not only that Scripture in the form of prophecy must be fulfilled (e.g., Matt. 26:24, 31, 54, 56). It is that God's Word is truth (John 17:17).

What kind of reliability does this teaching imply? Does Scripture function (as neoorthodoxy so frequently suggests) like a scratched record? The lyrics can still be clearly heard, even through the distortions. Is Scripture the fallible word of man, through which can be heard the eternal Word of God, who alone is infallible? More than this is claimed in Scripture. We have seen how Jesus assumes that an incidental statement in the psalms (and by parity of reasoning, the rest of the Scripture) is absolutely reliable and trustworthy. His debate with the Pharisees proceeds on the issue not of Scripture's reliability but of its meaning. This same principle lies behind the conviction that Scripture must be fulfilled—simply because it is Scripture.

The kind of reliability claimed for Scripture, therefore, is an infallible, inerrant reliability, precisely because Scripture is the Word of a God who cannot lie. Dewey Beegle calls this position the "syllogism of inerrancy."[16] If God is infalliable and if Scripture is God's word, then Scripture must also be divinely infallible. Beegle, in keeping with others, questions this "philosophical assumption."[17]

But such language simply clouds the issue; it is pejorative, not descriptive, and uses an honorable adjective in a dishonorable and emotive sense. It does not honestly admit what, for Christians who claim Scripture as God's Word in any sense, would be the alternative position:

God is infallible.

What God says is infallible.

But what God says through men is not and cannot be infallible.

The assumption here is that human fallibility stubbornly resists the infallible purpose of God. But the biblical witness contains no hint of this position. And with good reason, for this alternative syllogism is tanta-

15. Rudolf Bultmann, *The Theology of the New Testament*, 2 vols. (London: SCM, 1952), 1:16.
16. Dewey Beegle, *Scripture, Tradition, and Infallibility* (Ann Arbor: Pryor Pettengell, 1979), p. 198.
17. Ibid., p. 85.

mount to the denial of Scripture's own statements. Applied universally, this logic would repudiate God's sovereign, teleological rule of a fallen universe for his own perfect purpose (cf. Eph. 1:11b).

Having noted this point, however, our doctrine of Scripture's infallibility requires fine tuning. It will immediately be said that already the doctrine is exposed to "the death of a thousand qualifications." But this is to misunderstand. *Infallibility* is not a biblical term. It belongs to the realm of theology as a science and as such requires careful delineation and definition. In other sciences such definition or qualification is not a weakness but a matter of accuracy. We do not abandon any other Christian doctrine because it requires precision in its statement and even then retains elements of mystery. One needs to think only of the doctrines of providence or of the two natures of Christ, or the doctrine of the Trinity, to realize how important is the further elucidation, description, and qualification of principal statements. In the same way we need to describe and elucidate our definition of Scripture.

How can we further define Scripture's infallibility? What do we mean when we deduce that, as God's Word, it is free from error? Here, again, only a skeletal answer can be given. Three things should be noted. First, the nature of biblical infallibility cannot be described apart from the actual material of Scripture. As the canon of God's people's lives (not understood in any other category), it lays claim to infallibility. It would therefore be a mistake (made often enough in the past) to discuss whether the Hebrew and Greek of Scripture come to us as examples of perfect grammar. Such a topic is misleading, for grammar is a matter of custom and development, not (normally) a matter of truth and error. In any event, Scripture's infallibility could not be compromised by grammatical infelicities, any more than its meaning is altered by them. The presence of human idiosyncrasy (or eccentricity, for that matter) is not an argument against the infallibility of the product. Thus the young B. B. Warfield wrote:

> No one claims that inspiration secured the use of good Greek in Attic severity of taste, free from the exaggerations and looseness of current speech, but only that it secured the accurate expression of truth, even (if you will) through the medium of the worst Greek a fisherman of Galilee could write and the most startling figures of speech a peasant could invent.[18]

Second, the Bible, which claims such infallibility, speaks phenomenologically, according to the appearance of things, employing accepted customs of speech. In Scripture "the sun rises." That no more commits us to a three-decker view of the universe than does our saying, in the late twen-

18. A. A. Hodge and B. B. Warfield, *Inspiration* (Philadelphia: Presbyterian Board of Publication, 1881), p. 43.

tieth century, "the sun rises." The person who regards such language as erroneous is insensitive to the complexity of human language, the spheres in which it is used, and to the subtle nuances of human communication.

For some writers, these elements are what Abraham Kuyper called "innocent inaccuracies."[19] It is not difficult to understand what Kuyper is saying. Indeed, one may appreciate his desire to allow God's Word to stand just as it comes to us. But there is something infelicitous about such a statement in connection with God's Word. It brings Scripture to the wrong bar of judgment altogether. Scripture comes to us in the *koine*, the language of the world of the people. Its statements are to be assessed in that universe of discourse alone.

Third, in the very nature of the case, the Christian cannot prove the infallibility of Scripture. Many biblical statements are not amenable to proof of this kind, or if they were, they are no longer. We cannot prove that "Christ died for our sins according to the Scriptures" (1 Cor. 15:3) is an infallible statement. We do affirm that such a statement is coherent with itself, the rest of Scripture, and the universe in which we live. We subscribe to biblical infallibility not on the grounds of our ability to prove it but because of the persuasiveness of its testimony to be God's own Word.

This position is frequently accused of involving circular reasoning. So be it. We cannot abandon the ultimate authority for our faith when it comes to discussing the nature of that ultimate authority. It should, however, be noted that the argument here is not "Scripture is infallible because it claims to be infallible" (as, for example, Barr suggests).[20] Rather, Scripture testifies to its character as the infallible Word of God. The Christian is persuaded of that testimony (through the ministry of the Spirit); he or she recognizes it to be self-consistent and on that basis confesses it to be true. We know that the Word of God could be nothing less.

Belief in the infallibility of Scripture does not imply that we know how to resolve every prima-facie inconsistency in Scripture. Indeed, we are not under obligation to do this in order to believe in biblical inerrancy, although we will seek to do so for exegetical and apologetic reasons. We believe in the perfect love, righteousness, and sovereignty of God, although we cannot understand their operation in connection with every individual circumstance of life. So too our faith in the inerrancy of Scripture rests on the Bible's own testimony, and in view of the self-consistency of that testimony, we anticipate further resolutions to those passages which as yet we do not fully understand.

We ought not to be driven by the existence of some "problem passages"

19. Abraham Kuyper, *Principles of Sacred Theology* (Grand Rapids: Eerdmans, 1954), p. 457.
20. Barr, *Fundamentalism*, pp. 72–73.

into abandoning inerrancy, on the grounds that we are unable to prove it in every conceivable instance. It is important to recognize that "there are difficulties in Scripture which are at present insoluble and will probably remain so till the last day."[21] Failure to recognize this limitation has made some grasp at any solution to difficulties, however implausible, or has led others to abandon inerrancy altogether. Nor is it necessary, when a variety of resolutions is open to us, to commit ourselves dogmatically to any of them. One may be correct, or none may be correct. Our conviction of inerrancy does not depend on our possession of final answers to all questions.

Does this mean that the inerrantist ignores the "difficulties" for inerrancy present in Scripture and lives ostrichlike, with head in the sand? On the contrary, in our examination of the text and teaching of the Bible, we find no solid reason to yield up our conviction of Scripture's inerrancy any more than we find reason to yield up our conviction about God's perfect love for us because we cannot harmonize all the ways of the Lord in our own lives.

### Necessity

Why, then, is Scripture so necessary? It makes us wise for salvation through faith in Christ Jesus (2 Tim. 3:15). But there is a sense in which the existence of Scripture was not, in terms of strict logic, necessary for salvation. It is Christ and his work, not the Bible and its inspiration, that saves—according to Scripture's testimony.

Here, we return, therefore, to the practical function of Scripture. Consistently the church has recognized that the Bible is a gift of grace to humankind, who otherwise would forget, distort, and even destroy God's revelation of himself in space and history. The purpose of Scripture is to preserve for all people, in all places, the revelatory Word God has spoken. Its function is, in the fullest sense, evangelistic.

The perspicuity of Scripture is best understood within this framework. Scripture must be studied with the best tools at our disposal. Many of these are academic in nature (history, geography, foreign languages, etc.), although not necessarily in use. But this requirement should not lead us to conclude that a high level of preunderstanding is essential for grasping clearly the message of Scripture. Since Scripture was written for the common people, we should anticipate that its message about the things necessary for salvation is not difficult to understand (in terms of levels of education required): "The unlearned, in a due use of the ordinary means, may attain unto a sufficient understanding of them."[22]

---

21. A. Lecerf, *An Introduction to Reformed Dogmatics,* trans. A. Schlemmer (London: Lutterworth, 1949), p. 314.

22. *Westminster Confession of Faith,* chap. 1, sec. 7.

This principle of the perspicuity of Scripture is underlined by Jesus and the apostles. It is a source of disappointment to Jesus that the Scripture is misunderstood so seriously (see, e.g., Luke 24:25—"how foolish you are . . ."!). Scripture's message is clear enough; people's minds are darkened not by below average intelligence but by sin. The function of the testimony of the Holy Spirit is not to introduce perspicuity to Scripture but to bring illumination to our darkened understanding of it. In this process the Lord of the Scriptures rejoices, knowing that God has hidden the mystery of the kingdom from the wise and understanding and revealed it to babes (Matt. 11:25–27).

If we affirm the inspiration, authority, infallibility, and necessity of Scripture, we are by no means suggesting that to hold "Scripture's view of itself" is to have all the answers. We have already indicated that these are the first words, not the last word, about Scripture. We have many questions, even puzzles and unreconciled difficulties remaining, which indicate that the continued disciplined exegesis of Scripture is necessary. We therefore have the greatest of motives to learn how to handle God's Word correctly (2 Tim. 2:15). Such study is based on the recognition of what Scripture is: God's mouth, every word from which sustains us in daily life.

Those who study Scripture in such a humble spirit will find that there is yet more truth to break forth from God's Holy Word. This attitude has never been better expressed than in the words of John Murray:

> There is no doctrine of our Christian faith that does not confront us with unresolved difficulties here in this world, and the difficulties become all the greater just as we get nearer to the center. It is in connection with the most transcendent mysteries of our faith that the difficulties multiply. The person who thinks he has resolved all the mysteries surrounding our established faith in the Trinity has probably no faith in the Triune God. The person who encounters no unresolved mystery in the incarnation of the Son of God and in his death on Calvary's tree has not yet learned the meaning of 1 Timothy 3:16. Yet these unanswered questions are not incompatible with unshaken faith in the Triune God and in Jesus Christ the incarnate Son. The questions are often perplexing. But they are more often the questions of adoring wonder rather than the questions of painful perplexity.
>
> So there should be no surprise if faith in God's inerrant Word should be quite consonant with unresolved questions and difficulties with regard to the content of this faith.[23]

In such knowledge we rest on the testimony of God's Word to itself.

23. Murray, "Attestation of Scripture," pp. 7–8.

# 4

## Old Princeton, Westminster, and Inerrancy

### Moisés Silva

*A sounder attitude to most problems of harmonization . . .*
*is marked by the exercise of greater care in determining*
*what the Gospels as a whole and in detail actually say as*
*well as greater restraint in arriving at conclusions where*
*the available evidence does not justify ready answers. In*
*particular, there is the possibility of genuine progress if one*
*does not maintain that the trustworthiness of the Gospels*
*allows the evangelists no liberty of composition whatsoever,*
*and does not insist that in reporting the words of Jesus, for*
*example, they must have been characterized by a kind of*
*notarial exactitude or what Professor John Murray has*
*called "pedantic precision."*

—Ned B. Stonehouse, 1963

Warm devotion to the Reformed faith. Noble aggressiveness in the defense of historical orthodoxy. Emphasis on the exegesis of the original languages of Scripture. Commitment to the blending of piety and intel-

This chapter is a revised version of a lecture delivered by the author upon his inauguration as professor of New Testament at Westminster Theological Seminary, 19 February 1985, and published in *WTJ* 50 (1988): 65–80.

lect. Willingness to engage opposing viewpoints with scholarly courtesy and integrity. These and other qualities combined to give Princeton Theological Seminary, from its inception through the 1920s, a powerful distinctiveness in the ecclesiastical and academic worlds. It was this distinctiveness that the founders of Westminster Theological Seminary sought to preserve when the new institution was established in 1929.

We would betray the genius of this tradition if we were to identify any one issue as all-important or determinative. And yet, given the historical contexts that brought Princeton into new prominence in the late nineteenth century and that brought Westminster into existence over half a century ago, one must fully acknowledge the unique role played by the doctrine of inerrancy as that doctrine has been understood by its best exponents, notably B. B. Warfield. It may be an exaggeration, but only a mild one, to say that the infallibility of Scripture, with its implications, has provided Westminster's raison d'être. Indeed, as far as the present faculty is concerned, we would sooner pack up our books than abandon our conviction that the Scriptures are truly God's very breath.

I would like to stress in this chapter, however, the definition of inerrancy implied by the words in the previous paragraph: *as that doctrine has been understood by its best exponents.* The contemporary debate regarding inerrancy appears hopelessly vitiated by the failure—in both conservative and nonconservative camps—to mark how carefully nuanced were Warfield's formulations. The heat generated by today's controversies has not always been accompanied by the expected light, and for every truly helpful statement one will easily encounter ten that blur the issues. The unfortunate result is that large numbers of writers and students assume, quite incorrectly, that their ideas about inerrancy correspond with the classic conception.

One effective way to demonstrate this point would be to conduct a survey that asked people to identify selected quotations. Consider the following statement on biblical inspiration:

> It is not merely in the matter of verbal expression or literary composition that the personal idosyncracies of each author are freely manifested . . . , but the very substance of what they write is evidently for the most part the product of their own mental and spiritual activities. . . . [Each author of Scripture] gave evidence of his own special limitations of knowledge and mental power, and of his personal defects as well as of his powers.

Here is another one:

> [The Scriptures] are written in human languages, whose words, inflections, constructions and idioms bear everywhere indelible traces of error. The record itself furnishes evidence that the writers were in large measure

dependent for their knowledge upon sources and methods in themselves fallible, and that their personal knowledge and judgments were in many matters hesitating and defective, or even wrong.

Where do these remarks come from? A nineteenth-century liberal like Briggs? A radical theologian like Bultmann? Those words, it turns out, come from what is widely regarded as the classic formulation of biblical inerrancy by the two great Princeton theologians A. A. Hodge and B. B. Warfield.[1] Most evangelicals, I am sure, would be quite surprised to hear this. Some of them might even decide that Warfield did not really believe the Bible after all. The situation is even worse among nonevangelical writers, very few of whom would be able to understand that the quotations above are indeed consistent with a belief in inerrancy.

This widespread ignorance works to the detriment of the doctrine. For example, when modern conservative scholars seek to nuance the discussion, they are more often than not accused of putting the doctrine to death through a thousand qualifications. Indeed, these scholars are perceived as backing away from their commitment to inerrancy and redefining its boundaries more or less after the fact—as though they were making up the rules as they go along. Sadly, that assessment is accurate enough in certain cases, and one can fully understand (and even share) the concern expressed in some quarters.

The passages quoted above, however, should make it plain that, in its original form, the Princetonian doctrine was carefully qualified. Contemporary scholars who do the same, therefore, are not necessarily undermining inerrancy but possibly preserving it. The common conception of Warfield is that he proposed a "deductive" approach to inspiration which did not take into account the phenomena of Scripture. Such an approach would in any case have been unlikely when one considers Warfield's expertise in the fine points of textual criticism and exegesis,[2] and our two quotations leave no doubt that the common view is a grotesque misconception. Similarly, it makes little sense to accuse modern evangelical scholars of (1) being insensitive to the text if they happen to believe in inerrancy, or (2) being untrue to inerrancy if they take fully into account the human qualities of Scripture.

1. A. A. Hodge and B. B. Warfield, *Inspiration* (1881; reprint, Grand Rapids: Baker, 1979), pp. 12–13, 28. Interestingly, the second quotation was attacked at the time of publication as reflecting a lowered view of inspiration. See Warfield's responses, included as appendixes 1 and 2 in *Inspiration*, pp. 73–82.

2. Warfield became a member of the Society of Biblical Literature and Exegesis as early as 1882 and contributed a number of technical articles to *Journal of Biblical Literature* and other periodicals. One interesting example is "Notes on the *Didache*," *Journal of Biblical Literature* (no vol., June 1886): 86–98. For other material, see John E. Meeter and Roger Nicole, *A Bibliography of Benjamin Breckinridge Warfield, 1851–1921* (N.p.: Presbyterian and Reformed, 1974).

Before proceeding any further, however, it is crucial to point out that the two passages quoted above cannot be taken, by themselves, as an adequate representation of the Hodge/Warfield view. The whole thesis of their famous work is that the Bible, whose primary author is God, teaches no errors. That thesis is the broad context necessary to understand their qualifications. One can easily imagine how some contemporaries who wish to preserve their identity as evangelicals while abandoning the doctrine of inerrancy might gleefully inscribe those two quotations on their personal banners and announce to the world their solidarity with Warfield.

But that is hardly fair to the Old Princeton theology. Indeed, it would constitute one more example of the kind of shoddy use of sources that got us into our present confusion to begin with. Writers (liberals and conservatives) who like to quote Warfield's strongest expressions of inerrancy without paying attention to the nuances that accompany them are no worse than individuals who look for the qualifications alone and ignore the very thesis that is being qualified.

Without seeking to exegete those two quotations, we should at least identify the basic qualification that the authors have in view, namely, the need to distinguish between official teaching and personal opinion. Elsewhere Warfield stated that such a distinction

> seems, in general, a reasonable one. No one is likely to assert infallibility for the apostles in aught else than in their official teaching. And whatever they may be shown to have held apart from their official teaching, may readily be looked upon with only that respect which we certainly must accord to the opinions of men of such exceptional intellectual and spiritual insight....
>
> ... A presumption may be held to lie also that [Paul] shared the ordinary opinions of his day in certain matters laying outside the scope of his teachings, as, for example, with reference to the form of the earth, or its relation to the sun; and it is not inconceivable that the form of his language, when incidentally adverting to such matters, might occasionally play into the hands of such a presumption.[3]

Warfield did not mean, of course, that every chapter of the Bible may well contain erroneous personal opinions and that we are left to our subjective judgment regarding the authoritative character of each proposition. Such an interpretation of Warfield's words would be a complete

---

3. B. B. Warfield, *The Inspiration and Authority of the Bible* (Philadelphia: Presbyterian and Reformed, 1948), pp. 196–97. The passage comes from an article entitled "The Real Problem of Inspiration," originally published in *Presbyterian and Reformed Review* 4 (1893): 177–221.

travesty. What he surely had in view was the occasional occurrence of certain forms of expression, such as conventional phrases, that *reflect* commonly held views regarding history, nature, and so forth.

Inspiration does not convey omniscience, and since the personal limitations of any one biblical writer are not all miraculously suspended by virtue of his being inspired, we may expect to see here and there some evidences that he was indeed a limited human being. The marvel of inspiration resides precisely in the fact that the divine origin of Scripture ensures the preservation of both the divine truth being communicated and the unique personality of each writer. The Holy Spirit, in other words, prevents the authors from teaching falsehood or error, without overriding their personal traits.

Warfield's distinction between the "official teaching" of Paul and, on the other hand, those "matters lying outside the scope of his teachings" is exceedingly important for our concerns. In effect, it forces us to consider the thorny issue of authorial purpose or intention.[4] And this issue in turn reminds us of the crucial role that exegesis must play in our discussion. Not everything found in the Scriptures is actually affirmed or taught by the biblical authors (e.g., "There is no God" [Ps. 14:1]). The text must therefore be studied so that we can determine what it teaches. Such is the task in view when we say that we must identify the author's intent. To put it simply, we must figure out what the writer wishes to communicate. Unfortunately, the words *intention* and *purpose* have become veritable shibboleths in the contemporary debate. Some writers, in fact, argue that the appeal to intention undermines biblical authority.[5]

Their concern is understandable, since these terms are a little vague. A theologian, for instance, may have in mind the broad purpose of Scripture and argue that, while the Bible could be full of errors, yet it is infalli-

---

4. One issue that cannot detain us here, however, is the distinction among such factors as divine meaning, author's meaning, audience meaning, and so on. I must assume that the readers of this chapter recognize the primary importance of ascertaining the original historical meaning of a document (whatever credence they may or may not give to the possibility of additional meanings intended by God or read into the text by later readers).

5. Nelson Kloosterman, for example, speaks pejoratively of those who "hold to a Bible whose authority is limited by the human author's intentions, intentions which can presumably be exposed and defended by a certain kind of theological scholarship" ("Why You Need Mid-America Theological Seminary," *Outlook* 31, no. 12 [December 1981]: 3). Similarly, Harold Lindsell, in *The Battle for the Bible* (Grand Rapids: Zondervan, 1976), makes the same point repeatedly. Even Lindsell, of course, finds it necessary to appeal to the concept of intention, as in his discussion of the parable of the mustard seed: "The *American Commentary* says of this passage that it was popular language, and it was the intention of the speaker to communicate the fact that the mustard seed was 'the smallest that his hearers were accustomed to sow.' And indeed this may well be the case. In that event there was no error" (p. 169).

ble in its explicit teachings about salvation. Again, another writer may suggest that the intention of the biblical author is a psychological element behind the text and to be distinguished from the text—a position reminiscent of the old argument that the thoughts, not the words, of Scripture are inspired and infallible. These and comparable formulations are indeed destructive of biblical authority and must be rejected.[6]

It would be a grave mistake, however, if we allowed these abuses to force us into the indefensible position of denying the crucial exegetical role played by an author's intention, for this is the fundamental element of the principle of *sensus literalis*. Grammatical-historical exegesis is simply the attempt to figure out what the biblical writer, under divine guidance, was saying. The basic question is, then, What did the author mean? The only evidence we have to answer that question is the text itself. In other words, we dare not speak about the Bible's infallibility in such a way that it legitimizes random and arbitrary interpretations of the text.

Our best theologians made it clear all along that inerrancy was being claimed for the Bible on the assumption that the Bible would be interpreted responsibly, and such a proper interpretation consists in determining what the original author meant, what he intended. As Hodge and Warfield stated it, the Bible gives us "a correct statement of facts or principles intended to be affirmed. . . . Every statement accurately corresponds to truth just as far forth as affirmed."[7]

It may be useful to illustrate our problem by referring to 1 Corinthians 10:8, where Paul mentions 23,000 Israelites who died because of their immorality, in apparent conflict with Numbers 25:9, where the figure given is 24,000. Notice the following attempt to solve the problem: "It is not unheard of, *when there is no intention* of making an exact count of individuals, to give an approximate number. . . . Moses gives the upper limits, Paul the lower." Another writer makes the same point.

6. Norman L. Geisler has rightly attempted to discredit these approaches in "The Relation of Purpose and Meaning in Interpreting Scripture," *Grace Theological Journal* 5 (1984): 229–45. Unfortunately, Geisler draws too sharp a distinction between meaning and purpose. Determining the purpose of a text is one of the elements necessary to identify the context of the document. On p. 231, Geisler attacks interpreters of Genesis 1–2 who believe that those chapters intend merely to draw people to worship God. Geisler seems unaware that his own understanding of those chapters (with which I concur) also assumes a certain purpose, namely, the intent to state certain historical facts. Cf. these comments by Hodge and Warfield: "No objection [to inspiration] is valid . . . which overlooks the prime question: What was the professed or implied purpose of the writer in making this statement? . . . Exegesis must be historical as well as grammatical, and must always seek the meaning *intended*, not any meaning that can be tortured out of a passage" (*Inspiration*, pp. 42–43).

7. Hodge and Warfield, *Inspiration*, pp. 28–29. It is very important to note that Warfield emphasized this particular qualification when he responded to criticisms of the article (see pp. 79–80).

Neither of the writers *intended to state* the exact number, this being of no consequence to their object. . . . It was not at all necessary, in order to maintain their character as men of veracity, that they should, when writing *for such a purpose,* mention the exact number. The particularity and length of the [exact] expression would have been inconvenient, and might have made a less desirable impression of the evil of sin, and the justice of God, than expressing it more briefly in a round number; as we often say, with a view merely to make a strong impression, that in such a battle ten thousand, or fifty thousand, or half a million were slain, no one supposing that we meant to state the number with arithmetical exactness, as *our object does not require this.* And who can doubt, that the divine Spirit might lead the sacred penman to make use of this principle of rhetoric, and to speak of those who were slain, according to the common practice in such a case, in round numbers?

Here is another author that takes a similar approach:

Are there errors in the Bible? Certainly not, so long as we are talking in terms *of the purpose of its authors* and the acceptable standards of precision of that day. . . . *For the purpose* that Paul had in mind [the variation] made no difference. His concern was to warn against immorality, not to give a flawless performance in statistics.

All three of these writers seem concerned to deny that the apostle is guilty of an error, yet none of them attempts some artificial harmonization (e.g., the view that Paul is speaking about those who fell "in one day," while Numbers includes the additional one thousand who died later). Moreover, all three of them assume that inerrancy does not necessarily demand mathematical exactness. Finally, all of them appeal to Paul's intention or purpose to use a round number. I am unable to see any substantive difference among these three explanations.

The three authors quoted here are John Calvin, the nineteenth-century American theologian Leonard Wood (one of the most forceful defenders of biblical inerrancy prior to B. B. Warfield), and our contemporary, Robert H. Mounce.[8] I bring these three quotations together in light of Harold Lindsell's quoting the third of those statements as evidence that Mounce does not believe in inerrancy. Yet a few pages

8. John Calvin, *The First Epistle of Paul the Apostle to the Corinthians* (Grand Rapids: Eerdmans, 1961), pp. 208–9; Leonard Wood, *The Works of Leonard Wood, D.D.,* 5 vols. (Boston: Congregational Board of Publications, 1854), 1:173; R. H. Mounce, "Clues to Understanding Biblical Accuracy," *Eternity* 17, no. 6 (June 1966): 18. (The italics in all quotations are mine, except for the phrase *for such a purpose* in the second quotation.) In connection with Wood, note the very helpful discussion of pre-Warfield inerrantists by Randall H. Balmer, "The Princetonians and Scripture: A Reconsideration," *Westminster Theological Journal* 44 (1982): 352–65.

later Lindsell presents the quotation from Calvin as giving an acceptable treatment of the problem![9] It may be that the tone of Mounce's brief
article (it sounds as though the author is apologizing for the evangelical
view) led Lindsell to believe that Mounce had indeed rejected the doctrine of inerrancy. It is impossible, however, to prove that point from the
quotation above (or, for that matter, from the other statements by
Mounce to which Lindsell refers).

In any case, we can see clearly how easy it is to misconstrue qualifying
statements, even when the qualification in view is very much a part of
the evangelical tradition. In short, the appeal to the author's intent, if
properly understood, is an integral element in the classical affirmations
of biblical inerrancy. We simply cannot claim to know what the Scripture
infallibly teaches unless we have done our exegetical homework.

Our discussion so far has made it apparent that one can hardly speak
of inerrancy without getting involved in hermeneutics. And yet, an exceedingly important caveat is necessary here, for while the two concepts
are closely related or even inseparable, they are also distinct. For inerrancy to function properly in our use of Scripture, an adequate hermeneutics is a prerequisite. But that is a far cry from suggesting that the
doctrine of inerrancy automatically provides us with the correct hermeneutics, except in the rather general sense that it precludes any interpretation that suggests that God lies or errs.

A few examples will clarify the issue. As recently as two decades ago it
was not unusual to come across devout Christians who were persuaded
that, when interpreting prophecy, a premillennialist eschatology was
the only approach consistent with the doctrine of infallibility. For many
of these brethren—of whom a few remain, I am sure—a so-called literal
interpretation of prophetic passages was taken as evidence, maybe even
as the most important piece of evidence, that an individual believed the
Bible; and it was taken for granted that amillennialists, therefore, were
"liberals." But such an equation is baseless, since the doctrine of inerrancy does not determine that any one prophecy (or set of prophecies) must be interpreted "literally." That can only be determined by an
exegesis of the passage(s) in question.

Let us consider a more disturbing example: the historicity of Genesis
1–3. All inerrantists, as far as I know, believe in the factual character of
that material. This state of affairs creates a certain presumption that
inerrancy by itself demands such an interpretation. But the presumption
is false; indeed, it is an equivocation. The doctrine of biblical infallibility
no more requires that certain narratives be interpreted literally than it
requires that certain prophetic passages be interpreted literally. That

9. Lindsell, *Battle for the Bible*, p. 168.

decision must be arrived at by textual evidence and exegetical argument.

Now I happen to believe that the essential historicity of Genesis 1–3 is a fundamental article of Christian orthodoxy. It would surely require hermeneutical prestidigitation to argue that the original writer intended those chapters as any less historical than the later patriarchal narratives (and could the original audience have discovered any such distinction between the early and the later chapters of the book?). For that reason and others, such as Paul's argumentation in Romans 5 and 1 Corinthians 15, I would want to argue very strongly that the proper interpretation of the Genesis material is one that does justice to its historical claim.

And yet I would want to argue just as strongly that such an interpretation is independent of my commitment to inerrancy. These are two distinct questions. Of course, once we have established exegetically that the first three chapters of Genesis teach historical facts, then our belief in infallibility requires us to accept those chapters as factual. But infallibility, apart from exegesis, does not by itself determine historicity. Otherwise we would be obligated to accept as historical Nathan's story in 2 Samuel 12:1–4 or even the parable of the trees in Judges 9:7–15.

I have deliberately chosen my two examples from polar opposites. Relatively few evangelicals would argue that inerrancy entails premillennialism, but many seem ready to argue that it does require a historical interpretation of Genesis 1–3. Between these two extremes are countless interpretations that have traditionally been held by conservatives and that are viewed as necessary consequences of accepting biblical infallibility. It may therefore prove worthwhile pointing out that the Princeton/Westminster tradition, though it has stood forcefully and unequivocally for biblical inerrancy, has never degenerated into the practice of assuming that this doctrine requires the adoption of particular interpretations.

My first example comes from the area of the relationship between the Bible and science. Students familiar with Warfield's writings are well aware of his positive attitude toward modern scientific theories regarding origins. Though it is a little difficult to determine specifically Warfield's position, it appears that his view came relatively close to what we call theistic evolution (without compromising, to be sure, the direct creation of humankind).[10]

J. Gresham Machen, in sharp contrast to the fundamentalism of his

10. See Mark A. Noll, *The Princeton Theology, 1812–1921: Scripture, Science, and Theological Method from Archibald Alexander to Benjamin Breckinridge Warfield* (Grand Rapids: Baker, 1983), pp. 289, 293–94.

day, refused to become involved in the evolution controversy.[11] More recently, Meredith G. Kline proposed an interpretation of Genesis 1 that parted company with traditional views. Kline's colleague on the Westminster faculty, E. J. Young, took issue with that interpretation, but at no point in his argument did he accuse Kline of abandoning the doctrine of infallibility. Nor did Young simply assume that such a doctrine entailed the traditional view of Genesis; rather, he sought to refute Kline through careful exegetical argumentation.[12]

A second example has to do with higher criticism. This is one area, it must be admitted, where a belief in inerrancy appears to have a direct bearing on interpretation. If the author of a New Testament epistle, for example, claims to be the apostle Paul, we would be questioning the moral integrity of the author if we were to argue that the letter was not in fact written by Paul. Yet this set of questions too has to be decided on exegetical grounds, not on the assumption that inerrancy entails a traditional view of authorship, date, and so on.

It is no secret that E. J. Young, who was uncompromisingly conservative on virtually every higher-critical issue, came to the conclusion that the Book of Ecclesiastes was not composed by Solomon, even though that appears to be the claim of the book itself.[13] Young was among the most conservative in the long line of biblical scholars in Old Princeton and Westminster. It is doubly significant, therefore, that he did not apparently see a necessary connection between a belief in inerrancy and the traditional view of Solomonic authorship for Ecclesiastes.

A third and particularly instructive example is the way different writers approach the difficult problem of Gospel harmonization. Consider the story of the rich young ruler. According to Mark 10:17–18 and Luke 18:18–19, this ruler addressed Jesus as "Good teacher" and asked what he could do to inherit eternal life; Jesus replied, "Why do you call me good?" In Matthew 19:16–17, however, the word *good* is transferred to the man's actual question ("Teacher, what good thing shall I do . . . ?"), and so Jesus' rebuke takes a different form: "Why do you ask me about what is good?" One author seeks to solve the problem by incorporating both versions into one account:

In all probability, the full question was, 'Good teacher, what good thing shall I do that I may possess eternal life?' To this the complete answer of the

11. See Ned. B. Stonehouse, *J. Gresham Machen: A Biographical Memoir* (Grand Rapids: Eerdmans, 1954), pp. 401–2.

12. E. J. Young, *Studies in Genesis One* (Philadelphia: Presbyterian and Reformed, 1964), pp. 58–64.

13. E. J. Young, *An Introduction to the Old Testament* (Grand Rapids: Eerdmans, 1949), p. 340. The revised 1964 edition omits the strongest paragraph, but it is clear that Young's position had not changed, in spite of the fact that not a few feathers had been ruffled by it.

Lord may have been, 'Why callest thou Me good and why askest thou Me concerning that which is good?' . . . No one of the evangelists, however, has seen fit to give the complete question or the complete answer.

The following quotation reflects quite a different approach:

One must allow for the possibility that Matthew in his formulation of 19:16, 17 has *not only been selective* as regards subject matter but also that he used some freedom in the precise language which he employed. The singular use of the adjective "good" might then be a particularly clear example of his use of that freedom. . . . One tendency [in the history of the harmonization of the Gospels], that is both conservative and simple, has been to join divergent features and to seek to weave them together into a harmonious whole. Where, however, the divergent elements are exceedingly difficult to combine in that way, it is insisted that the narratives must be regarded as reporting different events or different sayings. . . . [T]here is, in my judgment, a sounder attitude to most problems of harmonization than that which was characterized above as conservative and simple.

Neither of these writers is against harmonization in principle, but they differ rather substantively in what they consider necessary to defend the integrity of the narrative. One could certainly argue that the second writer is directly reacting against the viewpoint espoused by the first. Remarkably, these two passages were written by contemporaries on the Westminster faculty. The first one comes from E. J. Young's famous work on inerrancy, published in the late 1950s, while the second statement was written just a few years later by Ned B. Stonehouse.[14] One is intrigued by the question whether Stonehouse remembered Young's discussion; if so, was he deliberately distancing himself from that approach? In any case, the differences are most instructive.

What shall we infer from these examples?[15] Should evangelical

14. E. J. Young, *Thy Word Is Truth: Some Thoughts on the Biblical Doctrine of Inspiration* (Grand Rapids: Eerdmans, 1957), p. 131; Ned. B. Stonehouse, *Origins of the Synoptic Gospels: Some Basic Questions* (Grand Rapids: Eerdmans, 1963), pp. 108–9, emphasis added. Warfield's own approach, which seems close to Young's, may be found in *The Person and Work of Christ* (Philadelphia: Presbyterian and Reformed, 1950), p. 160: "It lies in the nature of the case that the two accounts of a conversation which agree as to the substance of what was said, but differ slightly in the details reported, are reporting different fragments of the conversation, selected according to the judgment of each writer as the best vehicles of its substance."

15. Other intriguing examples of diversity could be mentioned. Particularly important (because of its relation to the field of ethics) is the case of Paul Woolley, professor of church history, who took a rather liberal position on a wide variety of social and political issues. On many questions of this sort, Woolley stood alone or nearly alone within the Westminster faculty, but to the best of my knowledge his devotion and commitment to biblical authority was never called into question.

scholars be isolated from criticism if they appear to be bucking historic Christian tenets without clear biblical support? So far from it, that the Princeton/Westminster tradition has consistently deepened the evangelical conception of biblical authority within the framework of Reformed orthodoxy. No doubt, some may wish to appeal to these evidences of flexibility and argue that, therefore, "anything goes," that the increasingly positive attitude toward higher criticism by a number of contemporary evangelical scholars is quite consistent with the doctrine of inerrancy. Such a move would hardly be honest, however, especially when one considers that the Princetonian formulations of inerrancy were meant precisely to counteract the growing popularity of nineteenth-century critical theories. There are, nevertheless, some important lessons we can learn from the history we have briefly surveyed.

The hermeneutical flexibility that has characterized our tradition would probably come as a surprise to many observers who view Westminster as excessively rigid. Ironically, our confessional documents, the Westminster Confession and Catechisms, are far more extensive and detailed than those found in most evangelical institutions. Our theological parameters are indeed very clearly defined, and yet those parameters themselves have made possible a diversity of viewpoints that would not have been tolerated in some other institutions.

It can even be argued, I think, that there is a direct connection between such a diversity and the fact that the Princeton/Westminster tradition has provided consistent leadership to the evangelical world in the area of biblical authority. Why is this so? The doctrine of infallibility assures us that we can have total confidence in God's revelation to us. It does not mean, however, that we may have total confidence in our particular interpretations of the Bible.

For many believers, unfortunately, assurance that the Bible is truth appears to be inseparable from assurance about traditional interpretive positions, so that if we question the latter we seem to be doubting the former. George E. Ladd is absolutely right when he states:

> "Thus saith the Lord" means that God has spoken His sure, infallible Word. A corollary of this in the minds of many Christians is that we must have absolute, infallible answers to every question raised in the historical study of the Bible. . . .
> This conclusion, as logical and persuasive as it may seem, does not square with the facts of God's Word; . . . the authority of the Word of God is not dependent upon infallible certainty in all matters of history and criticism.[16]

16. George E. Ladd, *The New Testament and Criticism* (Grand Rapids: Eerdmans, 1967), pp. 16–17.

I do not know to what extent Ladd agrees or disagrees with Warfield's position, but this quotation is perfectly consistent with it; more to the point, Ladd's qualification belongs to the very essence of the classical doctrine of inerrancy. Yet Lindsell quotes those words as evidence that Ladd has abandoned biblical infallibility.[17]

Uncertainty is not a pleasant thing, and our instinct to avoid it can lead us into trouble. Concerned not to leave the door open to excesses, we are tempted to raise artificial barriers. But this medicine can be worse than the disease. I mention these things because there is a strong current of opinion in evangelical circles that says we need to tie inerrancy down to certain hermeneutical boundary lines. But to speak in this way is once again to increase the conceptual confusion. It is of course true that a commitment to inerrancy entails that we will believe such interpretations are clearly demonstrable from the scriptural text, but inerrancy does not automatically settle interpretive debates, such as the mode of baptism, the doctrine of unconditional election, the practice of charismatic gifts, and so on.

Many evangelicals have awakened to the fact that belief in inerrancy does not ensure acceptance of traditional positions, and several recent writers have emphasized the wide and significant disagreements that exist within the evangelical community. Some infer, not surprisingly, that the doctrine of inerrancy is of little value for Christian living and should therefore be given up. Conservatives then tend to overreact and argue that we need to define inerrancy in such a way as to guarantee that evangelicals will agree on important issues.[18]

Nothing could be more wrong-headed. Forced hermeneutical unanimity is meaningless; worse, it would be destructive of biblical authority. To say that the doctrine of inerrancy demands acceptance of a particular interpretation is to raise human opinion to the level of divine infallibility; in such a case, the interpretation cannot be questioned and need not be defended. On the other hand, to acknowledge a measure of interpretive ambiguity, rattling though that may be, indicates our conviction that the Bible, and the Bible alone, is inerrant. To be sure, the Christian church may and must condemn hermeneutical approaches as well as specific interpretations that contradict the teaching of Scripture. But in doing so, the church cannot simply appeal to the infallibility of the Bible. The church is obligated to show persuasively that these interpretations are

---

17. Lindsell, *Battle for the Bible,* p. 114. In fairness to Lindsell, I should point out that Ladd's language (in the larger section from which the quotation is taken) does not seem designed to inspire confidence in biblical infallibility.

18. I have treated this matter more extensively in *Has the Church Misread the Bible? The History of Interpretation in the Light of Current Issues* (Grand Rapids: Zondervan, 1987).

wrong. In short, we must exegete that infallible Bible and demonstrate that we have understood its teachings.

Perhaps it is now clear why, in my opinion, the hermeneutical flexibility that has found expression on the faculties of Old Princeton and Westminster has actually contributed to (instead of undermining) the influence these institutions have exerted with regard to the doctrine of biblical authority. Precisely because we accept the reality of hermeneutical uncertainty, we work especially hard to remove that uncertainty through careful exegesis.

It is no accident that Old Princeton and Westminster have been so obnoxious in requiring students to learn Greek and Hebrew. It was not some methodological misconception that led John Murray to teach courses in systematic theology that looked more like courses in exegesis. It was no blunder that made a Warfield or a Machen or a Stonehouse pay an enormous amount of attention to the work of liberal and radical scholars. These and other "oddities" are direct consequences of a commitment not to leave any stones unturned to find out what the Bible really says. Our whole ministry is, in its own way, a response to our Lord's penetrating criticism, "You err because you do not know the Scriptures." With Warfield we devote ourselves to the task of knowing the Scriptures so that we will not err.

# 5

## What Does God Say Through Human Authors?

### Vern Sheridan Poythress

*The fact that the Old Testament is both preliminary and preparatory to the New Testament is too obvious to require proof. In referring the Corinthian Christians by way of warning and admonition to the events of the Exodus, the apostle Paul declared that these things were "ensamples" (types). That is, they prefigured things to come. This gives to much that is in the Old Testament a special significance and importance. Thus, when Hosea and Ezekiel foretell the return of Israel to "David their king," most Christians have understood these passages to refer to the Messiah. . . . Such an interpretation recognizes, in the light of the New Testament fulfillment, a deeper and far more wonderful meaning in the words of many an Old Testament passage than, taken in their Old Testament context and connection, they seem to contain.*

— Oswald T. Allis, 1945

What is the relation between God and the human authors of the Bible? Does God's meaning at every point coincide with the intention of the human author? Can we use the same procedures of interpretation as we would with a noninspired book? A recent article by Darrell Bock delineates no less than four distinct approaches among evangelicals.[1] The specific issue that Bock discusses is the question of New Testament interpretation of the Old Testament. Does the New Testament use of Old Testament texts sometimes imply that God meant more than what the human author thought of? Walter C. Kaiser, Jr., says no, while S. Lewis Johnson, James I. Packer, and Elliott Johnson say yes.[2] Bruce K. Waltke introduces still a third approach, emphasizing the canon as the final context for interpretation. A fourth approach, represented by E. Earle Ellis, Richard Longenecker, and Walter Dunnett, emphasizes the close relation between apostolic hermeneutics and Jewish hermeneutics of the first century. Thus it appears that even among evangelicals there are disagreements concerning the relationship between the divine and human meanings of a biblical text. We will concentrate on this problem of dual authorship, rather than on the question of the New Testament use of the Old Testament.

## Situations with One and with Two Authors

Let us begin with the simple situation of a single human author. When we read a letter from a friend, we read it using our previous knowledge of the friend and our previous knowledge of earlier correspondence. A postcard with only the words "Success at last" may have very different implications, depending on who sent it and under what circumstances. Correct interpretation certainly depends on our paying attention to the wording of the letter, but we also must bear in mind what we know of the author and the circumstances.

Now what may we say about a particular book of the Bible, such as Amos? God commissions Amos to prophesy. There are two authors, God and Amos. The Bible makes it very clear that what God says does not cease to be what God says just because a human intermediary is introduced (Deut. 5:22–33). After all, it is God who chose the human intermediary and who fashioned his personality (Ps. 139:13–16). Hence in interpreting the Book of Amos, we must bear in mind what we know about God as the divine author.

Conversely, what human beings say to us does not cease to be what they say when they become spokesmen of God. Hence, it would appear, we must interpret the Book of Amos also as Amos's words.

This chapter is a condensation of "Divine Meaning of Scripture," *Westminster Theological Journal* 48, no. 2 (Fall 1986): 241–79. Readers interested in a fuller exposition of my view should consult this article.

1. Darrell Bock, "Evangelicals and the Use of the Old Testament in the New," *Bibliotheca Sacra* 142 (1985): 209–23.

2. Elliott Johnson, however, wishes to express this "more" as more references ("references plenior"), not as more sense ("sensus plenior").

But now we have a complex situation. For we have just argued that interpretation of a piece of writing must consider the words in the light of what is known of the author and the situation. If the same words happen to be said by two authors, there are two separate interpretations. The interpretations may have very similar results, or they may not, depending on the differences between the two authors and the way in which those differences mesh with the wording of the text. But, in principle, there may be differences, even if only very subtle differences in nuances.

Hence it would seem to be the case that we have two separate interpretations of any particular biblical text. The first interpretation sees the words entirely in the light of the human author—his characteristics, his knowledge, his social status. The second sees the same words entirely in the light of the divine author—his characteristics, his knowledge, his status. In principle, the results of these two interpretations may differ. We cannot simply and automatically collapse the two interpretations into one. Any such move would overlook the basic principle that words have to be interpreted in the light of their author.

What does this imply? Do we conclude that the two interpretations simply exist side by side, with no necessary relation to one another? Might they even contradict one another? If so, it introduces the danger that we could attribute to God something entirely unrelated to the meaning of the human author. And then, what would keep us from arbitrarily twisting a text?

The Bible itself shows the way to a more satisfactory resolution of the difficulty. In the Bible, the human and divine authors do not simply stand side by side. Rather, each points to the other and affirms the presence and operation of the other.

First, God himself points out the importance of the human authors. For example, when God establishes Moses as the regular channel for conveying his Word to the people of Israel, he makes it clear that Moses is to be active in teaching the people (Deut. 5:31; 6:1). Similarly, the commissioning of prophets in the Old Testament often includes a mention of their own active role, not only in speaking God's Word to the people, but in actively absorbing it (Ezek. 2:8–3:3; Dan. 10; Jer. 23:18). This is still more clear in the case of Paul's writings, where his own personality is so actively involved. Now, what happens when we pay careful attention to God as the divine author? We find that we must pay attention to what he says about the role of the human authors. Sometimes he directly affirms the significance of their involvement; sometimes this affirmation is only implied. But whichever is the case, it means that God himself requires us to interpret the words of Scripture against the background of what we know about the human author. We cannot simply ignore the human author and try to concentrate only on what God is saying.

Conversely, the human authors of the Bible indicate that they intend us to interpret their words as not merely words that they speak as ordinary persons. For example, the Book of Isaiah explicitly indicates that it is a message from God, not just the personal thoughts of Isaiah (1:1; 2:1). Isaiah reinforces this point by using the phrase "thus says the Lord." What is the effect of a phrase like this one? Would the inhabitants of Jerusalem in Isaiah's time say, "Now we must interpret what our friend Isaiah is saying simply in terms of everything we know about him: his relations with his family, his opinions about agriculture and politics, and so on." Certainly not. When Isaiah says, "Thus says the Lord," it is no doubt still Isaiah who is speaking. But Isaiah himself, by using these words, has told people to create a certain distance between himself, merely viewed as a private individual, and what the Lord has commissioned him to convey. In addition, consider what happens when Isaiah makes detailed predictions about the distant future. If the hearers treat him simply as a private human being, they would say, "Well, we know Isaiah, and we know the limits of his knowledge of the future. So, because of what we know about him, it is obvious that he is simply expressing his hopes or making artistically interesting guesses." Again, such a reaction misunderstands Isaiah's claims.

We may try to focus as much as possible on Isaiah as a human author. The more carefully we do our job, the more we will realize that he is not just any human author. He is one through whom God speaks. He himself intends us to reckon with this dimension. It is not a denial of human authorship, but an affirmation of it, when we pay attention to God speaking. In particular, in the case of predictions, we pay attention to all that we know of God, God's knowledge of the future, the wisdom of his plan, and the righteousness of his intentions. This procedure is in accord with Isaiah's intention, not contrary to it. In fact, we might say that Isaiah intended that we should understand whatever God intended by Isaiah's words.[3] Hence there is a unity of meaning and a unity of application here. We do not have two diverse meanings, Isaiah's and God's, simply placed side by side with no relation to one another.

But the matter is complex. We have here a situation of personal communion between God and prophet. Each person affirms the significance of the other's presence for proper interpretation. On the one hand, God has formed the personality of the prophet, has spoken to him in the heavenly council (Jer. 23:18), and has brought him into inner sympathy with the thrust of his message. What the prophet says using his own particu-

---

3. See, e.g., Ben F. Meyer, *The Aims of Jesus* (London: SCM, 1979), p. 246: "In prophecy what the symbol intends is identical with what God, for whom the prophet speaks, intends. This may enter the prophet's own horizon only partially and imperfectly."

lar idiom fits exactly what God decided to say. On the other hand, the prophet affirms that what God is saying is true, even where the prophet cannot see all its implications.

This situation therefore leaves open the question of how far a prophet understood God's words at any particular point. The Bible affirms the prophets' inner participation in the message. In addition, extraordinary psychological experiences were sometimes involved. It would therefore be presumptuous to limit dogmatically a prophet's understanding to what is "ordinarily" possible. On the other hand, it seems to me equally presumptuous to insist that at every point there must be complete understanding on the part of the prophet. Particularly this is so for cases of visionary material (Dan. 7; 10; Zech. 1–6; Rev. 4:1–22:5) or historical records of divine speech (e.g., the Gospel records of Jesus' parables). Why should we have to say, in the face of Daniel 7:16, Zechariah 4:4–5, Revelation 7:14, and the like, that the prophets came to understand everything that there was to understand, by the time that they wrote their visions down? Is it not enough to stick with what is clear? It is clear that the prophet faithfully recorded what he saw and heard. He intended that we should understand from it whatever there is to understand when we treat it as a vision from God. Similarly, there is no need to insist that Luke understood all the ramifications of each of Jesus' parables. He may or may not have. The results for our interpretation of the parables in the Gospel of Luke will be the same.

I have spoken primarily about the role of prophets in speaking the Word of God. But, of course, prophecy is not the only form in which the Bible is written. The different genres of biblical writings—prophecy, law, history, wisdom, song—each call for different nuances in our approach. The relation between divine and human participation in the writing is not always exactly the same.[4]

For instance, consider the case of Mosaic law. The background of the meeting at Mount Sinai forms a framework for Moses' later writings and leads us to reckon more directly with the divine source of the Law. On the other hand, Moses' close communion with God (Num. 12:6–8) hints at his inner understanding of the Law.

In the case of prophecy, narrowly speaking, the prophet's pronouncement "thus says the Lord" and the predictive elements in his message frequently have the effect of highlighting the distinction between the prophet as mere human being and the prophet as channel for the Lord's

---

4. Abraham Kuyper notices some of these differences and argues for a division into the categories of lyric, chokmatic, (i.e., wisdom), prophetic, and apostolic inspiration (*Principles of Sacred Theology* [Grand Rapids: Eerdmans, 1968], pp. 520–44, the section entitled "The Forms of Inspiration").

message. The prophet himself steps into the background, as it were, in order to put all the emphasis on God's speaking. In visionary experiences this may be all the more the case, inasmuch as it is often not clear how much the prophet understands.

With the psalms and the New Testament epistles, on the other hand, the human author and his understanding come much more to the fore. Paul does not continually say, "Thus says the Lord." That is not because he has no divine message. Rather, it is (largely) because he has so thoroughly absorbed the message into his own person. He has "the mind of Christ" (1 Cor. 2:13, 16), as a man indwelt by the Spirit.[5]

Here we confront still another complexity. What is human nature, and what does it mean to analyze a biblical passage as the expression of a human author? If the human author is Paul, that means Paul filled with the Holy Spirit. We are not dealing with "bare" human nature (as if human beings ever existed outside of a relationship to God of one kind or another). We are already dealing with the divine, namely, the Holy Spirit. Paul as a human being may not be immediately, analytically self-conscious of all the implications of what he is saying. But people always know more and imply more than what they are perfectly self-conscious of. How far does this "more" extend? We are dealing with a person restored in the image of Christ, filled with the Holy Spirit, having the mind of Christ. There are incalculable depths here. We cannot calculate the limits of the Holy Spirit and the wisdom of Christ. Neither can we perform a perfect analytical separation of our knowledge from our union with Christ through the Holy Spirit.

## Christological Fulness in Interpretation

The complexities that we meet here are only a shadow of the greatest complexity of all: the speeches of the incarnate Christ. Here God is speaking, not through a mere human being distinct from God, but in his own person. The eternal Word of God, the Second Person of the Trinity, speaks. Hence we must interpret what he says in the light of all that we know of God the author. At the same time, a man speaks—Jesus of Nazareth. With respect to his human nature, he has limited knowledge (note Luke 2:52). Hence we must interpret what he says in the light of all that we know of Jesus of Nazareth in his humanity.

This is a permanent mystery. Yet we know that we do not have two

5. See Peter R. Jones, "The Apostle Paul: A Second Moses According to II Corinthians 2:14–4:7" (Ph.D. diss., Princeton University, 1974); idem, "The Apostle Paul: Second Moses to the New Covenant Community, a Study in Pauline Apostolic Authority," in *God's Inerrant Word*, ed. John Warwick Montgomery (Minneapolis: Bethany Fellowship, 1974), pp. 219–44.

antithetical interpretations, one for the human nature speaking and one for the divine nature speaking. We know that there is a unity, based on the unity of the one person of Christ. However, it is possible, with respect to his human nature, that Jesus Christ is not exhaustively self-conscious of all the ramifications, nuances, and implications of what he says. He nevertheless does take the responsibility for those ramifications, as does any other human speaker. As the divine Son, Jesus Christ does know all things, including all ramifications, applications, and so forth of his speech. There is a distinction here, but nevertheless no disharmony.

Furthermore, we may say that Jesus in his human nature was especially endowed with the Spirit to perform his prophetic work, as planned by God the Father (Luke 3:22; 4:18–19). When we interpret his speech, we should take into account that the Holy Spirit speaks through him. Thus, we are saying that we must take into account the ultimately trinitarian character of revelation,[6] as well as the unique fulness of the Spirit's endowment in Christ's messianic calling.

In short, when we interpret Christ's speech, we interpret it (as we do all speech) in the light of the author. That is, we interpret it as the speech of the divine Son. But Christ says that the Father speaks through him (John 12:48–50; 14:10). Hence it is the speech of the Father. Since the Holy Spirit comes upon Jesus to equip him for his messianic work, we also conclude that it is the speech of the Spirit. And of course it is the speech of the man Jesus of Nazareth. Each of these aspects of interpretation is in harmony with the others. But they are distinct, at least in nuance.

In Christ, we meet verbal communication undergirded by a communion and fellowship of understanding. In Christ's being there is no pure mathematical identity of divine persons or identity of two natures, but harmony. The result is that there is no pure mathematical identity in the interpretive product. That is, we cannot in a pure way analyze simply what the words mean as (for instance) proceeding from the human nature of Christ, and then say that our results precisely and exhaustively interpret his words.

The case of divine speech through apostles and prophets is, of course, secondary, but none the less analogous. The revelation of Jesus Christ is the pinnacle (Heb. 1:1–3). All other revelations through prophets and apostles are secondary to this supreme revelation. There is ultimately no other way to gain deeper insight into the secondary than through the pinnacle. Hence we cannot expect to collapse the richness of divine presence into a mathematical point, when we are dealing with the words of the Bible.

6. Vern S. Poythress, *Symphonic Theology: The Validity of Multiple Perspectives in Theology* (Grand Rapids: Zondervan, 1987), pp. 47–51.

## Progressive Revelation

A further complication arises because the many human authors of the Bible wrote over a long period of time. None of the human authors except the very last can survey the entire product in order to arrive at an interpretation of the whole.

Once again, we may throw light on the situation by starting with a simpler case. Suppose that we have a single uninspired human author speaking or writing to a single audience over a period of time. Even if we are dealing with only a single long oral discourse, the discourse is spread out in time. Individual statements and individual paragraphs near the beginning of the discourse are understood first, then those near the end. Moreover, an audience is in a better position to draw more inferences from earlier parts of a discourse once they have reached the end. Typically, all the parts of a discourse qualify and color each other. We understand more by reading the whole than we do from reading any one part, or even from all the parts separately. The effect is somewhat like the effect of different parts of an artist's picture. If we just attend to small bits of paint within the picture, one by one, we may miss many implications of the whole. The "meaning" of the picture does not reside merely in a mechanical, mathematical sum of the blobs of paint. Rather, it arises from the joint effect of the individual pieces. Their joint effect arises from the relations between the pieces. Likewise, the import of an author's discourse arises partly from the reinforcements, qualifications, tensions, complementations, and other relations between the individual words and sentences, as well as from the effects of each individual sentence. The overall effect of this process is that an audience may understand what the first part of a discourse means and then have that understanding modified and deepened by the last of the discourse.

Now consider a particular example of two people communicating over a long period of time. Suppose a father teaches his young son to sing "Jesus Loves Me." Later on, he tells the story of the life of Christ from a children's Bible storybook. Still later, he explains how the Old Testament sacrificial system depicted aspects of Christ's purpose in dying for us. Finally, the son becomes an adult and does extended Bible study for himself. Suppose then that the son remembers how his father taught him "Jesus Loves Me." He asks, "What was my father saying in telling me the words of the song? At the time, did I understand what he was saying?" The answer may well be yes. The son understood what the father expected that he would have the capacity to understand at that point. But the father knew as well that the child's initial understanding was not the end point. The father intended that the earlier words should be recalled later. He intended that the son should understand his father's mind better and better by comparing those earlier words with later words that the father would share.

Now, suppose that there was no misunderstanding or misjudgment at any point. There is still more than one level of understanding of the father's words. There is what one may understand on the basis of those words more or less by themselves, when not supplemented by further words, and when seen as words adapted to the capacity of the young child. And there is what one may understand on the basis of comparing and relating those words to many later words (and actions) of the father. The first of these understandings is a legitimate one, an understanding not to be underestimated. As long as the child has only those words of the father, and not all the later history, it would be unfair of him to build up an exact, elaborate analysis of all the ramified implications of the statements. But once the father has said a lot more, it throws more light on what the father intended all along that those words should do: they should contribute along with many other words to form and engender an enormously rich understanding of Christ's love, an understanding capable of being evoked and alluded to by the words of the song.

The complexity arises, as before, from the dynamic and relational character of communicative meaning. The understanding we achieve from listening arises not only from individual words or sentences in the discourse but from the complex relations that they have to one another and to the larger situation, including what we know of the author himself. In particular, the song "Jesus Loves Me" conveys meaning not simply in virtue of the internal arrangement of the words, but also in virtue of the context of who is saying it, what else is being said by way of explanation, and so on. There is indeed something like a "common core" of meaning shared by all or nearly all uses of the song. But the implications that we may see around that common core may differ. Imagine the song being used by a liberal who believes that in fact Jesus is merely human and therefore still dead. In his mouth, the song is only a metaphorical expression of an ideal of human love.

Now we are ready to raise the crucial question: Does something analogous to this Father-son communication happen with God's communication to his people over the period of time from Adam onward? Is God like a human father speaking to his child? The basic answer is obviously yes. Those who do not think it is so obvious should consider the following. First, Israel is called God's son (Exod. 4:22; Deut. 8:5), and Paul explicitly likens the Old Testament period to the time when a child is still a minor (Gal. 4:3–4). These passages are not directly discussing the question of biblical interpretation, but they are nevertheless suggestive.

Second, from very early in the history of the human race, God indicates that more is to come. History and the promises of God are forward looking. The story is yet to be completed. It is altogether natural to construe this feature as implying that earlier promissory statements of God may be more deeply understood once the promises begin to be fulfilled, and especially when they are completely fulfilled. Similar reflections evidently apply even to the hope we now have as Christians (1 Cor. 13:12).

Third, in at least a few cases in the Old Testament, we find prophecies whose fulfilments take unexpected form. One of the most striking is Jacob's prophecy about the dispersion of Simeon and Levi (Gen. 49:7b).[7] If we attend only to the immediate context (v. 7a), we are bound to conclude that God undertakes to disgrace both tribes by giving them no connected spot of settlement. The actual fulfilment is therefore quite surprising in the case of Levi. But it is not out of accord with God's character of turning cursings into blessings. What we know about him includes his right to exceed our expectations. This whole affair is more easily understood when we take into account the fact that Genesis 49:7 is not an isolated word of God but part of a long history of God's communications, yet to be completed. We cannot expect to draw all our conclusions until we have heard the whole.

In short, God's actual ways of bringing fulfilments may vary. Some of them may be straightforward; others quite surprising. An author likewise may continue a discourse in a straightforward way, or in a surprising way that causes us to reassess the exact point of the first part of what he says.

Fourth, the symbolic aspects of Old Testament institutions proclaim their own inadequacy (Heb. 10:1, 4). They are not only analogous to the final revelation of God, but at some points disanalogous (v. 4). Suppose that people stand in the Old Testament situation, trying to understand what is symbolized. They will inevitably continue with some questions unanswered until they are able to relate what is said and done earlier to what God does at the coming of Christ. Until the point of completion, the interpretation must remain open ended (but not without content).

Fifth, the speech of God is not complete until the coming of Christ (Heb. 1:1–3). We must, as it were, hear the end of the discourse before we are in a position to weigh the total context, in terms of which we may achieve the most profound understanding of each part of the discourse.

I conclude, then, that any particular passage of the Bible is to be read in three progressively larger contexts, as follows:

1. Any passage is to be read *in the context of the particular book of the Bible in which it appears,* that is, in the context of the human author

---

7. Oswald T. Allis, *Prophecy and the Church* (Philadelphia: Presbyterian and Reformed, 1945) p. 30.

and historical circumstances of the book. God speaks truly to the people in particular times and circumstances.

2. Any passage is to be read *in the context of the total canon of Scripture available up to that point in time.*[8] The people originally addressed by God must take into account that God's speech does not start with them but presupposes and builds on previous utterances of God.

3. Any passage is to be read *in the context of the entire Bible* (the completed canon). God intended from the beginning that his later words should build on and enrich earlier words, so that in some sense the whole of the Bible represents one long, complex process of communication from one author.

For example, Ezekiel 34 is to be understood (1) in terms of the immediate context of the Book of Ezekiel and the historical circumstances in which the book first appeared; (2) in terms of its continuation of the Word of God recorded in the law of Moses and the preexilic prophets; (3) in terms of what we can understand in the light of the whole completed Bible, including the New Testament.[9]

In addition to these three analyses of the passage, we may, in more fine-grained reflection, distinguish still other possibilities. In principle, we may ask what the passage contributes at any point during the progressive additions to canon through further revelation. For example, Bruce K. Waltke argues that, in the case of the Book of Psalms (and presumably many other Old Testament books), it is illuminating to ask about its meaning at the time when the Old Testament canon was complete but before the dawn of the New Testament era.[10] This is still another approach alongside all the rest. For simplicity we confine the subsequent discussion to the three contexts distinguished here.

As we have stressed, our understanding of a passage depends not only on the sequence of words of the passage but on the context in which it occurs. Hence, consideration of the three contexts can, in principle, lead to three different results. Some people might want to speak of three meanings. One meaning would be the meaning obtained from focusing

---

8. This point is rightly emphasized in Kaiser, *Exegetical Theology,* pp. 79–83.

9. My approach is virtually identical with that of Bruce K. Waltke, "A Canonical Process Approach to the Psalms," in *Tradition and Testament: Essays in Honor of Charles Lee Feinberg,* ed. John S. Feinberg and Paul D. Feinberg (Chicago: Moody, 1981), pp. 3–18. My arguments rest more on the general features of communication, whereas Waltke's arguments rely more on the concrete texture of Old Testament revelation. Hence the two articles should be seen as complementary. See also William Sanford LaSor, "The *Sensus Plenior* and Biblical Interpretation," in *Scripture, Tradition, and Interpretation,* ed. W. Ward Gasque and William Sanford LaSor (Grand Rapids: Eerdmans, 1978), pp. 260–77.

10. Waltke, "Canonical Process Approach," p. 9.

primarily on the human author and his circumstances. Another meaning would derive from focusing on what is known about all the divine author's utterances up until the time in which he causes the particular passage to be written. The final meaning would obtain from focusing primarily on the divine author and all that we know about him from the whole of the Bible.

However, for most purposes I would prefer to avoid calling these three results three "meanings." Otherwise we might suggest that three unrelated and perhaps even contradictory things are being said. But these three approaches are complementary, not contradictory. The difference between these three approaches is quite like the difference between reading one chapter of a book and reading the whole of the book. After taking into account the whole book, we understand the one chapter as well as the whole book more deeply. But it does not mean that our understanding of the one chapter by itself was incorrect. Remember again the example of a child's understanding of "Jesus Loves Me."

## Psalm 22:12–18

Consider these three contexts in our understanding of Psalm 22:12–18. In the first approach, we focus on the human author. The passage speaks of the distress of a person who trusts in God (note vv. 2–5, 8–10) but who is nevertheless abandoned to his enemies. In a series of shifting metaphors the psalmist compares his suffering to being surrounded by bulls and lions (vv. 12–13), to being sick or weak in body through emotional distress (vv. 14–15), to being caught by ravening dogs (v. 16), and to being treated virtually like a carcass (vv. 17–18).[11] The psalmist's words evidently spring from his own experience of a situation of abandonment.

We encounter a special complexity in the case of Psalms. The actual author (David, according to the title of Psalm 22)[12] and the collector or collectors who under inspiration included Psalm 22 in the larger collection both have a role. The psalm receives a new setting when it is in-

11. See Charles A. Briggs and Emilie G. Briggs, *A Critical and Exegetical Commentary on the Book of Psalms*, 2 vols. (Edinburgh: T. and T. Clark, 1906), 1:196–97; A. A. Anderson, *The Book of Psalms*, 2 vols. (London: Marshall, Morgan and Scott, 1972), 1:190–91; Derek Kidner, *Psalms 1–72* (London: Inter-Varsity, 1973), pp. 107–8; Joseph A. Alexander, *The Psalms* (1864; reprint, Grand Rapids: Zondervan, 1955), pp. 101–3. Commentators have some disagreements over the details of the picture, particularly over the interpretation of v. 16, "they have pierced my hands and feet." But it is clear that, in the original context, the speech is dominated by metaphorical comparisons between the psalmist's enemies and fierce animals.

12. We need not at this point discuss whether the superscriptions are inspired.

cluded in the Book of Psalms. This setting provides a new context for interpretation. In my opinion, it means that the collector invites us to see Psalm 22 not simply as the experience of an individual at one time but as a typical or model experience with which the whole congregation of Israel is to identify as they sing and meditate on the psalm.[13] Hence, in the context of the Book of Psalms (the context with divine authority), we compare this psalm of lament and praise (see vv. 25–31) with other psalms. We understand that there is a general pattern of suffering, trust, vindication, and praise that is to characterize the people of Israel.

Now we move to the second approach, considering Psalm 22 in the light of the entire canon of Scripture given up until the time when the Book of Psalms was compiled. But there is some problem with this. The Book of Psalms may have been compiled in stages (e.g., many scholars think that Book 1, Psalms 1–41, may have been gathered into a single collection before some of the other psalms had been written). Whatever the details, we do not know exactly when the compilation took place. Hence we do not know exactly what other canonical books had already been written.

We may still proceed in a general way. We read Psalm 22 in the light of the promise to David (2 Sam. 7:8–16) and its relation to the earlier promises through Abraham and Moses. Then we understand that the people of Israel are represented preeminently by a king in the line of David. The deficiencies and failures of David's immediate descendants also point to the need for a perfect, righteous king who will truly establish David's line forever. Old Testament prophecies make it progressively clear that the hopes centered in David's line will ultimately be fulfilled in a single great descendant, the Branch (Isa. 11:1–5; Zech. 6:12; see also Isa. 9:6–7). The experiences of suffering, trust, and vindication expressed in Psalm 22 and other psalms we expect to be fulfilled in a climactic way in a messianic figure, the Branch, who is the kingly Davidic representative of all Israel.[14]

What the messianic mediator will be like becomes progressively revealed in the course of the Old Testament. Yet, it is never made very clear just how the experience of the Messiah ties in with Psalm 22 in detail. We know that Psalm 22 is related to the prophetic passages, but just how is not so clear.

Finally, let us consider Psalm 22 in the light of the completed canon. In this light, we know that Christ has come to fulfil all righteousness (Matt. 3:15), to fulfil all God's promises (2 Cor. 1:20; Rom. 15:8; Luke 24:45–48). We know too that Christ used the opening words of Psalm 22

13. See, e.g., Anderson, *Psalms* 1:30.
14. See Waltke, "Canonical Process Approach," pp. 10–14.

when he was on the cross (Matt. 27:46). This reference suggests that he is indicating the relevance of the whole psalm to himself. If we remain in doubt, other New Testament passages assure us that that is indeed the case (Matt. 27:35; John 19:24; Heb. 2:12).

We proceed, then, to read through Psalm 22 afresh. We compare it with the accounts of the crucifixion in the New Testament and with New Testament theology explaining the significance of Christ's death. We see that in verses 12–18 Christ describes his own distress, and in verses 25–31 he expresses the "fruit of the travail of his soul" (Isa. 53:11 RSV), or the benefits that will follow. In particular, certain details in the psalm which appeared to be simply metaphorical in the original Old Testament context strike home with particular vividness (Ps. 22:16, 18).[15]

## What Is "in" a Verse

Now let us ask, "What is the correct understanding of what God is saying in verses like Psalm 22:1, 16, 18?" Is it the understanding that we gain from the first approach, or the understanding that we gain in considering the context of the whole Bible? The answer, I think, is both. If we simply confine ourselves to the immediate context, or even to the canon up through psalms, we neglect what can be learned by reading the whole of the Bible as the Word of the single divine author. On the other hand, if we simply confine ourselves to this third approach, we neglect the fact that God's revelation was progressive. We need to remember that God was interested in edifying people in Old Testament times. Moreover, what he made clear and what he did not make so clear are both of interest to us because they show us the ways in which our own understanding agrees with and sometimes exceeds previous understanding, due to the progress in revelation and the progress in the execution of God's redemptive program.

Moreover, certain dangers arise if we simply confine ourselves to only one approach. If we neglect the first approach, we miss the advantage of having the control of a rigorous attention to the historical particulars associated with each text of the Bible. Then we run the danger that

15. See Kidner, *Psalm 1–72*, p. 107: "While verses 14, 15, taken alone, could describe merely a desperate illness, the context is of collective animosity and the symptoms could be those of Christ's scourging and crucifixion; in fact verses 16–18 had to wait for that event to unfold their meaning with any clarity." Many commentators in the classical historical-critical tradition, by contrast, refuse in principle to let the New Testament cast further light on the implications of the verses because they do not allow the principle of unified divine authorship to exercise an influence on interpretation.

our systematic understanding of the Bible as a whole, or our subjective hunches, will simply dictate what any particular text means.

On the other hand, if we neglect the third approach, we miss the advantage of having the rest of the Bible to control the inferences that we may draw in applying a particular text. Perhaps we may refuse to apply the text at all, saying to ourselves, "It was just written for those people back there." Or we may apply it woodenly, not reckoning with the way in which it is qualified by the larger purposes of God. We may miss the Christocentric character of the Bible, proclaimed in Luke 24:45–48. We could refuse to see the particulars in the light of the whole and thus repeat an error of the Pharisees, who meticulously attended to detail but neglected "justice and the love of God" (Luke 11:42).

These approaches combine in a way analogous to the way in which a human son combines earlier and later understandings of "Jesus Loves Me." There is a complex interplay.

But I think that we can be more precise. There are several legitimate ways of organizing our research. In a typical case of scholarly research, we may begin with the first approach as a control. For Psalm 22, we focus narrowly on the original historical context and what is known within that context. We do grammatical-historical exegesis as the foundation for all later systematizing reflection. We try to avoid simply "reading in" our total knowledge of Scripture, or else we lose the opportunity for the Bible to criticize our views. As a second, later step, we relate Psalm 22 to earlier canonical books and finally to the New Testament. Whatever we find at this stage must harmonize with the results of the first approach. But we come to additional insights and deeper understanding as we relate Psalm 22 to the New Testament. These extra things are not "in" Psalm 22 in itself. They are not somehow mystically hidden in the psalm, so that someone with some esoteric key to interpretation could have come up with them just by reading the psalm in isolation from the rest of the Bible. Psalm 22 in itself gives us only what we get from the first approach. The additional understandings arise from the relations that Psalm 22 has with earlier canonical books, with the New Testament, and with the events of Christ's death. These relations, established by God, provide the basis for our advancing forward in understanding.

Suppose, now, that we are not scholars ourselves, but that we have been Christians for many years. Suppose that, through the aid of the Holy Spirit, we have been growing spiritually and studying the Bible diligently for the whole time. From our pastors and from other scholarly sources we have gained some knowledge of Old and New Testament times, but not elaborate knowledge. But we have gained a thorough knowledge of the Bible as a whole. Much of this knowledge might be called unconscious or subconscious knowledge. Especially when it is a matter of large themes of the Bible, we may not be able to say clearly what we know or exactly what texts of the Bible have given us our knowledge.

When we read Psalm 22, we read it against the background of all that unconscious knowledge of biblical truths. When we see the opening words in verse 1, we naturally assume that the psalm speaks of Christ's suffering. We read the rest of the psalm as a psalm about Christ. In each verse we see Christ's love, his suffering, and his rejection by his enemies.

The results we gain may be very similar to the results gained by scholars who go through all the distinct "steps." But scholars know that their understanding arises from the relations of Psalm 22 to the rest of the Bible. They self-consciously distinguish between what arises from the psalm viewed more or less in itself and what arises from other passages of the Bible as they illumine the significance of the psalm. Laypeople may have the same results, but without being able to say exactly what all the stages were by which they could logically come to those results.

The psychological perception of what is "in" the text of Psalm 22 may also be different. Lay readers are not consciously aware of the immense and important role played by our general knowledge of the rest of the Bible. Hence it seems that all the depth of insight that laypeople receive as they read Psalm 22 comes from the psalm itself. It is all "in" the psalm. By contrast, the scholar knows where things come from and prefers to speak of the depth of insight as arising from the relations between many, many individual texts of the whole Bible, as these are brought systematically into relation to Psalm 22.

But now consider once more the central question: What is God saying in Psalm 22? He is saying what he said to the original Old Testament readers of the psalm. He speaks the truth to them. Hence, scholars are correct in taking care to distinguish what comes from the psalm itself and what comes from the psalm seen in the light of the whole Bible.

But God also intends that we should read Psalm 22 in the light of the rest of what he says. Scholars are correct in going on to a second stage, in which they relate the psalm to the whole Bible. And laypeople are correct when they do the same thing. Of course, we must suppose that the laypeople are sober, godly readers, well versed in the Scripture. Then, as they read Psalm 22, all the depth that they receive is a depth that God intends them to receive. God is saying all that richness to them as they read. But that means that their psychological and spiritual perception is correct. All that richness is "in" the psalm as a speech that God is speaking to them now.

Hence, I believe that we are confronted with an extremely complex and rich process of communication from God. The scholarly psychological process of making the distinctions is important as a check and refinement of laypeople's understanding. But that lay understanding, at its best, is not to be despised. We are not to be elitists who insist that everyone become a self-conscious scholar in reading the Bible. Laypeople have a correct perception, even psychologically, of what God intends a passage like Psalm 22 to say. God does say more, now, through that passage, than he said to the Old Testament readers. The "more" arises from our present stage of fuller revelation and consequent fuller illumination of the Holy Spirit.

In this entire process, we have no need to postulate an extra, "mystical" sense. That is, we do not postulate an extra meaning which we can uncover only by using some esoteric hermeneutical method. Rather, our understanding is analogous to the way that a son's understanding of "Jesus Loves Me" arises and grows. At the end of a long period of reading and digesting a rich communication, we see each particular part of the communication through eyes of knowledge that have been enlightened by the whole. Through that enlightenment, each part of the whole is rich.

Our reflections up to this point also throw light on some of the problems arising from New Testament interpretation of the Old.[16] I would claim that the New Testament authors characteristically do not aim merely at grammatical-historical exegesis of the Old Testament. If we expect this of them, we expect something too narrow and pedantic. The New Testament authors are not scholars but church leaders. They are interested in showing how Old Testament passages apply to the church and to their present situation. Hence, when they discuss an Old Testament text, they consider it in the light of the rest of the Old Testament, the events of salvation that God has accomplished in Christ, and the teaching of Jesus himself during his earthly life. They bring all this knowledge to bear on their situation, in the light of all that they know about that situation. In this process they are not concerned, as scholars would be, to distinguish with nicety all the various sources that contribute to their understanding. Both they and their readers typically presuppose the context of later revelation. Hence, what they say using an Old Testament passage may not always be based on the text alone but may exploit relations that the text has with this greater context. There is nothing odd about this process, any more than there is anything odd about laypeople

16. Note similar concerns in the discussion of *sensus plenior* in Raymond E. Brown, "The *Sensus Plenior* of Sacred Scripture" (unpublished Ph.D. diss., St. Mary's University, 1955), pp. 68–71.

who read Psalm 22 in the light of their knowledge of the whole of Scripture.

## Scholarly Use of
## Grammatical-Historical Exegesis

In conclusion, let us ask what implications we may draw concerning scholarly grammatical-historical exegesis, that is, an approach like the first one, which self-consciously focuses on each biblical book as a product of a human author, in a particular historical setting. On the positive side, we have seen that grammatical-historical exegesis has an important illumining role. Several points can be mentioned.

First, in writing the Bible, God spoke to people in human language, in human situations, through human authors. God himself in the Bible indicates that we should pay attention to these human factors in order to understand what he is saying and doing.

Second, on a practical level, grammatical-historical exegesis serves to warn the church against being swallowed up by traditionalism, in which people merely read in a system of understanding that afterward is read out. It alerts us to nuances in meaning that we otherwise overlook or even misread.

Third, it serves to sensitize us to the genuinely progressive character of revelation. God did not say everything all at once. We understand him better the more we appreciate the wisdom involved in the partial and preliminary character of what came earlier (Heb. 1:1).

On the other hand, responsible biblical interpretation includes more than grammatical-historical exegesis. First, if grammatical-historical exegesis pretends to pay attention to the human author alone, it distorts the nature of the human author's intention. Whether or not they were perfectly self-conscious about it, the human authors intended that their words should be received as the words of the Spirit.

Second, it is legitimate to explore the relations between what God says in all parts of the Bible. When we perform such a synthesis, what we conclude may go beyond what we could derive from any one text in isolation. Yet, it should not be in tension with the results of a narrow grammatical-historical exegesis. Of course, sometimes because of the limitations of our knowledge, we may find no way to resolve all tensions.

Third, we are not to despise laypeople's understanding of the Bible. We are not to reject it just because on the surface it appears to "read in" too much. Of course, laypeople may sometimes have overworked imaginations. But sometimes their conclusions may be the result of a synthesis of Bible knowledge due to the work of the Holy Spirit. Scholars cannot reject such a possibility without having achieved a profound synthetic and even practical knowledge of the Bible for themselves.

Finally, when later human writers of Scripture interpret earlier parts of Scripture, they typically do so without making fine scholarly distinctions concerning the basis of their knowledge. Hence we ought not to require them to confine themselves to a narrow grammatical-historical exegesis. In many respects their interpretations may be similar to valid uses of Scripture by nonscholars today.

# 6

## The New Testament's Use of the Old Testament

### Dan G. McCartney

*The writers of the Bible did know what they were doing
when they wrote. I do not believe that they always knew all
that they were doing. I believe that there are mysterious
words of prophecy in the Prophets and the Psalms, for
example, which had a far richer and more glorious
fulfillment than the inspired writers knew when they wrote.
Yet even in the case of those mysterious words I do not think
that the sacred writers were mere automata. They did not
know the full meaning of what they wrote, but they did
know part of the meaning, and the full meaning was in no
contradiction with the partial meaning but was its glorious
unfolding.*

—J. Gresham Machen, 1936

It is often observed that a commitment to the inerrancy of Scripture is relatively meaningless unless this commitment entails some kind of hermeneutical principles by which one can have reasonable assurance of a correct understanding of what the text actually says. Obviously an incorrect understanding of an inerrant text is not inerrant.

A recent solution to this problem proposed by many evangelicals is to insist that only the "natural" or "literal" meaning derived by grammatical-historical exegesis is the genuine meaning of any text in Scripture. This restriction provides a clear means of control over interpretation and a starting point for discussion on the Bible's exact theological content.

While the advantages of this solution are appealing, the problem is that the Bible, when it interprets itself, does not always conform to the strict guidelines proposed by the grammatical-historical approach. Since the biblical writers were giving an inerrant interpretation, this failure to conform to our guidelines has been something of a "skeleton in the closet" for evangelicals. And of course many who do not share our convictions regarding the Bible point to this skeleton with delight.

We ought not be embarrassed by this "skeleton." The Bible's use of itself provides the richest path we have toward understanding the Bible's self-hermeneutic and gives us the material for establishing a genuinely biblical basis for our own hermeneutic. If the Bible's use of itself is a "skeleton," it ought to be regarded rather as a "skeleton *key*."

Admittedly, this is a difficult path. It is much easier to address the problem by taking the approach of Earle Ellis, who describes Paul's exegesis as "grammatical-historical exegesis *plus*,"[1] or Richard Longenecker, who suggests that where New Testament writers use historical exegesis we may follow them, but where non-grammatical-historical exegesis occurs the writers have spoken only by virtue of divine inspiration, and there we may not follow.[2]

But these solutions really skirt the issue of where we ought in the first place to find our hermeneutical principles. Furthermore, the very fact that there is a "plus" reminds us that the New Testament writers did not actually think in grammatical-historical terms at all. This fact becomes more apparent when we ask why the New Testament writers chose the particular texts they did. Was it because it was divinely revealed to them that these texts were special texts which, unlike most Old Testament texts, held a fuller meaning than grammatical-historical exegesis would establish? This answer seems unlikely, because it is probable that many, if not most, of the texts were liturgically familiar in the diaspora synagogues and may have been chosen simply for that very reason.[3] It was

---

1. Earle Ellis, *Paul's Use of the Old Testament* (Grand Rapids: Eerdmans, 1957).

2. R. Longenecker, *Biblical Exegesis in the Apostolic Period* (Grand Rapids: Eerdmans, 1975), pp. 218–19.

3. Cf. E. Werner, *The Sacred Bridge* (London: Dobson, 1959), and Simon Kistemaker, *Psalm Citations in the Epistle to the Hebrews* (Amsterdam: Van Soest, 1961). Kistemaker carefully demonstrates that most, and possibly all, of the Old Testament citations in Hebrews were liturgically familiar in the synagogues. This early Christian adherence to the

divinely revealed to them that the whole Old Testament spoke of Christ, and so the particular texts that happened to be liturgically familiar could certainly be understood in a Christocentric way. But this understanding often involved going beyond what we call the grammatical-historical meaning.

Certainly grammatical-historical exegesis is the most basic part of the foundation for understanding any biblical text. However, the conviction that the grammatical-historical meaning is the entire and exclusive meaning of the text seems to stem more from post-Enlightenment rationalistic presuppositions than from an analysis of the Bible's understanding and interpretation of itself. Since such analysis leads to "problems," I suggest that the problems are not really generated by the New Testament's use of the Old, but rather by our expectations as to what the New Testament's use of the Old ought to be. These precommitments not only yield difficulties but also have led to what in this writer's view is an impoverishment of hermeneutics.

I would like now to suggest four theses that we should bear in mind when striving for a hermeneutic that is genuinely harmonious with the Bible. First, hermeneutical method is a product of world view. Even for Christians, this world view is influenced not by Scripture alone but inescapably by cultural, intellectual, linguistic (pace Barr), spiritual, and even physical environment. Second, hermeneutical method is subservient to hermeneutical goal. That is, the method is simply the tool used to reach a goal which is at least vaguely known beforehand. Third, our world view must be compatible with the biblical writers' world view. An interpreter must recognize the function of world view, not only in the biblical writers but also in one's own interpretations, and must seek consciously to bring his or her world view into harmony with that of the Bible. Finally, our hermeneutical goal must maintain identity with the goal of the New Testament writers, namely, the focus on Jesus Christ and his redemptive program.

## Hermeneutical Method Is a Product of World View

World view is a person's way of looking at all reality. It is built up at first by exposure both to what we may call general revelation (which includes one's own self) and to the general societal interpretations of general revelation wherein one's thinking develops. It is therefore influenced

---

well-known liturgical texts may be why modern readers often ask, "Why did the author choose that Old Testament passage? Wouldn't another verse have been much better?"

and molded by such things as culture, social structure, and religious and philosophical assumptions within the society. When a person within a certain social context, who shares with the culture a certain way of thinking about reality, comes to a text, he or she understands that text in categories drawn from an already-extant understanding of everything. The difficulty is that humans can never really escape from their socially induced way of viewing reality. We may expand our categories by contact with other cultures, and we may have our world views continually modified by interactions with some text we seek to understand as well as by new experiences. But the very questions we ask a text, or expect it to answer, are generated by this world view. Hence, the method we use to understand a text will be bound up with our view of what that text ought to say (given our categories), or what questions it ought to answer. This expectation will also determine the way we expect a text to answer these questions.

This background enables us to understand better the history of hermeneutics. We tend to chuckle when we read of the wild interpretations of Origen, or the pedantic fourfold meaning sought by the scholastics. But perhaps we ought to ask, "Why did these men of obviously great learning and intellectual acumen engage in such activity?" It was because they expected a certain kind of teaching from the text, and expected it to be presented in a certain way.

Now to be fair to Origen, we should notice that, when it came to the actual establishment or proof of Christian doctrine, Origen reverted to what we might call a literal meaning. This may have been largely due to the fact that the church's tradition was based on the literal meaning of the New Testament. But whatever the reason, in facing the non-Christian or young Christian (as he did in *Contra Celsum*), Origen astutely avoids his usual allegorical method.[4]

But Origen's world view was heavily dominated by Alexandrian idealism. And since Origen believed that the Bible was the absolute Word of God, it must, given his idealistic framework, be a transhistorical book, treating divine truth (which of course is idealistic) as a whole, without historical development, or at least as though the historical development were of secondary importance. Accordingly he expected the language of the book to be idealistic, transcendent, and symbolic. He did not think of

---

4. See my "Literal and Allegorical Interpretation in Origen's *Contra Celsum*," *Westminster Theological Journal* 48 (1986): 281–301. Although Origen does not argue by means of allegorical interpretation, he does defend its appropriateness. Both Origen and Celsus as well as everybody else in that age assumed that any book worthy of the adjective *inspired* must be capable of yielding allegorical meanings.

himself as allegorizing; he was only uncovering the allegory which he was convinced God had intended in the text.

Now Origen stands at a safe distance. We are not usually affected directly by the kinds of assumptions that were predominant in his day. But let us give another example closer to home. The church in our century has struggled rather vigorously over the question of how to interpret Revelation 20. Stanley Gundry has observed that there seems to be a relationship between the political fortunes of the church, the philo-sophical outlook of the age, and the current predominating view of the millennium.[5] When the church is persecuted or composed of the disenfranchised, there is a tendency to premillennialism. In optimistic times, when the church is prospering materially and numerically but has little political clout, postmillennialism seems to predominate. And when the church is more comfortable or in league with the state, amillennialism is the favored option.

This correlation (and the correspondence is not exact—in every age there are people who do not accede to the popular opinion) does not help us attain the correct interpretation of Revelation 20. But we might be prompted to ask, "Are we unaffected in our methodological assumptions by our world view?" I suspect not. Even when we are sophisticated enough to recognize the function of world view, this recognition itself comes about by way of a certain world view. And whereas our world view may indeed be a legitimate perspective (as long as it is compatible with that of the Bible), it may not be, and in fact probably is not, an ultimate or absolute perspective. Thus, our approved method of exegesis is tied up with a certain view of reality. And for many American evangelicals as well as the liberal establishment, the view is not derived directly from Scripture but depends heavily on the Enlightenment construction of reality, and especially the eighteenth-century view of history as the reporting of things "as they were in themselves," or what we may call the videotape view of history.

Here is a representative statement that illustrates this point from the critical aide: "This juxtaposition of ancient and later traditional material in the gospel tradition creates difficulties for us, who because of our intellectual situation must attempt to separate the historical reality of the pre-Easter Jesus from the faith image of the post-Easter community. Yet this difficulty did not exist for the Palestinian primitive community."[6] This selection illustrates how a certain world view results (for

5. Stanley Gundry, "Hermeneutics or *Zeitgeist* as the Determining Factor in the History of Eschatologies?" *Journal of the Evangelical Theological Society* 20 (1977): 45–55.

6. W. G. Kümmel, *The Theology of the New Testament* (New York: Abingdon, 1973), p. 116.

Kümmel) in a critical attitude toward a text which he knows was never meant to be understood in that way. In his search for history "as it is in itself," he divorces it from the more strictly hermeneutical question, What does it really mean?

But we who believe that the Bible is direct revelation are also affected by this world view, albeit in a different way. Because we believe in inerrancy, we tend to see the two questions as identical, but we are still searching for some kind of history "as it is in itself." The two questions should not of course be divorced, as though one had nothing to do with the other. But they are different questions, and it is after all the *meaning* that is the Word of God, not the videotape reconstruction. Sometimes apparent discrepancies (as between Kings and Chronicles) drive us to recognize this distinction to a limited extent, but apart from these motivations brought on by our commitment to inerrancy, we still think primarily in terms of videotape history. Not surprisingly, we also then suppose that the writers of the Bible—even God himself—must have a strictly videotape view of history. And yet the biblical writers seldom attempt to give anything like a simple continuous and complete material description of an event, and they always either implicitly or explicitly look at the event theologically.

Similarly with respect to language, we assume that, since we are locked into what might be considered in some cultures a prosaic view of communication, the biblical writers must also have been prosaic, even if they were poets. So we end up stressing the literal meaning even of prophetic texts, to the exclusion of all else, unless the literal meaning is clearly discounted by some other literal statement in the text or by reason of its literal nonsensibility (to us).

Now, this is not to say that "what actually happened" is unimportant, but that all of what actually happened would not show up on video. The problem stems from a tendency still to think of facts independently from their interpretation by God. In order to describe a historical event properly, one must present the meaning of that event; the biblical writers are presenting a divinely inspired perspective on the meaning, not a sensory description. This meaning of a historical event in the mind of God may very well exist only in relation to a later historical event. (Perhaps this is the idea behind Hebrews 11:40— "only together with us would they [Old Testament believers] be made perfect"). Likewise, the so-called literal meaning of a text is not unimportant, but neither is it necessarily exhaustive of a text's meaning.

Such observations are no cause for despair. Our culture-boundedness is not necessarily bad. But we must recognize its effects, its values, and its limitations. Of first importance here is the truth that human beings cannot efface within them the image of God, which guarantees that in any human culture there is a context within which true communication can take place. Furthermore, the revelation of God's truth, even when imperfectly understood, can progressively transform the culture, so that even more truth can be communicated.

Actually, perspectives of some sort, however derived, are necessary to our understanding. One of the great problems of scholarly life is organizing material. Organization is necessary to understanding, and even more necessary to communication. It is a problem because every fact is related in some way to everything else. So to organize things one has to have a perspective, and a perspective naturally emphasizes certain relationships and downplays other relationships. Hence, the value of multiple perspectives if one wants to get a larger picture.

On the other hand, we must recognize that humans are also sinful, which means that any culture, and any individual's interpretive framework, is going to have some elements in it which distort the truth. Therefore, we cannot assume that what is obvious to us is necessarily true, and certainly not that it is the whole truth.

## Hermeneutical Method Is Subservient to Hermeneutical Goal

This thesis is consonant with and implied in the first, because world view generates the expectations brought to the text. This relationship became apparent when people began working on the Qumran literature and discovered that the exegetical methods of the New Testament, while usually quite dissimilar to rabbinical and Alexandrian exegesis, bear a close resemblance to the methods used at Qumran.[7]

For example, Isaiah 28:16 makes reference to a precious cornerstone. In its own context it refers to a prophesied act of God which will bring exposure and judgment to the falsehood of Judah, and this will give a true foundation for those who trust God. From the perspective of the New Testament, this act of God is a reference to the work of Jesus; the passage is accordingly applied to him in 1 Peter 2:6–8.

Qumran, however, took this act of God to be the founding of the community, and the "cornerstone" for them refers to the council of the community (*Manual of Discipline* [1QS] 8:4–8). Both 1QS and 1 Peter apply the Old Testament passage according to what the interpreters "knew" by contemporary experience and religious conviction to be the meaning of the text. Neither does violence to what we would call the grammatical-historical meaning, but neither distinguishes between an "original

7. See J. A. Fitzmyer, "The Use of Explicit Old Testament Quotations in Qumran Literature and in the New Testament," *New Testament Studies* 7 (1961): 297–333.

meaning" and "application of" the text. Apparently both regarded their applications as the first-order meaning of the text. And the method of interpretation is quite similar. The difference lay in the reference point of contemporary experience.

Paul uses this passage a third way. In Romans 9:30–33, he combines Isaiah 28:16 with Isaiah 8:14 and refers both the cornerstone and the stumbling stone to the principle of justification by faith, which the Jews rejected. It could perhaps be shown that, in Paul's mind, this principle is so closely connected with the actual work of Christ that we can say this is not really a different focus but rather a different emphasis or specialized perspective on that focus. But in any case, here again, as at Qumran, the known referent, the matter of present concern, is brought to the text, not taken from it. Paul's use also demonstrates a "catchword concatenation" technique that is similar to later rabbinical exegesis, and also to Qumran. *Damascus Document* (CD) 6:3–11, for example, connects Numbers 21:18 (the well dug by princes and nobles with a staff [*mĕḥōqēq*]) with Genesis 49:10 ("the scepter will not depart from Judah, nor the ruler's *staff* from between his feet") and then proceeds to give an almost allegorical interpretation based on the fact that the Hebrew word *mĕḥōqēq* can also mean "prescriber" or "lawgiver."

> God raised from Aaron men of discernment and from Israel men of wisdom, and He caused them to hear. And they dug the well: the well which the princes dug, which the nobles of the people delved with a staff *(mĕḥōqēq)*.
>     The well is the Law, and those who dug it were the converts of Israel who went out of the land of Judah to sojourn in the land of Damascus. God called them all princes because they sought him, and their renown was disputed by no man. The staff is the Interpreter of the Law of whom Isaiah said "he makes a tool for his work"; and the nobles of the people are those who come to dig the well with the staves which the staff ordained that they should walk in, all the age of wickedness.

Clearly, interpretive goal is ruling the day here. We have to admit that, on a surface level, this exegesis bears some resemblance to the concatenation of "stone" passages (Ps. 118:22; Isa. 8:14; 28:16) which Paul applies to justification (Rom. 9) and which Peter applies to Christ (1 Peter 2).

Another example is Isaiah 40:3. The New Testament consistently applies this passage to John the Baptist. The Gospel writers know that the "coming of the Lord" is the coming of Jesus, so the preparation spoken of here must be John the Baptist, who is known to have been the forerunner of Jesus. In the New Testament, the words *in the wilderness* are taken (as in the LXX) with the preceding clause *the voice of one crying out.* But the

Hebrew parallelism reflected in the NIV, suggests that it rather should go with "prepare."

| Prepare | in the desert | the way | for the LORD |
| Make straight | in the wilderness | a highway | for our God |

But the New Testament writers, having seen the fulfilment in John, know that it is not only the way of the Lord which was in the desert, but also the voice that was crying out. So the LXX interpretation fits well. Qumran, however, preserves the Hebrew parallelism because their community was literally in the desert wilderness and they "know" that the passage refers to the founding of their community. They also explain "highway" or "path" as the "study of the Law" (1QS 8:13–16), whereas for the New Testament the "way" is repentant hearts, prepared to receive the coming Messiah.

Both the New Testament writers and Qumran writers thus referred the Old Testament passage to a known referent, which was a present and important reality. Since from the context in Isaiah it would, on strictly grammatical-historical exegetical grounds, appear that the original author meant "desert" to be understood figuratively, we have here an example where both the New Testament and the Qumran use the method of "literalization" to achieve their interpretive goals. Literalization can be just as effective as "allegorization" in actualizing Scripture. This is not to say that such literalization was conscious, but it indicates that allegorization was probably equally unconscious, at least in Qumran and the New Testament. The method was never reflected on; only the hermeneutical goal was important.

We could compare other passages and methods, such as the allegorical approach already mentioned in CD 6:3–11 with Galatians 4, or the much more palatable typology that is characteristic of Qumran and the New Testament. But it might be better to ask at this point, Why are the interpretive techniques of the two communities similar? Probably it is because their interpretive goals are similar. Both groups regard the Old Testament as eschatologically oriented; both groups regard their own history as fulfilment of that eschatology. The difference lies in the particular character of their hermeneutic goal. The New Testament very consciously focuses the Old Testament on a single person, Jesus Christ, and his redemptive program. This is explicitly indicated in Luke 24:44–47 and is reflected in 1 Peter 1:10–12. Qumran's use of the Old Testament has no such coherent focus. Sometimes the Teacher of Righteousness, sometimes the future Messiah(s), sometimes the community or its council, is seen as the focus of Old Testament language. The methods are similar; the goal differs.

But then contrast Philo and the rabbis. Philo's interpretive goal is idealistic philosophy. Therefore his method not only seeks a certain outcome (viz, that the Old Testament speaks of idealistic philosophy) but seeks that outcome by idealistic method: the visible (the literal meaning) has an invisible reality (the allegory) lying behind it.

The rabbis' interpretive goal, on the other hand, is support for the legal tradition. Therefore their method not only seeks a certain outcome (viz., that the Old Testament gives support to the rabbinical legal tradition) but seeks that outcome by legalistic method. Even the nonlegal material is treated as containing (sometimes cryptically) legal directives, and the whole Old Testament is treated as one huge legal code. In these examples one can see both world view and interpretive goal at work in determining method. Such is also the case with the New Testament. The difference is that the New Testament has the right interpretive goal and a correct (though not necessarily exhaustively complete) world view, and therefore the right method.

We need to ask here, "How do we know which goal is the right one?" Although ultimately the question must be answered on the basis of God's self-evident voice in the New Testament as the Holy Spirit testifies in the heart, we can point to some other indications. First, the goal of the New Testament is a development of the Old Testament's own goal in its self-interpretation. And second, of all books claiming to provide a hermeneutical goal for interpreting Scripture (e.g., the Koran or the Book of Mormon), only the New Testament has a definite focus that is clearly compatible with the world view and goal of the Old Testament. But of course that "clearly" implies that I already know that the New Testament's goal is the right one.

## Our World View Must Be Compatible with the Biblical World View

The first thesis above notes that world view influences hermeneutical methodology. The implication is that if we are going to exercise the right method we must have the right world view. If we seek to interpret the Bible, we must first try to determine the world view of its writers, and then ourselves seek to be in harmony with it.

Now we must stress here that we are seeking compatibility, not identity, of world view. Compatibility of world view means primarily that the basic philosophical and theological outlook is shared. In other words, the communicator and the respondent are "on the same wavelength." Thus the biblical writers' world view is not compatible with the general modern non-Christian assumption that the sensate world is never affected by supernatural intrusion.

Identity of world view, on the other hand, would mean that our total impression of all of life, our categories for understanding everything, would be the same as that of the author. But the biblical writers themselves had different world views, which resulted in different, although always compatible, perspectives.[8] Furthermore, we cannot expunge from our awareness such things as developments in the study of the physical universe, world history since the New Testament was written, or even the increased sophistication in hermeneutical philosophy which led to the identification of the grammatical-historical method of exegesis.

Although the concept of a distinct grammatical-historical meaning may not have been part of the biblical writers' world views, grammatical-historical interpretation is certainly compatible with their world view (as long as the goal is right). But the compatibility requirement also demands that we not set up such a method as the exclusive tool for understanding Scripture.

I suggest that, by continual repeated application of the criterion of consistency, we become compatible with the world view of the Bible. This expectation is based on the assumption that all special and general revelation is completely consistent and that perceived or apparent inconsistencies indicate imperfections in perspective or imperfect compatibility with the divine total perspective. They are thus clues to problems in our hermeneutical methods. We must always be ready to modify our world view, as well as our interpretive method which depends on it. Generally, we learn the most from studying problems, that is, the difficult questions, the apparent contradictions, and so on. The seeming inconsistencies challenge our world view and help us expand our perspectives and grow.

If we are to achieve genuine understanding of God's intent in the Bible, we will have to be continually informing our world view both by general revelation and by special revelation.[9] We thus operate in a double hermeneutical circle. It may be disturbing to some to think of general revelation as in any way informing our understanding of special revelation, but it can hardly be otherwise. If nothing else, our knowledge of language and the meaning of words, even the development of concepts such as life, comes about by way of general revelation. We could not even read

---

8. The problem with James D. G. Dunn's analysis (*Unity and Diversity in the New Testament: An Inquiry into the Character of Earliest Christianity* [London: SCM, 1977]) is that, although he perceives many of the differences among the New Testament writers, he is satisfied to view them as in conflict rather than as complementary.

9. The term *general revelation* in this context should not be restricted to that in creation which directly indicates some characteristic of God; I am including everything in life which informs us of God and his truth, either directly or indirectly. Everything in life can tell us something about God and his interpretation of the world.

the Bible without some preunderstanding based on general revelation. Therefore we cannot afford to ignore data from outside the Bible. It too is valid, not by itself, but in relationship to the Bible.[10]

## A Focus on Christ and His Redemptive Program Must Be Maintained

Since interpretive method is subservient to interpretive goal, the goal we perceive in the New must be borne in mind at all times. We have already noticed that the New Testament focuses the Old on Christ, whereas the Qumran literature has no such coherency. Neither the community nor the Teacher of Righteousness serves as a central focus for the whole Old Testament in Qumran. And, as F. V. Filson noted, whereas both the New Testament and the Qumran communities regarded themselves as recipients of the new covenant, "in the New Testament it was really a *new* covenant . . . for the Qumran sect the new covenant was actually a renewal of the old covenant, which the sect now promised earnestly to observe by faithfully keeping the Mosaic law."[11]

But it was not hermeneutical methodology that determined this difference. Rather it was interpretive endpoint. Though their endpoints are similar in their eschatological orientation, the principal difference, which we have already observed and which was long ago observed by F. F. Bruce, is that "the New Testament interpretation of the Old Testament is not only eschatological but Christological."[12] This christological orientation provides the clear and definite focus for the New Testament's use of the Old. The vast majority of Old Testament references in the New refer to Christ directly, though some are applied to Christ's people or his redemptive work indirectly. And of course all the prophetic material in the Old Testament which the New Testament regards as fulfilled is fulfilled in Christ and his work.

Two passages in particular specifically spell out this connection. The first is Luke 24:44–47:

> He said to them, "This is what I told you while I was still with you: Everything must be fulfilled that is written about me in the Law of Moses, the Prophets, and the Psalms." Then he opened their minds so they could understand the Scriptures. He told them, "This is what is written: The Christ will suffer and rise from the dead on the third day, and repentance

10. There might be a third circle here: *self-understanding*.
11. Floyd V. Filson, "The Dead Sea Scrolls and the New Testament", *McCormick Quarterly* 21, no. 3 (1968): 315.
12. F. F. Bruce, *Biblical Exegesis in the Qumran Texts* (Grand Rapids: Eerdmans, 1960), p. 68.

and forgiveness of sins will be preached in his name to all nations, beginning at Jerusalem."

There is no single Old Testament passage where these elements all occur. Rather, it appears that Jesus is giving the disciples the key to understanding the Old Testament as a whole. (Note especially Jesus' reference in v. 44 to Moses, the prophets, and the psalms.) "This is what is written" equals "this is what the Old Testament is about."[13]

This approach is echoed in 1 Peter 1:10–12:

> Concerning this salvation, the prophets, who spoke of the grace that was to come to you, searched intently and with the greatest care, trying to find out the time and circumstances to which the Spirit of Christ in them was pointing when he predicted the sufferings of Christ [lit., the sufferings unto, or appointed for, Christ] and the glories that would follow. It was revealed to them that they were not serving themselves but you [Christians], when they spoke of the things that have now been told you by those who have preached the gospel to you by the Holy Spirit sent from heaven. Even angels long to look into these things.

Note that the same elements as mentioned in the previous quotation occur as being the subject matter of the Old Testament: the sufferings of Christ, the resurrection (glories that followed), and the preaching to the Gentiles as well as Jews.

Since the New Testament has such a definitive focus, it does evidence certain methodological preferences and characteristics which distinguish its hermeneutics from all other types of contemporary exegesis, including that of Qumran. Most notable is the occurrence of fulfilment patterns in the New Testament, observed by C. H. Dodd.[14] Matthew often introduces these in his Gospel with words like "this happened so that what was written might be fulfilled," followed by a quotation of a verse. A fulfilment use of Scripture can retain the original context of an Old Testament passage by focusing that whole context on Christ. Thus not just the quoted words but the whole context is being brought into view by the citation and, according to Dodd, even forms the theological "substructure" for the New Testament writers. Such things are altogether absent from the Qumran literature.

Furthermore, while individual Old Testament legal prescriptions are

13. This same idea seems to underlie Jesus' statement in John 5:46 that "Moses wrote about me."

14. C. H. Dodd, *According to the Scriptures: The Sub-structure of New Testament Theology* (1952; reprint, London: Fontana Books, 1965), esp. pp. 126–33. Dodd notes that a New Testament "testimony" includes its larger Old Testament context and sees a historical relationship between the cited text and its fulfilment in or by Christ.

reapplied at Qumran (note the extensive use of the Pentateuch and Ezekiel in 11Q Temple), in the New Testament the Law as a whole finds its focus and thus fulfilment in Christ. The idea of such a clear and unified personal focus for all Scripture, even the Law, was absent and even unthinkable at Qumran, and certainly for the rabbis and Philo.

Finally, not only is the christological focus of the New Testament a matter of the interpretive framework for the words of Scripture, but indeed Christ is regarded as the fulfilment of the very history itself. Thus this focus is the basis for typological interpretation in the New Testament. For example, in Luke 9:31, Moses and Elijah discuss with Jesus his *exodos* (exodus, departure), which he was about to fulfil in Jerusalem. The very history of Israel itself is here focused on Christ. Another example is Matthew's quotation of Hosea, "Out of Egypt I called my son" (2:15 = Hos. 11:1). Here the very history of Israel in Egypt, not just Hosea's statement, is regarded as ultimately speaking of the Christ. So there is no need in the New Testament to replace a historical meaning with the symbolic typological meaning (which Qumran frequently does); rather, the symbolic (eschatological) meaning is itself attached to the actual historical meaning. For this reason grammatical-historical exegesis is necessary for the beginning of understanding.

However, we need to bear in mind that these differences are due to the goal of New Testament exegesis of the Old, not some a priori attachment to method. And this goal was known prior to exegesis and demands something more than simply what we call grammatical-historical method.

This singleness of hermeneutic goal, with its focus on Christ, means that the Bible is primarily a book about God and humankind's relationship to him. Specific life problems are therefore only secondarily addressed. If we lose sight of the primary hermeneutical goal in order to seek for specific answers to our specific problems, we miss the mark, for very few of the "difficult" modern situational problems are directly addressed in the Bible. The Bible instills in us the knowledge of God. If we do know him, then our character is transformed, and we can confront the exigent contemporary problems as people of God, not as people armed with a comprehensive book of casuistic answers. This is not to say that the laws of God in the Bible no longer apply to us. It is quite the contrary. Such application of apodictic (as opposed to case) law must be *in relation to the God whose law it is;* the law is not a thing unto or for itself.

So we must maintain both of these factors—a compatible world view and a correct hermeneutical goal—if we hope to achieve true understanding of Scripture. If we keep one and not the other, we lose our way. As an example of some who keep the right goal but do not seek to make their world view compatible with that of the Bible, we might point to the neoorthodox and other modernists. The problem with Bultmann is not that he brought modern questions to the text but that he brought modern presuppositions which were not at all informed by special revelation and which were of greater authority to him than the text's presuppositions. He thus discarded and discredited the original framework of meaning as being unworkable. If one discards the native interpretive framework of a text, there is no meaning apart from the interpreter's own imported meaning. So Bultmann's "kernel" was of his own making. By explicitly rejecting the New Testament world view (and certainly the Old Testament world view) as inherently incompatible with any modern view, the modernists lose touch with the very Christ they are trying to maintain as a goal of exegesis. Instead they set up a Christ proceeding from their own world view.

On the other side, to try to maintain compatibility of world view without holding fast to the proper goal is a malady to which we evangelicals are sometimes prone. We may, for example, become overly anxious about the compatibility of our societal legal structure with the legal demands of parts of the Bible, without reference to the center and meaning of it all, Jesus Christ. The law, as well as prophecy, must have its focus in Christ. After all, as Hebrews 10:1 says, the law is but a shadow of the good things which were to come. Or, as another example, it is easy when immersing oneself in the Old Testament to dwell more upon the fortunes of physical Israel than upon Christ and his redemptive program and people of all ages.

We must conclude that we have not yet arrived. Even though what we call grammatical-historical exegesis is foundational to our interpretation of Scripture, we cannot rest content with it, because it does not take us far enough. It is not ultimately method that yields the true meaning. We must ask what interpretive framework, or world view, and what goal genuinely proceed from the world view and goal of the Bible itself.

Perhaps it has not escaped the reader that this understanding has certain implications for apologetics. Consider, for example, a book by Samuel Levine entitled *You Take Jesus; I'll Take God: How to Refute Christian Missionaries* (Los Angeles: Hamoroh, 1980). The book aims to equip Jews with a knowledge of the Old Testament which will enable them to escape the force of Christian references to Old Testament prophecy. It does so not by systematically interpreting all the passages that might be used by a Christian but by teaching a general method whereby any Christian reference to prophecy can be refuted.

This book is simply an elaboration of a few key procedures which will enable anyone to see the inadequacy or falseness of any Christian "proof." Here are the procedures:
1. If they quote from the Old Testament, then:

a) Look at the entire context of that verse—usually this alone will suffice.
b) See if the verse has been mistranslated—you should always try to look up every quote in the original Hebrew. If you do not know Hebrew, find a friend who does.
c) See if the verse seems to be mis-interpreted—see if the interpretation is forced into the words artificially.
d) See if the verse points exclusively to Jesus; see if the verse could apply to another person as well. (pp. 9ff.)

Do these words not echo the very words of our hermeneutical textbooks? The "method" of which we approve is here getting the wrong results. And how do we know they are wrong results? Only by the further revelation of the New Testament and the conviction of the Holy Spirit that the new revelation is revelation.

As Longenecker pointed out, we are not the recipients of direct new special revelation and therefore we cannot impose some category of theological preunderstanding that is not derived from already-existing revelation. Precisely for this reason, though, our hermeneutical goal in reading the Old Testament must remain that of the New. Furthermore, we are recipients of a new revelation, the New Testament, which expands our whole interpretive framework. So we may see things in the Old Testament that are really there but would not appear apart from the New. Special revelation in the New Testament clarifies the Christocentricity of Old Testament redemptive history. Furthermore, we have the whole New Testament, and thus can see relationships and perspectives on Christ that were unavailable to the original readers (e.g., we have Luke to help us understand Matthew).

Old Testament interpretation prior to the New Testament could still be compatible with the biblical world view and have a correct hermeneutical goal, as far as it was known. But without the New Testament, a complete and whole picture of the meaning of the Old was not possible. To reject the New Testament now, however, is to reject its hermeneutical goal, which consciously redirects interpretation away from even a partial proper understanding.

The New Testament writers did not have our problems; they knew that the Old Testament spoke of Jesus and proceeded to understand it in that light. We too know that the Old Testament speaks of Jesus. Did he not tell us so (Luke 24)? And are we not therefore justified in seeing him in its pages? This is no "skeleton in the closet." It is our skeleton key to open all the doors in the inerrant Word of God.

# 7

## Oral Tradition

### Bruce K. Waltke

*The defense of oral tradition is a rather difficult one for the Form Critics to make. If they claim that oral tradition was so accurate that these traditions did not need to be written down, but were so correctly transmitted for centuries that recording was unnecessary, then when they try to get back of the literary form to a quite different oral tradition, they virtually admit the importance and necessity of the written record. On the other hand if they insist that traditions were molded and altered in the course of oral tradition, they must admit that the desire for accuracy would make a written record desirable and necessary, provided such a record was possible. And archaeology has proved conclusively that it was both possible and probable in the time of Abraham and for centuries before his time.*

—Oswald T. Allis, 1972

Form criticism, tradition criticism, and canonical criticism are all based on at least two principles: (1) that much of the literature in the Pentateuch, especially the stories in Genesis, had a long prehistory before being written down, and (2) that during its oral stage this material was often transposed into new settings with new meanings. They differ about the extent of this material and about its relative fixity and fluidity. Most scholars grant greater fixity to material such as genealogies, laws, and cultic regulations, which gave social order to the community, than to stories about the fathers. Nevertheless, most source critics regard even the so-called sacred material as subject to accretions and change over an extended period of oral tradition. They also differ about the stages in the development of oral tradition from its fluid to its fixed stage. Scandinavian scholars such as Nyberg, Birkeland, Nielsen, and Engnell thought that the material floated in an oral stage until the time of the exile, when it was threatened with the danger of extinction. Other critics such as Noth and Mowinckel envision an early fluid stage followed by a later fixed, preliterary stage represented in the literary documents embedded in the Pentateuch. Both schools agree, however, that at some preliterary stage the biblical material was transmitted orally at local sanctuaries by tradents who preserved, reinterpreted, reformulated, and supplemented Israel's diverse traditions and theological heritage.

H. S. Nyberg expressed in a radical form the conviction that this material first existed in oral tradition:

Transmission in the East is seldom exclusively written; it is chiefly *oral* in character. The living speech from ancient times to the present plays a greater role in the East than the written presentation. Almost every written work in the Orient went through a longer or shorter oral transmission in its earliest history, and also even after it is written down the oral transmission remains the normal form in the preservation and use of the work.[1]

More popularly and less guardedly Gene M. Tucker expressed the concensus of form critics on this point: "All ancient . . . cultures had a body of oral 'literature'—that is, folklore—long before they developed written records and literature."[2]

After tracing the development of scholarly opinion regarding oral tradition from Hermann Gunkel through the views of Scandinavian scholars,[3] Walter E. Rast expressed the second principle of source critics who attempt to reconstruct the history of a text even in its oral stage: "Such study shows that the messages of the Old Testament texts have experienced development over long period of time. Different generations

1. H. S. Nyberg, *Studien zum Hoseabuche* (Uppsala: Lundequistska, 1935), p. 7 (my translation, Nyberg's emphasis).

2. Gene M. Tucker, *Form Criticism of the Old Testament* (Philadelphia: Fortress, 1971), p. 17.

3. For a full survey of the work of Scandinavian scholars, see Douglas A. Knight, *Rediscovering the Traditions of Israel*, Society of Biblical Literature Dissertation Series, 9 (Missoula, Mont.: Scholars, 1973).

have taken them up, either in oral or written form, and transposed them into fresh settings and understandings."[4]

These convictions of form critics and their successors profoundly influence the way in which they regard the historical accuracy of the Bible and its meaning. According to them, the stories contain only a kernel of historical accuracy. William F. Albright noted:

> In recent decades there has been steady increase of the use of aetiology (the analysis of stories explaining ancient names and practices) to identify legendary accretions in orally transmitted material. The discovery and application of the method of form criticism, especially by H. Gunkel, M. Dibelius, and their followers, have given a great impetus to the utilization of the aetiological method, which has now reached a point where its leading exponents are inclined to deny the historicity of nearly all early stories of both the Old and the New Testaments.[5]

In spite of Albright's caveat that this view has gone too far, it still prevails. Tucker's words are representative:

> Sagas usually tell us more about the life and time of the period in which they were circulated and written down than they do about the events they mean to describe. A careful form critical and traditio-historical analysis ... can help the historian to distinguish between the old and new and the historically reliable and the unreliable in those sagas.[6]

Also, the notion that Israel's sacred heritage was handed down in a fluid and very complicated process of redactional modification both before and after it was written down raises a complex of problems about authorial meaning during the changing loci of "revelation." If tradents reworked and reformulated the "literature" to meet ever-changing needs, then many meanings lie buried within the text. The view of some canonical critics such as Brevard Childs, who does not concern himself with the process of canonization but only with the product of canonization, relieves the problem to some extent. He contends that only the final meaning of a text in the Jewish canon matters. One is still left, however, with the uneasy feeling that the text's original meaning to the people of God has been deliberately obfuscated by the final redactor.

4. Walter E. Rast, *Tradition History and the Old Testament* (Philadelphia: Fortress, 1972), p. 18.

5. William F. Albright, *From the Stone Age to Christianity*, 2d ed. (Garden City, N.Y.: Doubleday, 1957), p. 70.

6. Tucker, *Form Criticism*, p. 20. For a survey of literature treating the relationship between historicity and oral tradition, see Jan Vansina, *Oral Tradition: A Study in Historical Methodology* (London: Routledge and Kegan Paul, 1965).

The documentary hypothesis, the pet theory of literary critics, has recently been attacked. Scholars such as Kikawada, Clines, Alter, Silberman, Berlin, and Longman, for example, have been demonstrating the artistic unity of Genesis, a unity that cannot be explained as a result of piecing together documents by redactors. Their apology for the unity of the books of the Bible contains also a polemic against all forms of source criticism. They explain doublets, for example, not as the result of a combination of sources but as a literary device to bind the work together, giving it shape and meaning. Form criticism, based on oral tradition, has also been coming under attack. Whybray, in his *Making of the Pentateuch: A Methodological Study* (1987), takes up and advances the earlier work of Van Seters. Whybray rightly insists that the alleged earlier forms of the material no longer exist and that there is no direct evidence of them. All arguments for and against form criticism and tradition criticism are indirect. Whybray, though granting that form criticism has made a distinctive contribution to the study of some books such as the Book of Psalms, attacked these five assumptions of form and tradition critics of the Pentateuch:

1. That Israel's traditions about its early history originated in circumstances in which the composition of written records is extremely improbable;
2. That the character and processes of oral tradition and composition as practiced by those who first composed and transmitted this early material can be deduced by comparison with the "oral literature" of other people which has been studied by modern folklorists;
3. That oral traditions of this kind, though subject to a degree of modification in the course of transmission, are capable of relatively faithful reproduction over a long period of time;
4. That there is reason to suppose that Israel had a tradition of storytelling which could have been the vehicle for the preservation of such traditions;
5. That it is possible by studying a written text to discover whether it is based on oral composition or not.[7]

This chapter, which disputes the view that the text underwent a long and often complicated oral prehistory, was written before Whybray's study appeared. Whybray's work, especially his polemic against the first two assumptions, will be used to enrich it. The first and major part of this

7. R. N. Whybray, *The Making of the Pentateuch: A Methodological Study,* Journal for the Study of the Old Testament Supplement Series, 53 (Sheffield: University of Sheffield, 1987), p. 139.

chapter attempts to demonstrate that the most important indirect evidence, the literature of the ancient Near East, does not support the principles on which form, tradition, and canonical criticisms of Pentateuch rests. In a second and briefer section it aims to show that even the more inferential evidence of literature from shortly after the time of the Old Testament's completion at about 400 B.C. and evidence from neighboring non-Semitic-speaking peoples does not suggest that oral traditions were transmitted in a fluid state. Finally, I address the question about material in Genesis that must antedate writing. It is hoped that, as a result of this study, the church will realize that it does not have to create a new memory, a new story, to understand itself and that the one it has memorized is not mistaken but reliable.

## Oral Tradition in the Ancient Near East

To decide whether the literature of the Old Testament was changed by tradents over a long period of oral transmission, it will be instructive to turn to the cultures of the ancient Near East, which undoubtedly influenced all of the Old Testament's literary genres: to Ebla in northern Syria (ca. 2350 B.C.); then successively to Mesopotamia, whose coherent culture can be traced with confidence for over two millennia until it was dealt what proved to be a fatal blow by Alexander the Great (ca. 330 B.C.); to the Hittites (1450 to 1250 B.C.); to Ugarit (ca. 1400 B.C.); to the Egyptian culture, whose literatures stretch from about 2500 to 500 B.C.; and finally to the Northwest Semites. In this last connection the Hebrews will be considered, including the internal evidence of the Old Testament itself. Recent archaeological and sociological research has validated the biblical presentation that Israel and its patriarchs lived in contact with its neighbors. The view that they had little contact with the centers of culture is an anachronism based on a false analogy between Israel and modern Bedouin. In this wide-ranging survey a single question is asked: "Did the people under investigation preserve their cultural heritage through an oral tradition subject to alteration or through written texts precisely with a view that its heritage not be corrupted?" If the evidence for the former is negative, there is no reason to accept the first principle, along with the historical exegetical difficulties entailed, on which form, tradition, and canonical critics construct their methods.

### Ebla

According to Giovanni Pettinato, the texts unearthed from the royal archives of Ebla include the following types: economic and administrative texts (regarding the various branches of industry, such as metals, wood, and textiles), historical and historical-juridical texts, lexical texts ("scientific" lists of animals in general, fishes and birds in particular; lists of professions and personal names; of objects in stone, metal, and wood; various lexical texts; grammatical texts with verbal paradigms; and finally bilingual vocabularies in Sumerian and Eblaite), and true literary texts (myths, epic tales, hymns to divinities, incantations, rituals, and collections of proverbs).[8] This ancient city, which antedates the Hebrew patriarchs by three to five centuries and Moses by about a millennium, was highly literate and preserved its culture and heritage in writing. So far as they have been translated and published, the Ebla texts make no mention of oral tradition or tradents. But much still remains to be deciphered.

### Mesopotamia

In Mesopotamia there is much evidence that the Akkadian culture conservatively transmitted its heritage in writing. By comparing collections of Sumerian proverbs that achieved canonical status among the Akkadians as early as circa 1500 B.C. with later collections dated to the Neo-Babylonian period (ca. 600 B.C.), it can be shown that they were transmitted in writing with relatively little modification.[9] The great Akkadian creation epic, *Enuma elish,* was probably composed during the time of Hammurabi (ca. 1700 B.C.), and its earliest extant copy, clearly not the original, is dated only a hundred years later.

The law codes of Lipit-Ishtar, Eshnunna, Hammurabi, and others antedate Moses by centuries. Moreover, they promised blessing to those who preserved the written laws and threatened judgment against those who altered them. The stele containing Lipit-Ishtar's law code reads: "May he who will not commit any evil deed with regard to it, who will not damage my handiwork, who will (not) erase its inscription, who will not write his own name upon it—be presented with life and breath of long days."[10] The epilogue to Hammurabi's code is similar:

If that man heeded my words which I wrote, on my stela,
and did not rescind my law,
has not distorted my words,
did not alter my statutes,
may Shamash make that man reign. . . .

If that man did not heed my words . . .

8. Giovanni Pettinato, *The Archives of Ebla: An Empire Inscribed on Clay* (Garden City, N.Y.: Doubleday, 1981), pp. 42–48.

9. Bruce K. Waltke, "The Book of Proverbs and Ancient Wisdom Literature," *Bibliotheca Sacra* 136 (1979): 221–38.

10. J. B. Pritchard, ed., *Ancient Near Eastern Texts Relating to the Old Testament,* 3d ed. (Princeton: Princeton University Press, 1969), p. 161 (hereafter cited as *ANET*).

and disregarded my curses, . . .
but has abolished the law which I enacted,
has distorted my words,
has altered my statutes, . . .
may mighty Anum . . .
deprive him of the glory of sovereignty . . .
the disappearance of his name and memory from the land.[11]

According to Otto Weber, it was the rule among the Akkadians that only an agreement fixed in writing was juridically valid.[12]

Hymns from the early Sumerian period (ca. 1900 B.C.) are also found in Mesopotamia. What arrests our attention about them here is that, though they were intended to be sung at cultic centers, they were written down. In fact their technical terms, probably related to their liturgical use, have not as yet been deciphered by Sumerologists, even as the same kind of notices in the biblical psalms cannot at present be deciphered by Hebraists.[13]

Letters were read from written texts, as evidenced by letters from Mari. These typically state: "Your tablet which you did send forth, I have heard."[14]

Representing the historical literary genre in Mesopotamia we have the famous Sumerian king lists and the later and equally famous Assyrian annals. Representatives of the religious genre include rituals, incantations, and descriptions of festivals. We may infer that events referred to in this literature that occurred before the invention of writing were transmitted by word of mouth, but we cannot reconstruct its nature. After writing evolved to communicate effectively, there is no indication that a fluid oral transmission alone was the principal means of preserving memory in Mesopotamia. In this literature there is no mention of either tradents or oral tradition. Eduard Nielsen, contending for oral tradition in the Near East, conceded: "The fact that religious and epic texts of major importance in the high cultures of the Ancient Near East were ordinarily put into written form has already been stressed in the case of Egyptian literature."[15]

What evidence is there for oral tradition after the invention and evolution of writing? The best Nielsen can offer against George Widengren's

11. Ibid., pp. 178–79.
12. Otto Weber, *Die Literatur der Babylonier und Assyrer* (Leipzig: J. C. Hinrichs, 1970), p. 249.
13. Samuel N. Kramer, *The Sumerians* (Chicago: University of Chicago Press, 1963), p. 207.
14. See Archives Royales de Mari (Paris: P. Geuthner, 1941), 1. 6:5, 9:5, and others.
15. Eduard Nielsen, *Oral Tradition: A Modern Problem in Old Testament Introduction* (London: SCM, 1954), pp. 28–29.

contention that texts were always written is one example, which may introduce a minor correction. A colophon in a hymn reads: "Written from the scholar's dictation, the old edition I have not seen."[16] In fact, however, Nielsen's one exception actually proves Widengren's rule. It would appear that oral tradition was only reluctantly relied upon, and in this particular case because an original written document was not available. The situation reflected by this colophon differs *toto caelo* from that supposed by source critics, who presuppose a long and often complex oral tradition. The scribe is a faithful copyist, not a tradent manipulating his heritage.

There is evidence, however, that redaction of older written sources into later ones did occur. As Donald J. Wiseman pointed out,

> Tigay has shown that redactors completed the remoulding of the earlier Sumerian poems into one "Gilgamesh" tradition (ca. 1800 B.C.) about the same time as the Hittites made a summary of 5 tablets of Gilgamesh into one; and about the same time as the Kassite period of Babylonia (1540–1250) when scribes began copying the Gilgamesh, and other epics, in a traditional way which was to hand them on virtually unchanged for more than a thousand years.[17]

Some texts show that the written tradition was to be accompanied with memorization for oral recital. Nielsen called attention to the following: (1) from the Irra myth: "The scribe who learns this text by heart escapes the enemy"; (2) from Ashurbanipal's prayer to Shamash: "Whosoever shall learn this text [by heart and] glorify the gods"; (3) from tablet 7 of *Enuma elish:* "The sage and the learned shall together ponder [them], father shall tell [of them] to son and teach [them to] him."[18] These texts, however, do not argue for a long and complicated oral prehistory before the material in view was written down. Rather they suggest that oral recitation accompanied the written texts. R. K. Harrison rightly commented:

> Modern scholars have largely misunderstood the purpose and function of oral transmission in the ancient Near East. The firm tradition of the Mosaic period, as well as of ancient peoples other than the Hebrews, was that any events of importance were generally recorded in written form quite soon after they had taken place. . . . The principal purpose of oral transmission was the dissemination of the pertinent information . . . . It

16. Ibid., pp. 28–29.
17. Donald J. Wiseman, "Israel's Literary Neighbours in the 13th Century B.C.," *Journal of Northwest Semitic Languages* 5 (1977): 82.
18. Nielsen, *Oral Tradition,* pp. 19–20.

is entirely fallacious to assume . . .that an oral form of a narrative was the necessary and normal precursor of the written stage. There can be little doubt that in many cases both oral and written traditions existed side by side for lengthy periods.[19]

Bendt Alster explored the possibility that, because poetic lines turn up in the same form in several Sumerian poems, these may be traditional formulas of an oral tradition.[20] In fact, however, traditional formulas may point to oral composition, not to a long and flexible oral tradition, and there is no direct evidence about how such texts were composed. Ruth Finnegan argued against any fundamental, qualitative difference between oral and written literature.[21]

In sum, from Mesopotamia there is evidence of redaction from earlier written sources into later complexes followed by a conservative transmission of the literary achievement with an accompanying oral recital, but there is no evidence of a preliterary and/or flexible oral tradition.

### Hittites

The Hittite literature and history are mostly known from the archives recovered from its capital at Hattusilis (modern Bogazköy). These archives yielded texts similar to those encountered elsewhere in the ancient Near East. Its international suzerainty treaties, which are remarkably parallel to the Book of Deuteronomy, according to George Mendenhall,[22] Klaus Baltzer,[23] and Meredith Kline,[24] enjoyed canonical status. A treaty between Suppululiumas and Mattiwaza contains the following provision:

In the Mitanni land (a duplicate) has been deposited before Tessub . . . . At regular intervals shall they read it in the presence of the king . . . . Whoever will remove this tablet from before Tessub . . . and put in a hidden place, if

19. R. K. Harrison, *Introduction to the Old Testament* (Grand Rapids: Eerdmans, 1969), pp. 209–10.
20. Bendt Alster, *Dumuzi's Dream: Aspects of Oral Poetry in a Sumerian Myth* (Copenhagen: Akademisk Forlag, 1972).
21. Ruth Finnegan, *Oral Literature in Africa* (Oxford: Clarendon, 1970), p. 61, cited by R. C. Culley, "Oral Tradition and the OT: Some Recent Discussion," *Semeia* 5 (= *Oral Tradition and Old Testament Studies;* 1976). The title of this issue of *Semeia* may cause confusion by confounding oral composition with oral tradition. Evidence for the first is not evidence for the second, as that term has been traditionally understood in Old Testament studies.
22. George E. Mendenhall, *Law and Covenant in Israel and the Ancient Near East* (Pittsburgh: Biblical Colloquium, 1955).
23. Klaus Baltzer, *The Covenant Formulary* (Oxford: Blackwell, 1971).
24. Meredith Kline, *Treaty of the Great King* (Grand Rapids: Eerdmans, 1963).

he breaks it or causes anyone else to change the wording of the tablet—at the conclusion of this treaty we have called the gods to be assembled and the gods of the contracting parties to be present, to listen and to serve as witnesses.[25]

In sum, the Hittites, like the other great peoples of the ancient Near East, committed their important literature to sure writing instead of an oral tradition.

### Ugarit

Richard E. Whitaker discovered that 82 percent of the language of the Ugaritic poems is formulaic. This high frequency of formulae and formulaic structures led him to suppose that "we are dealing here with an orally created poetry."[26] But once again it is necessary to note that he is talking about oral composition, not about a long and complicated prehistory before its transposition to writing. The fact is that the peoples of ancient Ugarit wrote down their hymns and myths celebrating their nature deities and recited them at their sanctuaries. Moreover, a sharp distinction between written and oral forms of communication cannot be made, because written texts were meant to be read aloud. Whybray cites with approval Ruth Finnegan's point that it has been forgotten that ancient literature was intended to be read aloud:

> The relationship between oral and written literature . . . is a difference of degree and not of kind . . . . The literature of the classical world . . . laid far more stress on the oral aspect than does more recent literatures . . . . The presence of writing can coexist with an emphasis on the significance of performance as one of the main means of the effective transmission of a literary work . . . . Throughout much of antiquity even written works were normally read aloud rather than silently, and one means of transmitting and, as it were, "publishing" a literary composition was to deliver it aloud to a group of friends.[27]

Recall Augustine's astonishment as late as circa A.D. 400 in finding Ambrose in his study reading a text by merely moving his eyes down the page and not reading it aloud. Nothing in the Ugaritic texts suggests that oral recitation existed apart from written texts or that it had priority over the written witnesses to their beliefs. It seems plausible to suppose that these potent, magical words were considered as unalterable

---

25. *ANET,* p. 205.
26. Richard E. Whitaker, "A Formulaic Analysis of Ugaritic Poetry" (Ph.D. diss., Harvard University, 1969), p. 157.
27. Whybray, *Making of the Pentateuch,* p. 182.

and written down either at the time of composition or shortly thereafter.

## Egypt

From Egypt have come numerous texts of many of the literary genres represented in the Bible. These texts demonstrate that Egyptian scribes attempted to preserve their heritage in writing as accurately as possible. Albright wrote:

> The prolonged and intimate study of the many scores of thousands of pertinent documents from the ancient Near East proves that sacred and profane documents were copied with greater care than is true of scribal copying in Graeco-Roman times. Even documents which were never intended to be seen by other human eyes, such as mortuary texts, manuscripts of the Book of the Dead, and magical texts, are copied so that we can nearly always read them without difficulty if the state of preservation permits.[28]

Kenneth A. Kitchen called attention to the colophon of a text dated circa 1400 B.C. in which a scribe boasted: "[This book] is completed from its beginning to its end, having been copied, revised, compared, and verified sign by sign."[29]

Is there any evidence of oral tradition among the Egyptians? Boudoun van de Walle laid an excellent foundation for understanding the development of textual criticism of Egyptian literary works.[30] Askel Volten in his editions of the Teaching of *Any*[31] and *Insinger*[32] identified the main types of error to be encountered: (1) entirely graphic error, (2) auricular errors, (3) slips of memory, and (4) the usual unintentional slips due to carelessness. Gunter Burkard took issue with Volten's thesis that by far the majority of errors were *Hörfehler,* "mistakes of hearing," but argued rather that the most common type of mistake, apart from simple carelessness, arose from copying directly from a written text and that the next largest group of errors was caused by writing texts from memory.[33] This procedure led to omission of verses, transpositions of maxims or lines, the substitution of synonyms, and on occasion the intermingling and confusion

---

28. Albright, *Stone Age,* p. 79.

29. Kenneth A. Kitchen, *Ancient Orient and Old Testament* (Chicago: Inter-Varsity, 1966), p. 140.

30. Boudon van de Walle, *La transmission des textes littéraires égyptiens* (Brussels: Fondation égyptologique reine Elisabeth, 1948), p. 12.

31. Aksel P. F. Volten, *Studien zum Weisheitsbuch des Ani* (Copenhagen: Levin and Munksgaard, 1937).

32. Aksel P. F. Volten, *Das demotische Weisheitsbuch: Studien und Bearbeitung,* Analecta Aegyptica, v. 1, 2 (Copenhagen, 1941).

33. G. Burkard, *Textkritische Untersuchungen zu ägyptischen Weisheitslehre des Alten und Mittleren Reiches,* Ade. Abh. 34 (Wiesbaden, 1977).

of maxims or pericopes. Such scribal errors do not provide a foundation for building a theory that the Egyptians transmitted their heritage in a pliable oral tradition. All three scholars describe these changes as errors in *the writing of the texts,* assuming that the scribe intended to preserve and transmit the written heritage in writing and that the material was memorized for personal edification and dissemination. By contrast the hypothetical tradents imagined by modern source critics do not accidentally change the text through faulty memory that accompanies the written tradition but intentionally alter it, sometimes drastically, to keep the traditions contemporary with changing historical conditions.

### Northwest Semitic

Apart from the Ugaritic texts, treated above, and the Old Testament itself, the literature from the Northwest Semitic cultures is poorly preserved, probably because of the perishable nature of materials other than clay and rock in a hostile climate. What evidence exists suggests widespread literacy in this part of the ancient Near East due to the invention of the alphabet based on the acrophonic principle at circa 1600 B.C. Whybray notes: "The author of the Egyptian story of *Wen-Amon* from the eleventh century B.C. represents the prince of Byblos as consulting the 'books of the days of his fathers' in which the past relations between Byblos and Egypt were recorded: a recognition by an Egyptian of an established Phoenician practice of recording past events in writing."[34] The Proto-Sinaitic inscriptions (ca. 1475 B.C.) represent the written prayers of Semites enslaved by the Egyptians,[35] giving us strong reason to think that Abraham's descendants, though lowly slaves in Egypt, were literate.

The Old Testament witness about the manner of its transmission comports favorably with what has been found elsewhere in the ancient Near East, namely, that its sacred literature was transmitted in writing with oral dissemination. Its authors appeal to literary sources: "The Book of Songs" (3 Kings 8:53 LXX); "The Book of the Upright" (Josh. 10:13); "The Book of the Wars of Yahweh" (Num. 21:14); "The Diaries of the Kings" (Kings and Chronicles). The Hebrew Scriptures represent its laws as having been written down in books at the time of composition (Exod. 24:7; Deut. 31:9; Josh. 24:25–27; 1 Sam. 10:25) that must not be changed (Deut. 4:2; 12:32). The prophets refer to the law as a written document (Hos. 8:12). And to judge from Isaiah 8:16 and Jeremiah 36, the originally

34. Whybray, *Making of the Pentateuch,* pp. 140–41.
35. William F. Albright, *The Proto-Sinaitic Inscriptions* (Cambridge: Harvard University Press, 1969).

oral messages of the prophets were written down shortly after their delivery, exactly in the same way as happened in the case of the Koran (as we shall see shortly). Even Moses' song was written down at the time of its original recitation (Deut. 31:19, 30). From this evidence may we not assume that the same was true of other songs mentioned in the Hebrew Scriptures (cf. Num. 21:17 and elsewhere)?

By comparing the Ugaritic poetry and the Amarna glosses (ca. 1400 B.C.) as his *terminus a quo* for the earliest forms of Hebrew poetry and Amos and Micah as his *terminus ad quem* for the later standard forms, David A. Robertson concluded (with the qualification that each one contains standard forms) that Exodus 15 is unqualifiedly early and that Deuteronomy 32, Judges 5, 2 Samuel 22 (Ps. 18), Habakkuk 3, and Job are qualifiedly early.[36] Even if they were passed on through the generations by word of mouth, they were not drastically reformulated.

A man must write a bill of divorce (Deut. 24:3); kings had secretaries to assist them in their writing (2 Sam. 8:17). According to Judges 8:14, a young man wrote down for Gideon the names of the seventy-seven officials of Succoth. This text assumes the literacy of Israel's youth. On the basis of ancient Hebrew inscriptional evidence uncovered by archaeologists, A. R. Millard draws the conclusion that writing was available to all Israel[37] and that prophets could have recorded and edited their words themselves.[38]

Regarding the stories in the Pentateuch, Whybray notes:

Whatever their origins, the stories have been anonymously recorded in writing and are simply "there." There is, rather strangely, no word in the Hebrew of the Old Testament equivalent to "story" in the sense of a simple tale. Words like *dābār*, "saying, report," *māšāl*, "proverb, saying, parable," *midrāš*, "didactic story, commentary" (very rare, and only in Chronicles), *tōlēdōt* (usually "genealogy," very occasionally "history, account," e.g. Gen. 37.2) are all either too general or denote some special kind of communication.

There are, it is true, scenes in the narrative books of the Old Testament in the course of which stories are told: where someone makes a report, or gives an account, to another person about something which has occurred. But these are not events of the remote past like those of the Pentateuch:

36. David A. Robertson, *Linguistic Evidence in Dating Early Hebrew Poetry* (Missoula, Mont.: Society for Biblical Literature, 1972), p. 154. For the problems involved in dating documents, see my *Intermediate Hebrew Grammar* (Winona Lake, Ind.: Eisenbrauns, forthcoming), par. 2.8.
37. Alan R. Millard, "The Question of Isarelite Literacy," *Bible Review* 3 (1987): 26.
38. Ibid., p. 31.

they are practical reports, each made with a specific purpose, of very recent
events, usually events witnessed by the speaker himself . . . .

There is in fact no evidence to support either of Gunkel's suggestions for
a *Sitz im Leben* of the *"Sage"* . . . or the visit of the itinerant, "professional"
storyteller.[39]

To be sure, the laws were to be memorized and recited orally (Exod.
12:24–26; Deut. 6:6, 20–25; Josh. 1:8; Ps. 1:2), as were the proverbs (e.g.,
Prov. 22:18) and Israel's sacred history (see Ps. 44:1), but we must not pit
this oral activity against a stable written tradition. None of these texts,
some of which pertain to parental replies, can be called narratives, and
they are all recorded. The evidence from the surrounding countries
strongly suggests that the two kinds of tradition complemented one another: the written to preserve Israel's religious treasure, the oral to dis-
seminate it. Whybray noted: "They do not in themselves witness to a
practice of the oral transmission of narrative."[40]

Regarding the form critic's claim that stories were passed down by tradents at sanctuaries, often as aetiologies legitimatizing the sanctuary,
Whybray noted: "Not a word is said in the Old Testament about the way
in which *narratives* (as distinct from laws) might have been used in worship practiced at these sanctuaries, or about functionaries who might
have been the agents of the transmission."[41]

By comparing synoptic passages in the Bible, Helmer Ringgren demonstrated that variants crept into the text in the same ways as Volten and
van de Walle uncovered in Egypt.[42] But he too speaks of them as "mistakes," assuming that copyists were attempting to preserve the tradition
rather than that tradents were at work deliberately reformulating and
re-presenting it. In sum, these changes introduced by copyists are both
qualitatively and quantitatively different from that supposed by critics
who base their theories on a protracted and complicated oral tradition.

Robert C. Culley thought that formulaic language found in the psalms
pointed to their origin in a tradition of oral formulaic composition. He
wisely left open the question, however, of whether any of the present
psalms were originally oral compositions.[43] In any case his study pertains to poetry and to oral composition, not to a pliable oral tradition.

---

39. Whybray, *Making of the Pentateuch*, p. 174.
40. Ibid., p. 175.
41. Ibid., p. 176.
42. Helmer Ringgren, "Oral and Written Transmission in the Old Testament," *Studia Theologica* 3 (1950–51): 34–59.
43. Robert C. Culley, *Oral Formulaic Language in the Biblical Psalms* (Toronto: University of Toronto Press, 1976).

# Oral Tradition Outside
# the Ancient Near East

Obviously analogies from the literature of non-Semitic-speaking peoples and/or from a time later than the composition of the Old Testament do not carry as much weight in deciding the issue addressed as analogies from the ancient Near Eastern literatures or from the Old Testament itself. Nevertheless, a consideration of this data is instructive.

### Homer and the Classics

According to Milman Parry, Homer composed poetic epics for easy oral recital in a preliterature society.[44] Once again, however, it is important to note that the topic here is oral composition in contrast to a complex oral transmission. Furthermore, according to Robert B. Coote, the material in Homer is altogether different in type and extent from that of the Bible,[45] and Parry's evidence for oral composition in Homer is not applicable in the case of the Bible. Coote wrote: "None of the characteristics . . . which make Parry's designation of repeated lines and phrases in Homer as oral formulas by analogy with the Yugoslav oral formula so compelling is to be found in the Hebrew '[tradition.]' "[46]

Some classicists are inclined to visualize a period of oral transmission in pre-Homeric times.[47] It is beyond my competence to make a judgment here. The fact that pupils were expected to memorize Homer and Virgil in classical antiquity is parallel to the use of oral tradition in the ancient Near East.

### The Jews and the Talmud

The Mishna and Gemara were both composed and transmitted orally for some period of time. But it may be supposed that these interpretations of the written laws found in the Bible were regarded at first during their oral stage as qualitatively different from the Scriptures themselves. In fact, they were probably put into writing only after they achieved an authoritative status among the Jews. Whybray wrote: "Comparisons with written material from other periods such as the rabbinic literature are of doubtful value because of their different back-

44. M. Parry, "Studies in the Epic Technique of Oral Verse-Making. I: Homer and Homeric Style," *Harvard Studies in Classical Philology* 41 (1930): 43–147.
45. Robert B. Coote, "The Application of the Oral Theory to Biblical Hebrew Literature," *Semeia* 5 (1976): 52.
46. Ibid., pp. 56–57.
47. Albert B. Lord, *The Singer of Tales* (Cambridge: Harvard University Press, 1960).

ground: the rabbinic traditions, for example, were first transmitted orally in the midst of a literate society for quite special reasons."[48]

### The Hindus and the Rig-Veda

The Rig-Veda is the most striking example of a religious tradition passed on by word of mouth over centuries, from probably before 1200 B.C. to no earlier than about the fifth century B.C. The oral transmission of the later Vedas and the Brahmanas also embraced centuries. This manner of preserving religious literature in the environs of the Indus River stands in striking contrast to what is known of the civilizations along the Nile and Tigris-Euphrates rivers. But even this more remote evidence does not support the second principle of modern source critics that the text underwent complex reformulations. Projecting back from the modern Hindu practice where thousands of Brahmins still accurately learn the Rig-Veda by heart (153,826 words!)[49] to the earlier centuries, it may be supposed that those reciting this tradition aimed not to change it. And, of course, what is disconcerting about modern source critics is not so much their theory of oral transmission as their presumption that an oral tradition in the case of the Bible entailed a complex development of the literature, calling into question both its historical reliability and the clarity of authorial intention.

### The Arabs and the Koran

Arabic literatures provide us with a much closer analogy to the Hebrew Scriptures. South Arabic inscriptions, which are notoriously difficult to date, show that even Bedouin were literate. From a much later period Widengren demonstrated that Muhammad not only contributed directly or indirectly to putting the Koran into writing but even made some interpolations into the text.[50] Regarding the role of oral tradition in the composition of the Koran, Widengren wrote: "We are confronted with the fact that in the earliest Islamic period the first generation were the collectors of traditions."[51] The situation in Islam seems very similar to that of Christianity: within the generation or two that witnessed Jesus Christ, written testimonies about him were made.

Regarding pre-Islamic poetry, Bridget Connelly points to an article by

48. Whybray, *Making of the Pentateuch*, p. 142.
49. Max Muller, "Literature Before Letters," in *Last Essays* (1st ser.), pp. 123, 130, cited in Nielsen, *Oral Tradition*, p. 24.
50. George Widengren, *Literary and Psychological Aspects of the Hebrew Prophets* (Uppsala: Universitets Arsskriff, 1948), pp. 10, 49.
51. G. Widengren, "Oral Tradition and Written Literature Among the Hebrews in Light of Arabic Evidence, with Special Regard to Prose Narratives," in *Acta Orientalia* 23 (1959): 201–62.

James T. Monroe arguing that, on the basis of formulaic expressions, these poems were composed for oral recitation.[52] Once again, oral composition is not directly relevant to the present study. However, Mary C. Bateson's investigation of five pre-Islamic Arabic codes rejected even this possibility.[53]

## Old Icelandic and Serbo-Croatian

The best evidence for an oral tradition such as that proposed by modern source critics comes from Indo-European peoples of a much later time, especially from Old Icelandic (ca. A.D. 1300). Here one finds a mighty priesthood trained in the oral transmission of their religious heritage. But the objections to founding a theory on this sort of evidence ought not to require demonstration. In fact, to make an appeal to it appears to be an act of desperation and actually weakens the case. Widengren asked:

> Is it not queer to observe that in order to prove the predominant role of oral tradition among such a Semitic people in antiquity as the Hebrews all real evidence from their closely related neighbors, the Arabs, has been left out of consideration . . .whereas evidence from all kinds of Indo-European peoples was adduced, so that even the old Icelanders were called upon to render their service in which case neither the "great interval of time" nor that of space seems to have exercised any discouraging effect?![54]

The field of study of Parry and Albert Lord on a living oral tradition of Yugoslav narrative poetry showed that the poets did not memorize their traditional poems but freshly created them in each performance.[55] But the objections to applying their study to the Bible are obvious. First, the date is not comparable. Coote wrote: "The severest obstacle to the application of the theory to the OT is the lack of verse analogous in type and extent to that of Homer or Yugoslavia."[56] Whybray argued that, for a convincing parallel to be drawn between Old Testament narrative literature and modern oral narrative literature, three criteria must be met: (1) "the existence of an adequate body of reliable information about the charac-

---

52. Bridget Connelly, "Oral Poetics: The Arab Case" (paper prepared for the Oral Literature Seminar, Modern Language Association, 1974), cited in Culley, *Oral Formulaic Language*, p. 6.

53. Mary C. Bateson, *Structural Continuity in Poetry: A Linguisitic Study in Five Pre-Islamic Arabic Odes* (The Hague: Mouton, 1970), cited in Culley, *Oral Formulaic Language*, p. 6.

54. Widengren, "Oral Tradition," p. 225.

55. Lord, *Singer of Tales.* For a survey of field studies on oral poetry and oral prose in India, Africa, Mongolia, etc., see Culley, *Oral Formulaic Language*, esp. pp. 2–4, 9–12.

56. Coote, "Application of Oral Theory," p. 52.

ter of modern oral literature"; (2) establishing a significant parallel between it and the Old Testament; and (3) a detailed comparison between them. He noted that none of these has been met.[57] He wrote: "Old Testament form- and tradition-critics, who in general are less skilled in these matters, may well be living in a fools' paradise."[58] Whybray fails to develop adequately, however, the significant point that sacred literature was composed and received as the inspired Word of God, and therefore it would have been treasured as authoritative at the time of composition and less likely to be changed.

### Conclusion

Having examined the literatures of the ancient Near East and other literatures as well, we have found no evidence in any Semitic cultures, including Islam, that tradents molded an oral tradition to meet changing situations over the centuries. John van Seters hit the nail on the head when he said, "Gunkel, Alt, von Rad, Noth, Westermann, and others . . . have not made a case for regarding the traditions of Genesis as . . . deriving from an oral base."[59]

## The Source of the Patriarchal Narratives

On first reflection it may seem necessary to assume that the stories in Genesis about the patriarchs must have been handed down orally. William Sanford LaSor, David Allan Hubbard, and Frederic W. Bush assume that the patriarchal narratives (that is, family history) were handed down primarily by oral tradition. They see no objection to the hypothesis that the narratives were put into writing in Moses' time.[60] The case for oral tradition becomes most strong, however, for the stories in the first eleven chapters of Genesis, some of which must antedate by centuries the invention of writing. Though admitting that Israel's memory of the patriarchs was handed down by means of an uncertain oral tradition, Gleason Archer nevertheless pointed in the right direction: "The legacy of faith was handed down through the millennia from Adam to Moses in oral form, for the most part, but the final written form into

57. Whybray, *Making of the Pentateuch*, pp. 162–69.
58. Ibid., p. 157.
59. John van Seters, *Abraham in History and Tradition* (New Haven: Yale University Press, 1975), p. 148.
60. William Sanford LaSor, David Allan Hubbard, and Frederic W. Bush, *Old Testament Survey: The Message, Form, and Background of the Old Testament* (Grand Rapids: Eerdmans, 1982), pp. 108–9.

which Moses cast it must have been especially superintended by the Holy Spirit in order to insure its divine trustworthiness."[61]

The only reliable information we have about the antediluvian and postdiluvian patriarchs is not from oral tradition but from the written records preserved in the canon. It is gratuitous to assume that the biblical narrators depended on oral tradition for their information. The truth is, as Robert Alter pointed out so brilliantly, that every biblical narrator is omniscient.[62] They know the thoughts of God in heaven and characterize the earthly subjects not by adjectives, such as "the wily Jacob," but by telling us their most private thoughts and conversations. Such storytellers are not dependent on oral tradition. Did men and women originally learn either about the creation of the cosmos as recorded in Genesis 1, assigned by literary critics to P, or about the creation of the man out of the earth in Genesis 2, assigned by the same critics to J, from oral tradition? In the final analysis these creation stories derive either from unassisted creative imagination or from revelation. The Bible and Spirit affirm that we are dealing not with prose fiction but with true knowledge, and we have no reason to think that it was not revealed to the storyteller himself, who inscripturated it in Holy Writ. The biblical authors are surrogates for God and as such are not dependent on oral tradition. That is not to deny that the successive patriarchs knew God's earlier promises to their fathers, and there is nothing objectionable in thinking that the author of Genesis, who along with the other biblical narrators drew a veil of modesty over his identity, used them. It is inapposite, however to think that he (or any other of the omniscient narrators of the Bible) was dependent on oral tradition. Undoubtedly the successive patriarchs knew antecedent revelation, but we do not know the extent or form of it.

It is difficult to verify or refute the claim that oral tradition lies behind the patriarchal narratives referring to events before the invention of writing. Whatever be the types and extent of sources that our omniscient narrator may have used, and the manner in which he may have used them, the important point is that God's inspired spokesman told the sacred stories in his own way. For this reason there is no reason to doubt their historicity or to be uncertain about his meaning.[63]

61. Gleason L. Archer, Jr., A Survey of Old Testament Introduction (Chicago: Moody, 1964), p. 21 n. 4.

62. Robert Alter, The Art of Biblical Narrative (New York: Basic Books, 1981), p. 128.

63. Lest I be misunderstood, let me state that my objection to form criticism pertains not to the objective identification of literary genres and forms—this practice is an indispensable exegetical tool—but to the subjective practice of tracing the history of a tradition.

# 8

## Storytellers and Poets in the Bible
### Can Literary Artifice Be True?

**Tremper Longman III**

*If we accept the principle that the Bible is its own best interpreter, it becomes, of course, of prime importance that we should have as clear an understanding as possible not only of its factual content, but also of its literary forms, of the language and style of the Bible, or what is covered broadly by the words, biblical rhetoric.*

—Oswald T. Allis, 1972

## Literature Versus Truth?

In our culture we make a clear-cut distinction between nonfiction and fiction. We read nonfiction to learn, to gain information, to accumulate knowledge about the real world. Biography is one of the most popular forms of nonfiction available today. When we read about Chuck Yeager or Lee Iacocca, we expect to learn something true about their lives.[1] On the

---

1. This reference is to the two most popular autobiographies on the market at the time this article was written: Lee A. Iacocca, *Iacocca: An Autobiography* (New York: Bantam, 1984), and Chuck Yeager, *Yeager, an Autobiography* (New York: Bantam, 1985).

other hand, we read fiction for entertainment. We may learn from serious novels, but not on the same order as we do from nonfiction. For instance, one need not read long in *Lord Jim* by Joseph Conrad or *Robots and Empire* by Isaac Asimov before recognizing them as fictional.[2] The reader does not respond to Jim, Marlow, or R. Daneel Ovilaw in the same way as to Yeager or Iacocca.

The point is that fiction introduces literary artifice, which we "know" is "not true." We are all aware, however, that a typical biography and more especially an autobiography contains much conscious and unconscious fictionalizing.[3] On the other hand, in most fictions there is much that is true. For instance, Asimov frequently uses his science fiction as a vehicle to instruct on science and also to moralize; and as we read *Lord Jim*, we learn about seafaring customs at a particular time and in a particular locale. Nonetheless, most of us equate nonfiction with the real world and fiction with literary deception.

We make a second distinction as well, which more or less correlates with the first—that is, between ordinary language or straightforward prose and, on the other hand, literary artifice or simply literariness.[4] Ordinary language and literary artifice are best defined in contrast to one another. The distinction is based on the degree of ornamentation in the language. Prose tends to suppress ornamentation or figures of speech. A general principle is that, the more the author intends to inform about the real world, the more literariness decreases. Science, philosophy, and modern historiography avoid explicitly metaphorical language as much as possible.[5] On the other side, literature is often highly ornamental, highly figurative, highly structured. In other words, it is artificial language in the sense that it is distanced from our normal everyday patterns of communication.

In our own culture we recognize poetry as the most artificial form of literary communication. Literary figures like simile, metaphor, and personification abound in poetry. Normal word order is suspended. Unfamiliar words are used. Often a metrical system will force an alien pattern on a literary text.

2. Joseph Conrad, *Lord Jim* (1900; reprint, New York: Bantam, 1981), and Isaac Asimov, *Robots and Empire* (Garden City, N.Y.: Doubleday, 1985).

3. Roy Pascal, *Design and Truth in Autobiography* (Cambridge: Harvard University Press, 1960); James Olney, *Metaphors of Self: The Meaning of Autobiography* (Princeton: Princeton University Press, 1972); Georges C. May, *L'autobiographie* (Paris: Presses universitaires de France, 1979).

4. Meyer H. Abrams, *A Glossary of Literary Terms,* 4th ed. (New York: Holt, Rinehart, and Winston, 1981), p. 166.

5. This conclusion is highlighted and disputed by Vern S. Poythress in "Science as Allegory," *Journal of the American Scientific Affiliation* 35 (1983): 65–71.

These are our modern distinctions. There are nonfiction and plain prose, which speak the truth and are the proper channel for the communication of historical facts and scientific proof. On the other hand, there are fiction and literary prose or poetry, which speak in an artificial way and which are not primarily for the communication of history and science but for entertainment and fun (see fig.1). These distinctions are reflected in some of our common idioms that contrast fiction and truth: "Is it fact or fiction?" and "Truth is stranger than fiction."

### Figure 1
### False Literary Distinctions

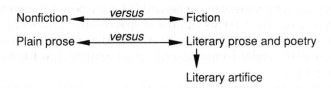

This distinction, however, is a modern prejudice, not an accurate analysis. Even as applied to modern literature, these distinctions are wrong, or at least not absolute.

## The Bible as Literature

As we examine the Bible, we see little in it that corresponds to what formally may be identified as nonfiction. Rather we encounter well-told stories and poems. We do not read straightforward prose like our modern historians, scientists, and philosophers (or theologians) write, but rather something more like literature.[6]

That there is literary artifice in the Bible is obvious from the nonnarrative poetry. Consider, for instance, Psalm 114:

> When Israel came out of Egypt,
>     the house of Jacob from a people of foreign tongue,
> Judah became God's sanctuary,
>     Israel his dominion.
>
> The sea looked and fled,
>     the Jordan turned back;

6. Robert Alter, *The Art of Biblical Narrative* (New York: Basic Books, 1981).

the mountains skipped like rams,
the hills like lambs.

Why was it, O sea, that you fled,
O Jordan, that you turned back,
you mountains, that you skipped like rams,
you hills, like lambs?

Tremble, O earth, at the presence of the Lord,
at the presence of the God of Jacob,
who turned the rock into a pool,
the hard rock into springs of water.

It is obvious that the language of this poem is highly ornamented. In the first place, we observe repetition between clauses (parallelism) that is unnecessary and sometimes undesirable for purposes of communicating information.[7] The various figures of speech—the simile of the hills leaping like lambs and the personification of the sea—communicate by indirection to the reader. In summary, literary artifice characterizes nonnarrative poetry.

It is also incontestable that there is literary artifice in narrative poetry. The Book of Job is clearly a narrative, usually taken by conservative scholars as historical. It relates the story of Job's suffering and his struggle over the theological implications of his suffering. The dialogues between Job and his three friends are taken by many as the height of literary art in the Old Testament.[8] Certainly the literary artifice cannot be denied: it is very unlikely that Job and his three friends flung beautiful poetic lines back and forth to each other as they were locked in a heated debate and as Job suffered.

Also it is well known that the dialogues themselves are highly structured into cycles.[9] Each of the three friends speaks in turn to Job, who invariably answers after each attacking speech (see fig. 2). Our conclusion, then, is that narrative poetry, of which Job is an example, is like nonnarrative poetry in that it is characterized by literary artifice.

As we move on to what we consider to be straightforward prose, the same situation pertains. Literary studies have shown how highly ornamented Old Testament and New Testament prose texts are. My point could be illustrated by literally any portion of the Bible, but I will choose

7. For parallelism and other literary devices associated with Hebrew poetry, see James L. Kugel, *The Idea of Biblical Poetry* (New Haven: Yale University Press, 1981); Robert Alter, *The Art of Biblical Poetry* (New York: Basic Books, 1985), and Tremper Longman III, *How to Read the Psalms* (Downers Grove, Ill.: Inter-Varsity, 1988).

8. Claus Westermann, *The Structure of the Book of Job: A Form–Critical Perspective* (Philadelphia: Fortress, 1981).

9. Peter Paul Zerafa, *The Wisdom of God in the Book of Job* (Rome: Herder, 1978).

## Figure 2
## The Literary Structure of Job

| 1st Cycle | 2d Cycle | 3d Cycle[a] |
|---|---|---|
| Eliphaz (4–5) | Eliphaz (15) | Eliphaz (22) |
| Job (6–7) | Job (16–17) | Job (23–24) |
| Bildad (8) | Bildad (18) | Bildad (25) |
| Job (9–10) | Job (19) | Job (27:1–12) |
| Zophar (11) | Zophar (20) | Zophar (27:13–23)[b] |
| Job (12–14) | Job (21) | Job (28–31) |

[a] The friends' speeches get much shorter in the last cycle, reflecting the fact that the three are, we might say, running out of steam.
[b] For Zophar's place in the 3d cycle, see Zerafa, *Wisdom of God,* pp. 1–28.

to analyze the flood story briefly, along the lines of Gordon Wenham, the noted evangelical scholar.[10]

Wenham's study is apologetic. He seeks to demonstrate the unity of the flood story over against the documentary hypothesis. He persuasively argues that the flood narrative is not a patchwork of two sources but rather a literary whole. Critics like Kikawada and Quinn have since followed him in this position.[11]

The point which is important for our concern is the recognition of literary artifice in the story of the flood. Wenham's major insight is that Genesis 6:10–9:19 appears to be a palistrophe containing 31 items.[12] In other words, the flood story is structured as a giant chiasm (the more common term for what Wenham calls a palistrophe). That is, the first episode of the story is paralleled by the last, the second by the next-to-last, and so forth. The chiasm as described by Wenham appears in figure 3.

As Wenham recognizes, the flood story naturally lends itself to such a structure.[13] After all, if the flood waters rise, they will also diminish. If the door of the ark is closed, it naturally will be opened. He is also correct, however, in his recognition that the chiasm extends beyond these features to produce a literary effect. In his words; "Though a palistrophe is an appropriate form for describing the flood, there are certain features in the story which reflect the large element of contrivance in casting the whole tale into this form . . . . There is clearly an element of artificiality here."[14]

10. Gordon J. Wenham, "The Coherence of the Flood Narrative," *Vetus Testamentum* 28 (1978): 336–48.

11. Isaac M. Kikawada and Arthur Quinn, *Before Abraham Was: The Unity of Genesis* (Nashville: Abingdon, 1985).

12. Wenham, "Coherence," p. 337.

13. Ibid., p. 338.

14. Ibid., pp. 338–39.

### Figure 3
### The Chiastic Structure of the Flood Narrative*

A  Noah (6:10a)
B    Shem, Ham, and Japeth (10b)
C      Ark to be built (14–16)
D        Flood announced (17)
E          Covenant with Noah (18–20)
F            Flood in the ark (21)
G              Command to enter ark (7:1–3)
H                7 days' waiting for flood (4–5)
I                  7 days' waiting for flood (7–10)
J                    Entry to ark (11–15)
K                      Yahweh shuts Noah in (16)
L                        40 days' flood (17a)
M                          Waters increase (17b–18)
N                            Mountains covered (19–20)
O                              150 days waters prevail ((21)–24)
P                                GOD REMEMBERS NOAH (8:1)
O'                             150 days waters abate (3)
N'                           Mountaintops visible (4–5)
M'                         Waters abate (5)
L'                       40 days (end of) (6a)
K'                     Noah opens window of ark (6b)
J'                   Raven and dove leave ark (7–9)
I'                 7 days' waiting for waters to subside (10–11)
H'               7 days' waiting for waters to subside (12–13)
G'             Command to leave ark (15–17 (22))
F'           Food outside the ark (9:1–4)
E'         Covenant with all flesh (8–10)
D'       No flood in future (11–17)
C'     Ark (18a)
B'   Shem, Ham, and Japeth (18b)
A' Noah (19)

*Gordon J. Wenham, "The Coherence of the Flood Narrative," *Vetus Testamentum* 28 (1978): 338.

The artificiality may be most readily seen in the dates given in the text. Twice the text mentions the seven-day wait for the flood (*H* and *I*), and twice the text mentions the seven days' waiting for the diminishment of the waters (*I'* and *H'*). Such symmetry is striking, particularly since a close reading of the relevant passages shows that *H* and *I* are referring to the same seven-day period (thus in actuality referring to one week), while *I'* and *H'* are actually referring to a three-week period. As Wenham comments, "Some of these time spans are mentioned purely in order to achieve symmetry in the palistrophe."[15]

The chiastic literary structure of the flood story highlights the middle verse—8:1, "But God remembered Noah." God's intervention was the turning point. The flood story is just a single example of a very common literary pattern in the Old Testament.

15. Ibid., p. 339.

## The Literary Approach to the Bible

Thus we have seen examples of literariness in two types of poetry and from a prose story. The literary nature of the Bible has come to the forefront of scholarly attention during the past two decades.[16] During this time there has arisen a whole new approach to the text called literary criticism, or aesthetic criticism. The literary approach is not just another method alongside of form, redaction, or tradition history but rather is a whole new approach, which in the eyes of some practitioners replaces all previous approaches.[17]

Very simply, the literary approach imports the insights, attitudes, and methods of the study of secular literature into the study of biblical literature. Of course, secular literary study is not a monolith. As a result, many different schools of literary study have been applied to the Bible. We cannot explore here the history of the relationship of literary studies and the Bible. But if we survey the secondary literature, we may easily find many examples of the close reading of New Criticism,[18] the rather esoteric method of structuralism,[19] and even the avant-garde approach of deconstruction.[20]

Apart from all of the variations in literary approaches, the literary approach in general presents quite a challenge to the evangelical, especially in the light of the obvious literary nature of the Bible. The challenge is not simple. On the one hand, the literary approach is potentially quite dangerous to the doctrine of Scripture. On the other hand, there is much in the approach which aids in interpretation.

The danger comes precisely in considering the question of this chapter's subtitle: Can literary artifice be true? The problem is that, in many people's opinion, literary artifice is incompatible with accurate historical representation. A text cannot be artfully constructed and historically reliable at the same time. The modern literary approach to the study of the Bible has a decided tendency to deny or severely limit any referential function in literature. Literature is art, and art is created for its own sake, not for any outside purpose. As the great English literary figure

16. See my *Literary Approaches to Biblical Interpretation* (Grand Rapids: Zondervan, 1987), esp. chap. 2.

17. A view presented, among others, by D. Robertson, "Literature, the Bible as," in *The Interpreter's Dictionary of the Bible,* supp. vol., ed. Keith Crim (Nashville: Abingdon, 1976), pp. 547–51.

18. One example is Adele Berlin, *Poetics and Interpretation of Biblical Narrative* (Sheffield: Almond, 1983).

19. An example is Robert M. Polzin, *Biblical Structuralism: Method and Subjectivity in the Study of Ancient Texts* (Philadelphia: Fortress, 1977).

20. An example is Peter D. Miscall, *The Workings of Old Testament Narrative* (Philadelphia: Fortress; Chico: Scholars, 1983).

Philip Sidney said, "The poet affirmith nothing." Frank Lentricchia has analyzed the history of secular literary theory over the course of the past four decades and has demonstrated that it is a period characterized by the progressive denial of any external reference for literature.[21] In short, literature has nothing to do with reality—past, present, or future. The rupture between the literary and the historical (which is one aspect of the referential function) is an element of modern literary theory. And, as one might expect, the recognition of the literary characteristics of the Bible has led to an equation of the Bible and literature on the part of some scholars. Then follows an acceptance of the view that literary texts do not refer outside of themselves; particularly they do not make any reference to history. This leads, on the part of some, to a complete or substantial denial of a historical approach to the text. Most often this position takes the form of a denial or denigration of traditional historical-critical methods. Source and form criticism particularly are attacked. The following quotations may be taken as representative of some (but not all) who adopt the literary approach.

> Above all, we must keep in mind that narrative is a *form of representation.* Abraham in Genesis is not a real person any more than the painting of an apple is real fruit.[22]

> Once the unity of the story is experienced, one is able to participate in the world of the story. Although the author of the Gospel of Mark certainly used sources rooted in the historical events surrounding the life of Jesus, the final text is a literary creation with an autonomous integrity, just as Leonardo's portrait of the Mona Lisa exists independently as a vision of life apart from any resemblance or nonresemblance to the person who posed for it or as a play of Shakespeare has integrity apart from reference to the historical characters depicted there . . . . Thus, Mark's narrative contains a closed and self-sufficient world with its own integrity . . . . When viewed as a literary achievement the statements in Mark's narrative, rather than being a representation of historical events, refer to the people, places, and events *in the story.*[23]

> As long as readers require the gospel to be a window to the ministry of Jesus before they will see truth in it, accepting the gospel will mean believing that the story it tells corresponds exactly to what actually happened during Jesus's ministry. When the gospel is viewed as a mirror, though of course not a mirror in which we see only ourselves, its meaning can be

---

21. Frank Lentricchia, *After the New Criticism* (Chicago: University of Chicago Press, 1980).
22. Berlin, *Poetics and Interpretation*, p. 13.
23. David Rhoads and Donald Michie, *Mark as Story: The Introduction to the Gospel as Narrative* (Philadelphia: Fortress, 1982), pp. 3–4.

found on this side of it, that is between text and reader, in the experience of reading the text, and belief in the gospel can mean openness to the ways it calls readers to interact with it, with life, and with their own world.[24]

R. Alan Culpepper further states, "The real issue is whether 'his story' can be true if it is not history."[25] For the author the answer is yes.

Similar evaluation may be seen in the hermeneutics of Hans Frei in his very influential book *Eclipse of Biblical Narrative*.[26] Frei argues that the major error in both traditional critical and conservative exegesis is the loss of the understanding that biblical narrative is historylike and not true history with a reference to the real world. Robert Alter, perhaps the best-known practitioner of the literary approach to the Bible and himself a literary critic, not a biblical scholar, argues that the nature of Old Testament narrative is "historicized fiction" or fictional history.[27] There has been a recent flurry of dissertations on the Book of Acts from a literary perspective. The tendency of these studies is to point to the highly structured form of the Book of Acts and to conclude that it does not convey true historical information.[28]

The result of this approach is a turning away from historical investigation of the text as impossible or irrelevant. The traditional methods of historical criticism are abandoned, radically modified, or given secondary consideration. Concern to discover the original *Sitz im Leben* or to discuss the tradition history of a text languishes among this new breed of scholar. This challenges traditional critical scholarship; articles like that of Leander Keck ask, "Will the Historical-Critical Method Survive?"[29] I personally hope that the historical-critical method will not survive, at least in terms of the destructive side that denies or doubts the Scripture's veracity. But we must realize that the danger cuts two ways.

---

24. R. Alan Culpepper, *Anatomy of the Fourth Gospel* (Philadelphia: Fortress, 1983), pp. 236–37.

25. Ibid., p. 236.

26. Hans Frei, *The Eclipse of Biblical Narrative* (New Haven: Yale University Press, 1974).

27. Alter, *Art of Biblical Narrative*, pp. 23–46.

28. Susan M. Praeder, "The Narrative Voyage: An Analysis and Interpretation of Acts 27–28" (Ph.D. diss., Graduate Theological Union, 1980); Charles B. Puskas, Jr., "The Conclusion of Luke-Acts: An Investigation of the Literary Function and Theological Significance of Acts 28:16–31" (Ph.D. diss., St. Louis University, 1980); William R. Long, "The Trial of Paul in the Book of Acts: Historical, Literary, and Theological Considerations" (Ph.D. diss., Brown University, 1982); Edwin S. Nelson, "Paul's First Missionary Journey as Paradigm: Literary-Critical Assessment of Acts 13–14" (Ph.D. diss., Brown University, 1982).

29. Leander Keck, "Will the Historical-Critical Method Survive?" in *Orientation by Disorientation*, ed. R. A. Spencer (Pittsburgh: Pickwick, 1980), pp. 115–27.

Both traditional criticism and evangelicalism have a high stake in the question of history.

The danger in brief is as follows. According to most secular literary critics, the distinguishing characteristics of literature are "fictionality," "invention," and "imagination."[30] To identify Genesis as a work of literature pure and simple is to move it out of the realm of history. This seems to be the tendency of some, if not much, of the literary approach to the study of the Bible.

But there is an easy defense. As Northrup Frye has said, "The Bible is as literary as it can well be without actually being literature."[31] On the one hand, Genesis is not reducible to a work of fiction. On the other hand, we are justified and required by the text itself to apply a literary approach because it possesses undeniable literary qualities. Another characteristic of literature is that it is self-consciously structured and expressed. In the terminology of Russian formalism, the language is foregrounded.[32] There is literary artifice in the parallelism between the first three days of creation and the last three (as the framework hypothesis has pointed out).[33] Whether this parallelism is mirroring the actual sequence of God's creative acts is a moot point here. There is artifice in the symmetrical structures of the flood story as pointed out by Wenham, and the Babel story, as pointed out by Fokkelman[34]—or to go a little more afield, the Solomon narrative, as indicated by Dillard.[35]

The point is that we do not have objective, neutral, unshaped reporting of events in the Bible. Of course, such objectivity is impossible anyway; there is no such thing as a brute fact, as Van Til has argued. An uninterpreted historical report is not even conceivable.

But it must be admitted by evangelicals that Genesis, for example, is not attempting to be as close as possible to a dispassionate reporting of events. Rather we have proclamation, with the result that the history is shaped to differing degrees. That is, the biblical narrators are not only concerned to tell us facts. They indeed intend to inform historically, but they also are concerned to guide our perspective and responses to events.

John says as much, referring to his Gospel. We do not get from him a

30. René Wellek and Austin Warren, *Theory of Literature* (New York: Harcourt Brace Jovanovich, 1942), p. 26.

31. Northrup Frye, *The Great Code: The Bible and Literature* (London: Ark, 1983), p. 62.

32. Abrams, *Glossary of Literary Terms*, p. 166.

33. Among others, Meredith G. Kline, "Because It Had Not Rained," *Westminster Theological Journal* 20 (1958): 146–57.

34. J. P. Fokkelman, *Narrative Art in Genesis* (Assen: Van Gorcum, 1975), pp. 11ff.

35. Raymond B. Dillard, "The Structure of the Chronicler's Solomon Narrative," *Journal for the Study of the Old Testament* 30 (1984): 85–93.

full report of the events of the life of Jesus, for "Jesus did many other things as well. If every one of them were written down, I suppose that even the whole world would not have room for the books that would be written" (21:25). That the selective nature of his account did not impinge on its truthfulness is indicated by the immediately preceding verse: "This is the disciple who testifies to these things and who wrote them down. We know that his testimony is true" (v. 24).

Biblical prose may thus be described as selective, structured, emphasized, and interpreted stories. The author/narrator controls the way we view the events. Here we can see how plot analysis, narrator studies, character studies, point-of-view analysis, and the like can be helpful to our exegesis of biblical texts. These are all methods of secular literary criticism, but as the fruit of common grace they can illumine the Word of God.

The question of the historical truth of the text boils down to the question of who ultimately is guiding us in our interpretation of these events. If human beings alone, then artifice may be deceptive. If God, then no. To recognize this difference is to recognize that a literary analysis of a historical book is not incompatible with a high view of the historicity of the text, even one which affirms the inerrancy and infallibility of Scripture in the area of history.

Note that not all of Scripture is historical in nature, although most is. After all, God worked our redemption in history. Nonetheless, the generic intention of each book and each section needs to be analyzed before attributing a historical reference to the book.[36]

Along with the dangers in the literary approach, there is also a reductive trend on the part of evangelical scholarship, that is, the tendency to reduce the text to history or to systematic theology. Except for Paul's letters, the Bible is mostly story and poetry.[37]

We thus cannot reduce the Scriptures to one function, whether aesthetic or historical. The Scriptures are both literary and are historically accurate. Indeed, the Scriptures are multifunctional.[38]

## Benefits of a Literary Approach

In considering the danger of literary criticism, the reader may ask, Why bother with it at all? Is there anything of value that we can learn

36. Tremper Longman III, "Form Criticism, Recent Developments in Genre Theory and the Evangelical," *Westminster Theological Journal* 47 (1985): 46–67.

37. For a literary analysis of Paul's letters, see Norman R. Petersen, *Rediscovering Paul* (Philadelphia: Fortress, 1985).

38. For a fuller explanation of this, consult my *Literary Approaches to Biblical Interpretation*, chap. 4.

from it? We have already touched on or hinted at a few benefits, but I would like to concentrate on one more, which I think is most compelling. A literary approach assists us in coming to an understanding of the conventions of biblical storytelling. Alter is correct when he says that "every culture, even every era in a particular culture, develops distinctive and sometimes intricate codes for telling its stories, involving everything from narrative point of view, procedures of description and characterization, the management of dialogue, to the ordering of time and the organization of plot."[39]

The literary text is an act of communication from writer to reader. The text is the message. For it to communicate, the sender and receiver have to speak the same language. The writer, through the use of conventional forms, sends signals to the reader to tell how he or she is to take the message. We all know the obvious generic signals in our own literature. When we read "once upon a time" or "a novel by . . . ," we immediately recognize the type of literature with which we are dealing and the type of reading strategy we should adopt in order to understand the text.

A literary approach explores and makes explicit the conventions of biblical literature to understand what message it intends to carry. To discover that Deuteronomy is in the form of a treaty, that the narrator shapes the reader's response to the characters of a text in different ways, that repetitions are not a sign of multiple sources but a literary device, is significant.

In ordinary reading, much of this understanding happens automatically. We passively let the narrator shape our interpretation of the event he or she is reporting to us; we make an unconscious genre identification. But as interpreters of the text, it is important to make these explicit. This is doubly so for the Bible, since it is an ancient text and the conventions employed are often not ones we are used to.[40]

## Conclusion

The point of this chapter is that much of the Bible is literature in the sense of story or poetry. Why is this the case? Why did God not reveal to us his mighty acts in history in the form of a *Cambridge Ancient History?* Or better, why is not the Bible in the form of a systematic theology? The ultimate answer to this question is to appeal to God's wisdom. But I can suggest two positive functions of the literary form of the Bible. The first one can be discussed under the rubric of defamiliarization, or distancia-

39. Robert Alter, "A Response to Critics," *Journal for the Study of the Old Testament* 27 (1983): 113–17.
40. Anthony C. Thiselton, *The Two Horizons* (Grand Rapids: Eerdmans, 1980).

tion. These are concepts discussed by Russian formalists, who describe the function of art as "the renewal of perception, the seeing of the world suddenly in a new light, in a new and unforeseen way."[41] To cast truth in the form of a story leads the reader/hearer to pay close attention to it, to be forced to reconsider what might easily become a truism by presenting it in an artistic fashion. A proverb is a good, focused example. Which communicates more powerfully, "Speak righteously" or "The mouth of the righteous flows with wisdom, but the perverted tongue will be cut out" (Prov. 10:31 NASB)? Which speaks more vividly, the statement "love your neighbor as yourself" or the story of the Good Samaritan? The second positive function is that literature appeals to the whole person. It involves our whole being—intellect, will, and emotions—to a greater extent than, say, the *Westminster Confession of Faith*.

In conclusion, we ask again: Can literary artifice be true? The answer is yes. To ask whether the Bible is literature or history is to set up a false dichotomy. The Bible is both—and much more.

41. Fredric Jameson, *The Prison-House of Language* (Princeton: Princeton University Press, 1972), p. 52.

# 9

# Harmonization
## A Help and a Hindrance

### Raymond B. Dillard

*It may very well be that there are some passages which, save
by strained and forced attempts, we cannot harmonize. If
such is the case, by all means let us be sufficiently honest
and candid to admit that we cannot harmonize the
particular passages in question; for to employ strained and
forced methods of harmonization is not intellectually
honest. If we do employ such methods, we shall only bring
upon our heads the deserved charge of intellectual
dishonesty. Far better it is to admit our inability than to
produce harmonization at the expense of honesty and
integrity. Much as we might wish that we could explain all
difficulties, we can console ourselves with the thought—and
a true thought it is—that those who have rejected the
Biblical doctrine of inspiration have far greater problems
and difficulties to solve, and that, upon the basis upon
which they proceed, these difficulties cannot be solved.*
> —Edward J. Young, 1957

Much of the debate about the integrity of the Bible has centered on
its apparent contradictions and discrepancies in matters of historical de-

tail. The synoptic portions of the Bible (Samuel–Kings and Chronicles; the Gospels) provide the primary exhibits of what are considered factual lapses, though the range of evidence is by no means confined to parallel passages.[1] Harmonization is the effort to provide scenarios by which two apparently contradictory statements or one improbable statement can be considered historically accurate.[2] Where one Gospel puts Jesus' sermon on a mountain (Matt. 5:1) and another on level ground (Luke 6:17), the harmonist replies by suggesting that there was a plateau on the side of the mountain or that Jesus gave the same sermon in different locales; the factuality of both texts is thereby preserved. Such apparent discrepancies are reasonably common in the Bible and characteristically involve numerical contradictions, chronological and geographical dislocations, different quotations of what appear to be the same speech, or similar types of problems. A number of handbooks attempt to provide a catalogue and an answer to many of these problems.[3]

Is a harmonistic component in exegesis a necessary and inevitable consequence of the doctrine of inerrancy? Or conversely, is rejection of harmonistic exegesis or reluctance to practice it equivalent to a rejection of inerrancy? What role should harmonization play in biblical studies? These are inherently difficult questions, and they are complicated by the considerable theological and emotional investment many have in the answers. Many evangelicals consider answers to questions in this area as somewhat of a theological watershed, a convenient touchstone or shibboleth dividing acceptable and unacceptable views about the Bible. I have a friend who is fond of saying that "for every difficult, complex, hard question there is always a simple, clear, unambiguous, wrong answer." It is tempting to want a quick and easy answer to these questions, but the set of issues involved requires more than a simple slogan. A summary of the assets and liabilities involved in harmonization will hopefully clarify the issues. I will draw primarily from Chronicles for illustrative purposes; it has been the focus of my own work for some time and presents some of the most interesting and difficult material.

---

1. For a history of preparing synopses of the parallel portions of the Bible, see Ronald Youngblood, "From Tatian to Swanson, from Calvin to Bendavid: The Harmonization of Biblical History," *Journal of the Evangelical Theological Society* 25 (1982): 415–23.

2. I am defining *harmonization* primarily in terms of what C. Blomberg has called "additive harmonization" ("The Legitimacy and Limits of Harmonization," in *Hermeneutics, Authority, and Canon,* ed. D. A. Carson and J. D. Woodbridge [Grand Rapids: Zondervan, 1986], pp. 135–74). The scope of his article is considerably wider than intended here, and the taxonomy of harmonistic solutions he offers is helpful.

3. As examples, see John W. Haley, *An Examination of the Alleged Discrepancies of the Bible* (Boston: Estes and Lauriat, 1881), and Gleason Archer, *An Encyclopedia of Bible Difficulties* (Grand Rapids: Zondervan, 1982).

## Harmonization as a Help—Its Assets

### Its Inevitability

The question is not "should we harmonize or not," for harmonization is a virtually universal and inevitable feature of daily life. At home parents confront sharply differing versions of a recent squabble between children, the children often sincerely believing their own accounts and arranging the data to make a particular point, usually their own innocence and the culpability of the other combatant. The parent hears both accounts and tries to create a scenario closer to "reality," that is, closer to what a more detached observer would have reported or what would have been recorded on videotape. A close and trusted friend who is a salesman calls on you at your office and extols the virtue of the equipment he would like to sell, while you are left trying to reconcile his account with the complaints of other friends who use this item regularly in their own offices. Encounters like these are regular features of daily life. You hope that, if a friend hears information that appears to be in tension with something that you have told him, he will at least mentally reconcile the discrepancies or investigate further before accusing you of falsehood or error. One must give the Scriptures the same benefit of doubt. This daily reconciliation of observed discrepancies is part and parcel with harmonization as a component of exegesis. It is an inevitable and natural reaction. One cannot a priori or simplistically repudiate harmonization of biblical data without contradicting what would be a routine and natural response to data in other areas of life. Harmonization in this sense appears to be a universal convention of human reasoning. Scholars writing from within almost any theological or critical stance in theory make allowance for harmonization in exegesis, though in practice factual difficulties are the grist from which scholars compose theories of sources, redaction, and so on, and efforts to harmonize are often dismissed with ridicule. Such facile rejection too often forgets the realities of daily life.

### Its Antiquity

Harmonization in biblical studies did not develop *de novo* among religious conservatives after the Enlightenment as a way of defending their view of Scripture. Quite to the contrary, if harmonization is a routine and universal activity applied to many facets of life, one would expect to find harmonization practiced in antiquity as well. There is ample evidence that this was so.

One could argue that a certain amount of intrabiblical exegesis reflects this effort.[4] In his treatment of Hezakiah, the Chronicler omits the

---

4. Michael A. Fishbane (*Biblical Interpretation in Ancient Israel* [Oxford: Clarendon,

report of Hezekiah's submission to Sennacherib and his despoliation of the temple (2 Kings 18:14–16); it is out of accord with his generally positive portrayal of Hezekiah and does not fit well with the deliverance of Jerusalem as reported in both Kings and Chronicles (19:35–37; 2 Chron. 32:20–23). The Chronicler also eliminates the double appearance of the Rab-shaqeh before the city (2 Kings 18:17–19:9a, 36–37; and 2 Kings 19:9b–35) and integrates these into a single appearance (2 Chron. 32:9–19), perhaps suggesting he recognized the accounts in Kings as parallel texts of the same event.[5] At a larger level, the Book of Kings, which explains the fall of the kingdoms and the end of the temple to an exilic audience (2 Kings 17:7–23; 21:1–15), has been viewed as harmonizing these events with the earlier promises of God to Israel concerning the temple and David's descendants. Kings is a theodicy—it justifies God's actions to human beings; theodicy is by its very nature a sort of harmonization. The ancient scribes also practiced harmonization with some regularity. Many textual variations reflect not copying errors but the efforts of the scribes to reconcile tension in historical details. Consider two examples, 1 Chronicles 29:22 and 2 Chronicles 22:8.

Chronicles contains a quite different account of the transfer of power from David to Solomon than that found in Kings.[7] In 1 Kings 1, an aged and bedridden David faces a coup supported by members of the royal household, cultic officers, and the military (vv. 7–9); the kingdom is saved for Solomon only by the intervention of Bathsheba and Nathan, just in the nick of time. Solomon's anointing as king was hastily done; David himself could not attend his own son's anointing (vv. 28–40). The picture in Chronicles contrasts sharply (1 Chron. 28–29). David presides over a national assembly (28:1) and specifically names his son Solomon as his successor and charges him with the construction of the temple. Solomon receives the immediate and wholehearted support of all the people (29:21–30), including specifically (v. 24) those who in 1 Kings 1:9 sup-

---

1985], pp. 221–28) suggests a process of harmonization and correction in Pentateuchal legal materials and other corpora of the Old Testament.

  5. This is one of the *cruxes* of modern Old Testament study. A recent article by Dana Fewell ("Sennacherib's Defeat: Words at War in 2 Kings 18:13–19:37," *Journal for the Study of the Old Testament* 34 [1986] 79–90) provides a fresh approach which views the mutiple accounts in Kings from the vantage of aesthetic or literary criticism; she presents an insightful reading of the pericope that concludes that the text is a cohesive unit.

  6. Raymond Dillard, "Reward and Punishment in Chronicles: The Theology of Immediate Retribution," *Westminster Theological Journal* 46 (1984): 164–72; or idem, *Second Chronicles*, Word Biblical Commentary, 15 (Waco: Word, 1987), pp. 76–81.

  7. Raymond Dillard, "The Chronicler's Solomon," *Westminster Theological Journal* 43 (1980): 289–300; or idem, *Second Chronicles*, chaps. 1–7.

ported Adonijah's attempt to seize power.[8] In the Masoretic text (MT) of 1 Chronicles 29:22, it is reported that Solomon was made king a *second* time. However, the word *second* is not found in LXX(B) or the Peshitta. Since 1 Chronicles does mention that Solomon was made king at an earlier point (23:1), the best explanation of this textual difficulty would be that a scribe inserted the word *second* to harmonize the two references in Chronicles to Solomon's being made king.

In 2 Chronicles 22:8, the LXX reports that Jehu found and killed the "brothers of Ahaziah," while the MT reports that he killed "the sons of the brothers of Ahaziah." A number of explanations for this small variation are possible. Perhaps the most compelling of these is that a scribe inserted the word for "sons" into the MT in order to harmonize this account with his awareness that the "brothers of Ahaziah" had already been killed (21:17; 22:1; cf. 2 Kings 10:13–14.)[9]

Examples from the period of the scribes could be multiplied many times. Some of the variations in the textual witnesses to the chronological notes in Kings probably represent harmonistic efforts on the part of the scribes. Their harmonizations were not confined to matters of historical detail. They included, for example, assimilating parallel passages in Jeremiah to one another, leveling differences in legal formulations, and so forth.[10]

### Its Contributions

Though it is ordinarily impossible to prove a harmonization right or wrong, in a few instances harmonistic approaches to biblical texts have led to fairly certain results. Nebuchadnezzar, king of Babylon, set siege to Jerusalem in the third year of Jehoiakim, according to Daniel 1:1, though Jeremiah 25:1 equates Jehoiakim's fourth year with Nebuchadnezzar's first. The reference to Nebuchadnezzar as king in Daniel 1:1 is readily explained as a prolepsis: he is given this title in anticipation of his accession. Few would quarrel that this is a satisfactory explanation. However, Edwin Thiele provided an alternate explanation for this and many similar phenomena in Old Testament chronologies.[11] Two distinctions crucial to his approach (the distinction between accession-year

---

8. It should be noted that 1 Kings 1:51 reports that Adonijah acceded to Solomon's rule after his abortive effort; presumably this change of heart included his supporters.

9. There was no need for the scribal correction; no contradiction exists if the Hebrew word for "brothers" is translated by another legitimate sense, "relatives." The same ambiguity attaches to the Greek term. Cf. the similar issue in 2 Chron. 36:10: Zedekiah was the uncle, rather than the brother, of Jehoiachin.

10. Fishbane, *Biblical Interpretation in Ancient Israel,* pp. 220–21.

11. Edwin Thiele, *The Mysterious Numbers of the Hebrew Kings,* rev. ed. (Grand Rapids: Zondervan, 1983).

reckoning and non-accession-year reckoning and between Nisan or Tishri as the first month of the year) have accounted for many problem passages and apparent discrepancies. Since the great empires around Israel varied in their calendrical and regnal reckoning, there is archaeological data making it reasonable to expect a mix of these systems in biblical chronologies. Though Thiele's system may not ultimately achieve consensus in all its particulars,[12] anyone working in Old Testament chronologies must grapple with his approach. Its explanatory power is sufficiently great that it cannot be simply dismissed as "unconscionably harmonistic."

### Its Respect for the Author

Oswald Allis cites with approval the advice of Coleridge that, "when we meet an apparent error in a good author, we are to presume ourselves ignorant of his understanding, until we are certain that we understand his ignorance."[13] In this regard, harmonistic exegesis has much in common with aesthetic or literary-critical approaches to the Bible. Phenomena which in the past were most frequently regarded as evidence of editorial bumbling now find their explanation as features of fairly sophisticated literary devices used by skilful authors. The Chronicler reports the appearance of the glory cloud twice at the dedication of Solomon's temple (2 Chron. 5:13–14 [note the parallel in 1 Kings 8:10–11] and 7:1–3). This fact is ordinarily explained as the forgetfulness of some later editor who inserted a second report of the appearance of the cloud at the same place where it is found in the parallel text of Kings. However, a far better explanation regards the double appearance of the glory cloud as one feature of a chiastic device the Chronicler has used to fashion his entire account of Solomon's reign.[14] Similar examples could be multiplied in other contexts or books of the Bible.

### Its Theological Warrant

Though all of the above considerations play a role, harmonization draws its principal operating strength from its theological warrant. God is true and cannot lie, and the Scriptures share in this attribute. The incarnational analogy is fundamental: just as the living Word was divine and without error, so also the written Word. More than any other single

---

12. Raymond Dillard, "The Reign of Asa (2 Chron. 14–16): An Example of the Chronicler's Theological Method," *Journal of the Evangelical Theological Society* 23 (1980): 207–18.

13. O. T. Allis, *The Five Books of Moses* (Nutley, N.J.: Presbyterian and Reformed, 1964), p. 125.

14. Raymond Dillard, "The Literary Structure of the Chronicler's Solomon Narrative," *Journal for the Study of the Old Testament* 30 (1984): 85–93. Cf. the briefer treatment in idem, *Second Chronicles,* chaps. 5–7.

factor, it is the belief in the divine origin and authority of the Bible that has given harmonization its hold in exegetical method. The work of exegesis is influenced or controlled by an overriding apologetic concern.

## Harmonization as a Hindrance— Its Liabilities

Harmonization is used primarily as a tool for solving problems; however, it is not itself free of difficulties.

### Its Arbitrariness

Harmonizations are too often offered almost cavalierly. Hackles are raised by what appears to be ad hoc invoking of any set of circumstances that will reconcile passages; to those steeped in higher-critical methods, such special pleading is rejected because it lacks any particular methodological control beyond the need for a quick solution. Nor are harmonizations readily amenable to proof or disproof; they may have varying degrees of probability, some more convincing than others, and some altogether too ingenious to commend the solution they attempt.

Again a few examples might help: (1) the large numbers in Chronicles; (2) places where the numbers in Chronicles differ with those in parallel texts; and (3) 2 Chronicles 2:13–14 and the parallel in 1 Kings 7:13–14. Each of these questions needs more discussion than space allows, but we can at least sketch an outline of the issues.

The large numbers in Chronicles have always been something of a stumbling block, especially the large numbers of troops under the command of the kings of the rather small kingdom of Judah (1 Chron. 12:23–40; 21; 27; 2 Chron. 12:3; 13:3–4, 17; 14:9; 17:12–19; 25:5–6; 26:12–13; 28:6–8); a small kingdom raised armies and inflicted casualties greater than in the mechanized battles of World War II. Almost everyone feels the need to reduce these numbers in some way; articles by J. Barton Payne and John Wenham represent fairly typical efforts to cope with these figures.[15] The Hebrew word *'elep*, "thousand," is also used for a subunit of a tribe, perhaps at the level of a clan or phratry (a group of clans). This use is almost certainly found in Judges 6:15; Numbers 1:16; Micah 5:2; 1 Samuel 10:19–21. These tribal units would have consisted of considerably less than a thousand individuals. Furthermore, by changing the vowels on the word *'elef*, one can create the word *'allûf*, "officer, warrior, leader of an *'alef*"; in this latter case the meaning "thousand" is reduced to a single individual. Both of these procedures transform the

---

15. J. Barton Payne, "The Validity of Numbers in Chronicles," *Biblicotheca Sacra* 136 (1979): 109–28, 206–20; John Wenham, "Large Numbers in the Old Testament," *Tyndale Bulletin* 18 (1967): 19–53.

large troop numbers in Chronicles radically, and this approach is rather widely adopted among evangelicals. When applied to the approximately 360,000 men who attended David's coronation (1 Chron. 12:23–40), this large number would be reduced to a more manageable 2000 (Wenham) or even 400 (Payne), numbers that can more readily be justified rationally. But there is a problem: What has become of "the army of God" (v. 22)? The numbers are reduced, but at the expense of the very point the biblical author is trying to make. It is hard to escape the conclusion that the Chronicler intends to be using plain numbers, not the number of tribal subunits or officers.

A similar issue can be raised in connection with 1 Chronicles 5:18–21. The Trans-Jordanian tribes captured 50,000 camels, 250,000 sheep, 2000 donkeys, and 100,000 captives. One cannot arbitrarily reduce the number of captives by appealing to "thousands" that are really subunits of tribes or individual soldiers in this context, without treating the other numbers similarly. But the other numbers are not amenable to this sort of reduction (sheep are not counted by phratries and are not officers!), suggesting that the Chronicler is using plain numbers. The drive for a solution to the issue of large numbers in Chronicles in these cases is at the expense of the biblical author.

In the second example, Chronicles often reports numbers that differ when compared with those found in Samuel–Kings. Payne provides an exhaustive survey and divides these differences into two basic classes, (1) those where no genuine difference exists, and (2) those where there is a difference. Under (1), Payne explains the apparent discrepancies by suggesting that in fact they report different instances—different items were being enumerated or different measures were being used that actually arrive at the same quantities. For example, where 2 Samuel 24:24 reports that David paid fifty shekels of silver for Araunah's threshing floor and oxen, 1 Chronicles 21:25 says David paid six hundred shekels of gold for "the place." No contradiction exists, since Samuel speaks of a fairly small parcel, while the Chronicler reports the price presumably for the whole area of Mount Moriah.[16] For (2), where a genuine difference between the two texts does exist, Payne appeals to errors in textual transmission primarily based on misread numerical notations using either the Canaanite alphabet, the later Aramaic alphabet, or a numeral system similar to Egyptian hieratic numerals. There is no direct evidence for the use of either of the alphanumeric systems before the Maccabean

---

16. Payne, "Validity of Numbers in Chronicles," p. 120. See also Raymond Dillard, "David's Census: Perspectives on 2 Samuel 24 and 1 Chronicles 21," in *Through Christ's Word*, ed. Robert Godfrey and Jesse Boyd III (Phillipsburg, N.J.: Presbyterian and Reformed, 1985), pp. 94–107.

period, nor is there direct evidence showing the use of a numeral system for writing numbers instead of spelling them out in biblical texts.[17] The harmonistic argument here shares the circularity of many hypotheses: explanatory systems are invoked to explain the discrepancies, and the discrepancies become the warrant for the suggested explanation. Though the suggested explanations may have been a factor in the transmission of the text, one has the feeling that they are invoked somewhat arbitrarily.

Finally, in 1 Kings 7:13–14, Hiram says that Huram-Abi's mother was from Naphtali, whereas in 2 Chronicles 2:13–14, she was from Dan. I once asked an adult Sunday school class consisting entirely of people without formal theological training if they could reconcile the differences. I received seven different scenarios that could have accounted for the two verses: some suggested that she was really from Dan but lived in Naphtali; others that his mother was born to parents from both tribes so that her own ancestry could be reckoned through either; another suggested that she may have lived in disputed territory contiguous to both tribes and claimed by both; one felt that Hiram of Tyre could have been mistaken in one case, and corrected by the biblical historian in another, and so forth. This was an interesting confirmation for me that harmonization is not hard to do, can always be done, can usually be done in several different ways, and cannot ordinarily be shown right or wrong. Nearly any conceivable scenario could be invoked, and for logicians it looks like unbridled special pleading.

Occasionally harmonization can become so ingenious as to undermine the very biblical authority it seeks to establish. Perhaps the most notorious example involves reconstructing the account of Peter's denial with the result that he denied Jesus six times before the cock crowed twice.[18] The account of the death of Ahaziah is quite different in 2 Kings 9:27–28 and 2 Chronicles 22:8–9. One can concoct an amalgam of the two passages, so that Ahaziah fled from Jehu in Jezreel south to hide in Samaria, where he was found and brought to Jehu, who fatally wounded him near Ibleam. Ahaziah then fled by chariot northwest toward Megiddo, where he died; his body was subsequently taken to Jerusalem for burial. But the uneasy feeling persists that this "solution" is forced and contrived.[19]

---

17. H. L. Allrik, "The Lists of Zerubbabel (Nehemiah 7 and Ezra 2) and the Hebrew Numeral Notation," *Bulletin of the American Schools of Oriental Research* 136 (1954): 21–27.

18. A convenient summary of this suggestion can be found in Harold Lindsell, *The Battle for the Bible* (Grand Rapids: Zondervan, 1976), pp. 174–76.

19. The Chronicler often uses death reports, particularly the honor accorded at death and the place of burial, as indicative of his judgment regarding a king. Cf. the similar issue

## Its Adequacy

At first glance the practice of harmonization appears to be a simple and straightforward way to deal with historical difficulties, but in actual application the approach becomes occasionally blurred and problematic. Intrabiblical quotations provide a case in point.

Most evangelicals adhering to the doctrine of inerrancy do not consider variations in reports of speech materials reason for harmonization. One Gospel may say that Jesus asked the rich young ruler, "Why do you ask me about what is good?" (Matt. 19:17), whereas another reports the question to have been, "Why do you call me good?" (Luke 18:19). The soldier at the cross said, "Surely this was a righteous man" (23:47), or "Surely he was the Son of God" (Matt. 27:54). Some may feel that Jesus or the centurion must have said both or that these are two different instances. But for the most part, evangelical theologians have seen variations like these as acceptable paraphrase and find no need to harmonize them.

New Testament citations of the Old Testament often follow the LXX instead of the MT. Hebrews 1:6 cites Deuteronomy 32:43 in a reading that is found in the LXX and a Qumran text, and it is difficult to be sure what the original text of the verse may have been. Some might insist that the New Testament has erroneously cited the Old Testament. Others might be tempted to say that the LXX represents the correct text. However, most evangelical theologians would say that inerrancy cannot be used to make text-critical decisions; the writer of Hebrews simply used the Bible he had before him. Nothing that he said was false, and his citation is no occasion for harmonization. Compare as other examples the citations of the Old Testament in Hebrews 2:6–8, James 4:6, and 1 Peter 4:18.

Galatians 3:17 presents a similar case in its allusion to Exodus 12:40, though the stakes appear to be a bit higher. Compare the text of Exodus 12:40 in the MT, LXX, and Samaritan Pentateuch (SP):

*MT:* The length of time the children of Israel lived in Egypt was 430 years.

---

regarding the death of Josiah (2 Kings 23:29–30; 2 Chron. 35:24). Some interpret the Chronicler's report of the death of Josiah in Jerusalem instead of Megiddo as an effort to ease the tension with the prophecy of Huldah that Josiah would go to his grave in peace (2 Kings 22:20; 2 Chron. 34:28) or as an effort to assign this righteous king death in the city of David instead of in defeat on a battlefield. See the discussions in H. Williamson, "The Death of Josiah and the Continuing Development of the Deuteronomic History," *Vetus Testamentum* 32 (1982): 242–48; idem, "Reliving the Death of Josiah: A Reply to C. T. Begg," ibid., 37 (1987): 9–15; C. Begg, "The Death of Josiah in Chronicles: Another View," ibid., pp. 1–8; see also my own *Second Chronicles,* pp. 292–93. A similar issue is raised by the Chronicler's treatment of the last four kings of Judah; see ibid., pp. 294–303.

*LXX:* The length of time the children of Israel lived in Egypt *and Canaan* was 430 years.

*SP:* The length of time the children of Israel *and their fathers* lived in Egypt *and Canaan* was 430 years.

In Galatians 3:17, Paul appears to be saying that the Law came 430 years after Abraham. Paul may have derived this information from a text of Exodus that agreed with either the LXX or the SP. Even if we were certain that the MT represented the correct text of the verse, one could argue that Paul has not been false. He has simply followed the Bible that he had before him; inerrancy does not require that the text-critical question be decided in favor of the LXX or the SP.[20]

Following in the same vein, one other illustration may heighten the difficulty a bit more. Ever since the Qumran discoveries, it has become clear that the Chronicler was following a version of Samuel that had numerous differences with the MT of that book. The MT and LXX of 2 Samuel 5:21 report that after a battle the Philistines "abandoned their gods there, and David and his men took them." The Lucianic recension of this verse reports that the Philistines left the idols but that David "gave orders to burn them in fire." When the Chronicler reports this incident (1 Chron. 14:12), he says that the Philistines abandoned their gods and that David "gave orders and they burned them in fire." David's actions conform to Deuteronomy 7:25 in the Lucianic edition of Samuel and in the Chronicles MT, but his actions are out of accord with the Law in the Samuel MT and the LXX. Assuming for the sake of the argument that the Samuel MT represents an earlier text,[21] it appears that the Lucianic revision and the Chronicler both worked from a text of Samuel in which a scribe had conformed David's actions to the Law. Once again one could argue that the Chronicler was simply using the Bible he had at hand. However, the historical character of the account has been modified by transmission history.[22] Similar illustrations could be drawn from other

---

20. There are, of course, other solutions to this difficulty. Some have suggested that, though the text appears to date the Law 430 years after Abraham, Paul in fact had the last time the promise was given in mind, so that the MT is correct, and the time between the last giving of the promise to Jacob and the Law is 430 years.

21. This is by no means to be taken for granted. The quality of the MT in Samuel has long been a matter of debate; the Qumran discoveries in general confirm that there are numerous difficulties in Samuel MT.

22. A typical harmonistic solution would be to suggest overlying the passages, e.g., "David took them up [Samuel MT] and burned them [Chronicles MT]." This solution would not give much weight to the fact that the Chronicler appears to be simply copying his source of Samuel at this point: the Chronicler would have had yet another version of the same event from which he chose this variant detail.

passages (e.g., 2 Sam. 8:4 and the parallel in 1 Chron. 18:4; or 2 Sam. 24:16–17 and its parallel in 1 Chron. 21:15–17).

The initial reluctance to harmonize intrabiblical citations when little is at stake leads inevitably to involvement in complicated historical questions. Considerable exegetical, theological, and hermeneutical work is needed to clarify the relationship between such intrabiblical citations and the doctrine of inerrancy.

### Its Focus

The goal of harmonistic exegesis is primarily to defend a doctrine of Scripture. That goal is immeasurably important. However, in actual practice, it has occasionally had unfortunate results. Too often, evangelical commentators on the historical books in particular have treated them as books full of problems and have commented on the Old Testament basically with an apologetic purpose in mind. This sort of focus tends to concentrate on minutiae and problem solving, and writers feel they can move on to the next passage once they have rebuffed critical opinion and thereby secured the faith of their readers in the Scriptures.

Though an apologetic component in writing about the Bible is laudable and necessary, the focus of exegesis is less defending a doctrine of Scripture than it is elucidating a text. The focus is on what the author and text say to a particular audience and to us; the text may not directly address the doctrine of Scripture at all.

Often the difficulties that are the grist for harmonization provide keys into the author's larger purpose. A later biblical author may provide an alternate account in order to portray an individual or event in a particular light. Matthew's reporting Jesus' sermon on a mountain may reflect his portraying Jesus as a second Moses, a second lawgiver on a mountain. When the Chronicler records Huram-Abi's ancestry in the tribe of Dan, he is carefully molding Huram-Abi as a kind of second Oholiab;[23] it is just one of a number of differences in his account that perfect a parallel between the building of the temple and Israel's original sanctuary, the tabernacle. The consistency with which the Chronicler portrays divine blessing through God's giving righteous kings large armies speaks to basic themes he wants his reader to understand. Read in this way, these "difficulties" are not so much problems as they are opportunities, open windows to the big picture.[24]

23. Dillard, "Chronicler's Solomon."
24. I have provided some further reflection on methodological questions in the introduction to *Second Chronicles,* pp. xviii–xix. The Chronicler was an individual, interacting with written texts at his disposal. I have described this interaction by saying that he "recasts, shapes, models, enhances, modifies, transforms, edits, rewrites" the material at his disposal. This vocabulary describes the Chronicler's activity and does not of itself prejudge

Good biblical study calls for a balance. We may not allow preoccupation with higher criticism and problems to cause us to miss what the biblical writer is trying to say, nor may we neglect attending to the outworking of the doctrine of Scripture in particular pericopes. We want to know all about the twigs and leaves on the branches, but we cannot afford to miss the forest.

We believe that the Scriptures are all that God wants them to be, without any compromise of his own glory and veracity. But the nature of Scripture is not established alone from the proof texts so often cited in reference to that doctrine, but also from the phenomena we observe there. The doctrine of Scripture, like all other doctrines, must be derived from Scripture itself and not subjected to some other more ultimate standard derived from modern philosophy.

In sum, harmonization as an exegetical method has a long history and has made many important contributions to biblical studies. But it has also been somewhat of a mixed blessing. When too facilely employed, it tends to lack credibility and does not commend the cause (the doctrine of Scripture) it seeks to uphold.

In those instances where no plausible harmonization offers itself, how should the theologian respond? Several avenues are open. E. J. Young's approach was essentially to wait patiently for better evidence and explanations and meanwhile to avoid making forced harmonizations.[25] The history of biblical studies has frequently ratified this approach.

A further avenue for addressing these problems is through genre criticism. After sober study one could conclude that a book of narrative prose in the Old Testament belongs to some other literary genre in which historical canons are suspended or modified. This approach is reflected in affirmation 13 of the Chicago Statement on Biblical Hermeneutics, issued by the International Council on Biblical Inerrancy: "We affirm that awareness of the literary categories, formal and stylistic, of the various parts of Scripture is essential for proper exegesis, and hence we value genre criticism as one of the many disciplines of biblical study."

The importance of genre criticism has long been recognized for books like Song of Songs and Ecclesiastes. One's reading strategy for Song of Songs is determined by whether it is identified as an allegory, a drama, or an anthology of love poems; all three positions and numerous variations have been advocated in the history of interpretation, and all three result in substantially different understandings of the book. Young himself ap-

---

historical questions. It is my own conviction that, understood within the allowable historiographical practices of his own culture and time, the Chronicler is a reliable and trustworthy historian.

25. E. J. Young, *Thy Word Is Truth* (Grand Rapids: Eerdmans, 1957), pp. 124–25.

proached the authorship of Ecclesiastes through questions of genre.[26] The writer of Ecclesiastes implies that he is Solomon by claiming to be king in Jerusalem and wiser than all before him—yet the oblique way in which this very claim is made suggests that the author is using pseudonymy, an accepted literary convention of his time, and that the book itself may be dated later in light of additional evidence.[27]

Making a determination of genre is itself problematic. A genre identification may not be sufficiently compelling so as to enable firm conclusions or to commend general adoption. In studying a particular narrative, we are able to make broad generalizations at the outset, while perfecting, modifying, and nuancing this identification through interaction with the phenomena of the text and through comparisons with other biblical literature and the literature of the geographically proximate and contemporary cultures.

Approaching biblical narratives with this tool is rife with difficulties; it has the potential of devouring much of the facticity of biblical historiography. Yet the fact that this method (along with almost any other) is capable of abuse is not sufficient reason for outright rejection. Rather than dismissal in one broad sweep of the hand, the appeal to genre identifications must be evaluated for the strength of the argument, as with any other aspect of exegesis.

Yet one further note needs to be added. Evangelical theologians must be ever wary of imposing on the Bible hermeneutical or exegetical principles derived from outside it. The Scriptures and the Scriptures alone are the ultimate canon for truth and must not be subjected to some other standard. This position raises a series of interesting and difficult hermeneutical questions. At the very least it requires that we scrutinize the historiosophical principles affecting our reading of the Bible. Should evangelical theology share the premises and canons for truthfulness dictated by the historical-critical method? Engaging the historical-critical method is unavoidable, but part of that engagement must be a transcendental criticism of the very methods and canons with which it operates, rather than adopting them wholesale into Christian theology. This area needs attention but unfortunately would take us far beyond the scope of this chapter.

26. E. J. Young, *An Introduction to the Old Testament* (London: Tyndale, 1966), pp. 347–49.
27. See chapter 8.

# 10

# The New Testament as Canon

## Richard B. Gaffin, Jr.

*To accept the New Testament as canonical is, in a word, to acknowledge the twenty-seven writings in the second part of the Holy Bible as possessing divine authority and as constituting, accordingly, an intregral part of the divine rule for faith and life. In attributing divine authority to these writings, the Christian church obviously judges that such authority is to be acknowledged only because these writings are held to possess inherently, that is, by virtue of what they actually are, the right to such a claim.*
                                        —Ned B. Stonehouse, 1946

Applied to the New Testament as the written Word of God, the word *canon* describes it as a collection of documents that, together with the Old Testament, possesses final authority in matters of faith and life.[1] This historic Christian confession is subject to scrutiny from two basic angles—historical and theological: (1) When and how did the church in fact come to accept these twenty-seven books as canon? (2) Was and is the church warranted in regarding them as canon? The second of these questions is the concern of this chapter.

1. See, e.g., *Westminster Confession of Faith*, chap. 1, secs. 2–3.

On its theological side, the canon question is, one may say, the crucial question of New Testament Introduction; the answer given to it decisively controls subsequent interpretation, especially in overall understanding of the New Testament. In the study of the Bible, however, historical and theological questions may not be divorced from each other; the answers to the two sorts of questions inevitably condition each other (because of the historical nature of the biblical documents). This is especially so for the issue of the New Testament canon. When theological reflection takes place in isolation from historical investigation, the former becomes abstract and speculative; in concentrating on the theological side of the canon question, we must be careful not to forget or distort the historical picture. It will be useful, then, to preface our discussion by noting, however briefly, the results of historical inquiry concerning the canon.

Contemporary scholarship, for the most part, is agreed that by the end of the second century (ca. A.D. 180) the four Gospels, Acts, the thirteen letters of Paul, 1 Peter, and 1 John were widely accepted throughout the church as canonical, that is, as constituent parts of a "New Testament," on a par in revelatory character and authority with what by that acceptance became its "Old Testament." Among the primary evidence for this consensus are the writings of Irenaeus and the earliest extant list of books, the Muratorian Canon. The canonical status of other documents (some eventually included in the canon, some ultimately rejected) continued to be debated for approximately two centuries until, in the last third of the fourth century, the present twenty-seven-book canon, facilitated by several ecclesiastical decisions, secured its fixed and permanent place in the life of the church—although random, peripheral exceptions continued for a time.

Scholars are also largely agreed on the importance of Marcion and other second-century heretics in forcing the Great Church to give its attention to the canon question. Division of opinion persists, however, over the nature of that influence. Basically the issue is this: Did Marcion create the idea of the New Testament canon, introducing something previously foreign or at least nonexistent in the life of the church? Or did Marcion's canon have a catalytic effect, forcing the mainstream of the church to account more explicitly for what it already possessed (and was already aware of possessing)? Does the New Testament canon antedate the middle of the second century or not?[2]

---

2. A helpful survey of the history of the recognition, formation, and closing of the canon is provided by A. B. du Toit, "The Canon of the New Testament," in *Guide to the New Testament*, vol. 1 (Pretoria: N. G. Kerkboekhandel, 1979), pp. 184–257; see also E. F. Harrison, *Introduction to the New Testament* (Grand Rapids: Eerdmans, 1971), pp. 98–134; more

Noncanonical materials available from before that time are relatively sparse and do not yield a decisive answer to this question. Consequently, scholarly attention has shifted to the New Testament documents themselves in order to clarify the historical picture. With that shift canon has ceased to be purely an issue in New Testament Introduction. Increasingly in this century, especially within the historical-critical tradition, the question of canon has become as much an exegetical/hermeneutical as an introductory one. Accordingly, historical and theological considerations patently intertwine. Concern with the New Testament as canon has become inseparable from (and in some cases virtually identical to) concern with the theology/theologies of the New Testament and various efforts to specify its presumably normative center (the "canon within the canon").[3] Invariably, it seems, attention to the canon question brings to light one's own basic presuppositions and theological commitments. That is true as well of the discussion that follows.

## The Problem

On the assumption, substantiated below, that inscripturated revelation was given in conjunction with the completion of Christ's work and the founding of the church, the real problem of the New Testament as canon is its completed or closed character. Why does the church accept this concrete collection, just these twenty-seven books and no others? How do we know that there is not some document, now unknown, which may some day be discovered and consequently deserve to be included? Alternatively, how do we know that something has not slipped in which really does not belong?

The status of these questions, it should be noted, differs in important respects from the situation of the Old Testament. The canonical standing of the Old Testament as a whole (see, e.g., Luke 24:44–45) and of most of the individual books is clearly established on the inspired authority of Christ and the New Testament writers and also corroborated in Judaism by the end of the first century A.D. For the New Testament, however, there is no such subsequent inspired, authoritative testimony to its constituent documents and their canonicity.

---

briefly, B. M. Metzger, "Canon of the New Testament," in *Hastings Dictionary of the Bible*, rev. ed., ed. F. C. Grant and H. H. Rowley (New York: Scribner's, 1963), pp. 123–27; most recent is Metzger's magisterial treatment in *The Canon of the New Testament* (Oxford: Clarendon, 1987), pp. 39–247; cf. pp. 289–93, 305–15.

3. This trend is especially clear in the collection of essays in E. Käsemann, ed., *Das Neue Testament als Kanon* (Göttingen: Vandenhoeck and Ruprecht, 1970); cf. H. Y. Gamble, *The New Testament Canon* (Philadelphia: Fortress, 1985), pp. 73–92.

The questions just raised can take on a pressing, perhaps even distressing, character when we pose them in the light of what we know about the actual course of developments in the early church. As noted above, it was a slow process, covering roughly three hundred years, before the canon accepted in the church was the same as our twenty-seven-book canon. Athanasius's so-called Easter Letter of 367 is apparently the first official, ecclesiastical decision to that effect. And there were significant differences at earlier stages (for example, over Hebrews and Revelation), even among orthodox figures. Why, for instance, did the Shepherd of Hermas, despite initial support, eventually go by the board, while 2 Peter, at first subject to much uncertainty, ultimately find a secure place in the canon?

All told, how do we know that in accepting the present New Testament—and the authority that goes with it—we are not simply following well-intentioned but nonetheless fallible decisions of people like ourselves?

## Criteria of Canonicity?

It may seem that the solution to this problem lies in the direction of establishing or distinguishing certain criteria—an index or mark that, by its presence or absence, demonstrates the canonicity or the noncanonical status of a book in question. That, notice carefully, would have to be a criterion in the sense of a *sufficient* as well as necessary condition for canonicity—that is, not simply any characteristic, no matter how essential, but a mark distinguishing each of the documents in the canon and just these documents alone.

This approach, promising at a first glance, is not viable. History shows that in fact the church has not been able to establish the criterion or set of criteria *(notae canonicitatis)* required. Nor, as I will try to show, can the church ever do so.

The most frequent proposal by far has been *apostolicity*. Certainly, as we will note below, there is a close connection between the apostles and the canon. But the difficulties for apostolic authorship or origin as a criterion are apparent.

Mark, Luke-Acts, Hebrews, Jude, and most likely James do not have apostles for authors. This objection has been countered by expanding the notion of apostolicity to include those who were close to the circle of apostles, so that what they wrote was associated with the authority of a particular apostle. But such an expansion fatally weakens apostolicity as a criterion of canonicity. There were no doubt other materials that would qualify as apostolic in an expanded sense but have not been included in the New Testament (see Luke 1:1). And an apostolic matrix for Hebrews is at best uncertain.

An even greater difficulty is posed by the references to Paul's "previous" letter to the Corinthians (1 Cor. 5:9) and his letter to the church at Laodicea (Col. 4:16). There is perhaps as well an allusion to previous written communication in Philippians 3:1. These documents, though evidently on a par with the canonical letters of Paul in apostolic authority, are not in the New Testament.

Other criteria that have been proposed are antiquity, public lection, and inspiration. *Antiquity*—only the earliest documents have been included in the canon—is really a variation on apostolicity, and it founders on the same difficulties; the "previous" letter of 1 Corinthians 5:9 is earlier, say, than Hebrews. *Public lection*—only those documents first read aloud in public worship are canonical—encounters the obstacle that, at an early point, documents like the Shepherd of Hermas and the Didache were used in public worship, while no evidence exists for such early usage of 2 Peter, 2 and 3 John, or Jude.

*Inspiration,* though necessary to canonicity, does not coincide with it. Paul's previous letter to the Corinthians and his letter to the Laodiceans carry full apostolic authority and are therefore presumably inspired. Without unduly multiplying nonextant documents, those letters suggest that he, along with at least some of the other apostles, produced a somewhat larger volume of inspired material (exactly how much is difficult to say) than has subsequently been included in the canon. Furthermore, there would be the insuperable difficulty of having to *demonstrate* inspiration for each New Testament document—if it is to serve as a criterion of canonicity.

This classical quest for criteria of canonicity should not be confused with what went on in the early church; the two differ markedly from each other. The former considers the New Testament as a completed entity already accepted by the church; it seeks to account, after the fact, for the inclusion of the twenty-seven books and those alone. In contrast, until late in the fourth century and beyond, the church was still in the process of reaching a consensus concerning which documents belong to the New Testament.

That earlier effort also made use of criteria—notably apostolic authorship and conformity to apostolic teaching (orthodoxy). Yet here, too, the application of criteria (in the strict sense) was defective. Hebrews, for instance, was accepted only when and where the church concluded that Paul was its author. In this case, ultimately, the early church made the right decision for the wrong reason.

Within the so-called historical-critical tradition, to comment briefly, the canon question has been approached along radically different lines. As the work of J. S. Semler (1725–91) already made unmistakably clear,[4] that approach, premised on the assumed rational autonomy of the interpreter/historian, has resulted in rejecting the church's historic conception of the canon (along with its accompanying understanding of biblical inspiration) as an outdated, unenlightened piece of supernaturalism. Operating characteristically with a radicalized version of Luther's criterion *was Christum treibet* ("what urges/promotes/inculcates Christ"), the formal authority of the New Testament documents as a collective entity is rejected, and the search goes on for some element of material authority within them (a "canon within the canon").

Increasingly in this century the impact of activistic, nonverbal conceptions of revelation (e.g., that of Karl Barth) has given rise to views of canonicity in which a normative center is played off in an activistic, more or less dialectical fashion against the competing, even contradictory teaching and theologies allegedly contained in the New Testament as a whole (see, e.g., the views of E. Käsemann: the New Testament itself is an ongoing "battleground" [*Kampfplatz*] for the gospel, wherein Christ and Antichrist, faith and superstition, struggle against each other).[5]

The church, as we have seen, has in fact failed to establish criteria of canonicity. Even more telling, however, is the recognition that, in principle, all attempts to demonstrate such criteria must fail and threaten to undermine the canonicity of Scripture. For example, suppose we take $X$ (say, apostolicity) to be a criterion of canonicity. That would mean entering into a historical investigation to identify and circumscribe $X$. But such a procedure could only mean subjecting the canon to the relativity of historical study and our fallible human insight. That is, it would destroy the New Testament as canon, as absolute authority.

In the final analysis the attempt to demonstrate criteria (the necessary and sufficient conditions) of canonicity seeks, from a position above the canon, to rationalize or generalize about the canon as a unique, particular historical state of affairs. It relativizes the authority of the canon by attempting to contain it *(kanōn)* within an all-embracing criterion *(kritērion)*.

Instead we must recognize that we are shut up to the New Testament canon as a self-establishing, self-validating entity. Canonicity is a unique concept. It neither coincides with what is apostolic nor even with what is inspired. Rather, canonical is what belongs to the New Testament, and what belongs to the New Testament is canonical. (The evident circularity of the last sentence is not unintended!)

4. J. S. Semler, *Abhandlung von der freien Untersuchung des Kanons* . . . (Halle, 1771–75).

5. E. Käsemann, "Zusammenfassung," in *Das Neue Testament als Kanon*, pp. 407–8.

# God Is Canon

We ought not, then, to try to secure for ourselves an Archimedean point outside or above the New Testament canon. Yet, in another respect, the canon does point back beyond itself—to God, its origin and author. When we think of the idea of canon (supreme authority), we may not think of anything or any other person than God. God is canon; God is supreme authority.

In dealing with the question of the canon and its closing, we must not lose sight of this personal reference in the notion of canon. Otherwise we will fall into some form of viewing history as, at least to some degree, an autonomous, impersonal process. Here (as in all historical studies)[6] we are to think concretely, "personalistically," so that history is recognized for what it is—down to its most minute details the realization of God's eternal, predeterminate counsel and good pleasure.

The collection of New Testament documents is not a historical phenomenon to be explained in terms of purely immanent factors—contingent factors, in turn, without an ultimate explanation. The New Testament is not a collection that "just happened," a kind of brute fact hanging there on the horizon of the past. Rather, it is the historical phenomenon by which God, the sovereign Architect and Lord of history, asserts and maintains himself as canon, that is, by which his supreme authority comes to expression.

With these observations we have arrived at a provisional answer to the question of an opened or closed canon, though that answer needs to be elaborated and further substantiated. How can we avoid confessing that God is the author of the Bible (the New Testament) as a whole, the architect of the collective entity? The only other alternative, on the assumption of inscripturated verbal revelation, is that the Bible (the New Testament) is a human anthology of divinely inspired writings and, if so, is open, in principle, to revision and requires verification. But such a human-anthology view of the canon, as we will presently see, runs counter to the witness of the New Testament documents themselves. In the sense that God is the author of the whole as well as the constituent parts, the New Testament canon is closed or complete.

This conclusion involves an important distinction. The origin of the New Testament canon is not the same as its reception by the church. We must avoid confusing the existence of the canon with its recognition, what is constitutive (God's action) with what is reflexive (the church's action). The activity of the church—statements of church fathers, decrees

---

6. See the valuable discussion by C. Van Til, "The Christian Philosophy of History," in *Common Grace and the Gospel* (Philadelphia: Presbyterian and Reformed, 1947), pp. 1–13.

of councils, and so forth concerning the contents of the New Testament—
does not create the canon.

## The New Testament Canon and
## the History of Redemption
## (Apostolicity and Canonicity)

The viewpoint just expressed is sometimes called the a priori of faith.
But that a priori, as so far stated, is not the last word, which would make
further discussion of the canon issue unnecessary.[7]

"Faith comes by hearing and hearing by the word of Christ" (Rom.
10:17). Taken in the context of verses 14–16, this statement reminds us
that true faith is nothing apart from its content, the content given to it
and that it receives. Only this content-full faith provides a biblically warranted a priori.

That involves, among other things, recognizing that the New Testament canon is bound up with the giving of revelation in history. Scripture has not been dropped straight down from heaven, as it were. As
much as possible, then, our statements about the canon should be qualified historically. Without, on the one hand, abandoning our a priori
or, on the other, trying to make faith (or redemptive history) a criterion
of canonicity in a strict sense, we need to reflect further on that faith
a priori in the light of Scripture. We will seek to explicate within the
circle of faith, without leaving that circle.

*The apostles as representatives of Christ: the christological dimension.*
The Greek noun *apostolos,* related to the much more common verb *apos-
tellō* (to send, send out), refers in general to a messenger or, more formally,
to an envoy or delegate. Traditionally, then, the New Testament apostle
has been understood primarily as a religious figure like a missionary,
someone sent to communicate the gospel. That understanding no doubt
has a large element of truth.

More recently, however, studies in the background of the New Testament have shed new light on the figure of the apostle in the New Testament. In particular, a line has been drawn to the figure of the *šālîaḥ* in
intertestamental Judaism. In fact, that relationship and the extent to
which the latter influenced the former continue to be debated. But that
debate does not have to be settled here for us to recognize that the Jewish

---

7. For the discussion in this section, see esp. H. Ridderbos, *Redemptive History and the
New Testament Scriptures* (Phillipsburg, N.J.: Presbyterian and Reformed, 1988), pt. 1;
N. B. Stonehouse, "The Authority of the New Testament," in *The Infallible Word* ed. N. B.
Stonehouse and Paul Woolley (Phillipsburg, N.J.: Presbyterian and Reformed, 1980),
pp. 92–140; du Toit, "Canon of the New Testament," pp. 91–170.

institution does at least serve as a backdrop to illumine an important point of New Testament teaching about apostolicity.

In the Judaism contemporary to the writing of the New Testament, the šālîaḥ (from šālaḥ, "to send") has a significance that is legal, not religious.[8] The šālîaḥ is someone authorized to execute a task in the interests of another person or group. The content of this commission can vary greatly (from economic tasks like carrying out a business deal to social activities like arranging a marriage). The fact of his authorization rather than a particular content distinguishes the šālîaḥ. He is an authorized, authoritative representative, akin to someone today who exercises power of attorney. Furthermore, the šālîaḥ was identified fully with the one who commissioned him; in some instances he was free to take initiatives in discharging his commission. This full authority, the fulness of empowered representation, is reflected in the Talmudic formula that "a man's šālîaḥ is the same as himself."

Something of this background is reflected in the figure of the apostle in the New Testament. In John 13:12–20, the issue of authority is prominent (the point, paradoxically, is the authority to serve others, exemplified in Jesus' washing the disciples' feet). The focus of verse 16 is the derivative nature of the apostles' authority—"no servant is greater than his master, nor is an *apostolos* greater than the one who sent him" (cf. Heb. 3:1–2, where Jesus is "appointed" by God as *apostolos*). Verse 20 not only expresses this point of derivation but accents the identification of the sender and the one sent: "whoever accepts anyone I send accepts me; and whoever accepts me accepts the one who sent me."

At issue, then, is the uniqueness and fulness of apostolic authority. The apostles encountered in the New Testament, with the few exceptions noted in the next paragraph, are "apostles of Christ." As such they are authorized representatives of Christ, deputized personal exemplifications of his authority. Note, for instance, Galatians 4:14, where Paul says of himself as an angel-apostle (cf. 1:1–2:10) that the Galatians received him "as if I were Christ Jesus himself."

A certain elasticity does attach to the New Testament usage of *apostolos*. Second Corinthians 8:23 ("apostles of the churches") and Philippians 2:23 (perhaps, too, Acts 14:4, 14) refer in a looser, most likely temporary, ad hoc sense to messengers or representatives sent by a local church for a specific task. This usage is in distinction from the apostles of Christ in the strict sense, who are "first" in the (one, universal) church (1 Cor. 12:28; cf. Eph. 4:11). In which sense the reference in Romans 16:7 is to be taken is difficult to say.

8. See e.g., K. H. Rengstorf, in G. Kittel, ed., *Theological Dictionary of the New Testament*, trans. and ed. G. W. Bromiley, 10 vols. (Grand Rapids: Eerdmans, 1964–76), 1:414–20.

*The apostles as foundation of the church: the ecclesiological dimension.*
The apostle of Christ does not operate on his own. He is not an unusually resourceful, charismatic free-lancer. Rather, he has his apostolic identity and function only as part of a group, a unified structure that the New Testament itself describes with the abstract noun *apostolē* (apostleship, apostolate—Acts 1:25; Rom. 1:5; 1 Cor. 9:2; Gal. 2:8). That function is always in the interests of the church.

This point can be amplified by considering the basic New Testament figure of the church as a house. This is a dynamic-historical figure: the church results from the construction activity of God as architect-builder in the period between the resurrection and return of Christ.

In terms of this house model, the apostles are the foundation of the church structure. Note Matthew 16:18, "You are Peter, and on this rock I will build my church." Peter is the foundation on which Christ, looking to the future beyond his resurrection and ascension, will build the church. This promise is not made to Peter in the abstract but in view of his confession (vv. 16–17) and as he, with that confession, represents the other apostles (the apostolate). The rock foundation of the church is to be confessing Peter as primus inter pares, first among apostolic equals.

See also Ephesians 2:20, "built on the foundation of the apostles and prophets, with Christ Jesus himself as the chief cornerstone." In the immediate context (vv. 19–22), the house model is even more explicit (cf. 1 Peter 2:4–8). Christ is the cornerstone; in the foundation his is the critical place that supports everything. In fact, in view of his unique, once-for-all work of redemption there is "no other foundation" (1 Cor. 3:11 RSV). Yet in some specific respect, still to be determined, the apostles are associated with Christ as the foundation; they, too, are constitutive for the foundation.

The redemptive-historical place and function of the apostolate bears emphasizing. The house building in view in the last half of Ephesians 2 is a comprehensive historical figure (see vv. 11–22). It is a dynamic model, taking in the church in its broadest unity, in every time and place. Accordingly, the foundation of the church-house is temporally qualified. It is a historical category: laying the foundation of a building is a one-time activity; the ensuing construction is on the superstructure, not the constant, repeated re-laying of the foundation. This temporal limitation ties in with the fact, already noted, that the foundation involves the work of Christ in its once-for-all historicity. Hence, we are pointed to the conclusion that in the church the office of apostle is not intended to be perpetual; the apostolate is a temporary institution.

Several other passages reinforce this conclusion. According to Acts 1:21–26, a prerequisite for being an apostle was to have been among Jesus' disciples during the entire period of his earthly ministry (v. 21) and especially to have been an eye and ear witness of the resurrected Christ (v. 22)—a prerequisite that Paul sees as being met, with an exception, in his own case (1 Cor. 9:1; see also 15:7–9). In other words, a historically limiting restriction attaches to who may be an apostle.

In 1 Corinthians 15:7–9, Paul states in effect that he is the last of the apostles (explicitly in 4:9, probably without the inclusion of Apollos): he is "the least of the apostles" (15:9), inasmuch as the resurrected Christ appeared to him "last of all," as one born abnormally (v. 8), after he had already appeared to "all the apostles" (v. 7; see also Gal. 1:17).

In the Pastoral Epistles Paul plainly views Timothy, as much as anyone else, as his personal successor; the task of gospel ministry about to be laid down by him is to be taken up by Timothy and others. Yet Paul never refers to Timothy or Titus as an apostle.

These considerations prompt the observation that in a personal sense the expression "apostolic succession" is a contradiction in terms. The New Testament maintains the once-for-all character of the apostolate. The presence of apostles in the church is foundational, that is, temporary.

Notice, in passing, that Ephesians 2:20 associates prophets with the apostles in the church's foundation, in the historical sense just indicated. That these are New Testament prophets follows (1) from the word order ("the apostles and prophets"—not "the [Old Testament] prophets and [New Testament] apostles"), (2) from 3:5, where "now" refers to "God's holy apostles and prophets," just in contrast to "other [Old Testament] generations," and (3) because they are prophets in the church seen as still in the future in Matthew 16:18.

Consequently, we are drawn to recognize that the New Testament prophets, included with the apostles as part of the foundation of the church, are, like the apostles, a temporary institution in its life. The presence of the prophets is limited, by God's architectural design, to the foundational, apostolic era of the church.

The only way to avoid this conclusion, apparently, is to argue either (1) that the New Testament teaches two kinds of prophecy in the church—foundational, noncontinuing prophecy and prophecy, like that mentioned in 1 Corinthians 12–14 and elsewhere, that continues until Christ's return—or (2) that in Ephesians 2:20 the prophets in view are actually apostles, that is, the apostles as prophets. Both these views, however, especially the second, rest on exegesis that seems unlikely, even forced. The "prophethood" of all believers, a truth taught in Acts 2:17–18, for instance, and recaptured especially by the Reformation, is another matter and is certainly not being denied here; in fact, as we will see, that universal prophetic office rests on the once-for-all, foundational ministry of "the apostles and prophets."

*The apostles as witnesses: the revelatory dimension.* The single most important function of the apostles is their witness-bearing *(marturia).* The focus of apostolic witness, especially in Acts, is Christ's resurrection (e.g., Acts 1:21; 2:32; 3:15; 10:40–41), not as an isolated event but in the context of his whole work, especially his death (e.g., 2:22–24; 1 Cor. 15:3–4), and as the consummation of redemptive history (e.g., Acts 3:12–26; 13:16–41). The apostles testify to the already-accomplished redemptive basis of the church. That testimony, specifically, makes the apostles the foundation of the church. Their witness is the foundational witness to the foundational work of Christ; to the once-for-all work of Christ is joined a once-for-all witness to that work (Eph. 2:20).

Apostolic witness is normative; the apostles are uniquely authorized and empowered to be witnesses of Christ. This binding, *šālîaḥ*-like character of the apostles' witness is seen in the equation of apostolic proclamation with the Word of God. Paul, for instance, says of the Thessalonians that they received his preaching "not as the word of men, but as it actually is, the word of God" (1 Thess. 2:13 NIV). Most likely, 1 Corinthians 11:23 ("For I received from the Lord what I also passed on to you") points to the exalted Lord himself as the author-bearer of apostolic tradition. According to Galatians 1:12, Paul's gospel is revelation received directly from Christ; yet, verse 18 intimates (in context) that revelation is on a par with the tradition he received through contact with the other apostles. Such an equation exists because, ultimately, both come from the exalted Christ (cf. Acts 9:26–27; 1 Cor. 15:1–4).

The promise of the coming of the Spirit as *paraklētos* (Counselor-Advocate, Helper) in John's Gospel (14:16, 26; 15:26–27; 16:7; cf. 16:13–15; Acts 1:8) is not given directly and indiscriminately to all believers. A specific historical qualification attaches to the "you" who are its immediate recipients. The "you" who are to testify are those who have been with Jesus during his earthly ministry "from the beginning," (John 15:27; note similar qualifications of "you" in 14:26; 16:7, 12). These promises are to be understood (at least primarily) in a foundational sense, that is, in terms of apostolic witness-bearing.

Apostolic witness, then, is not merely personal testimony. Instead, it is infallibly authoritative, legally binding deposition, the kind that stands up in a law court. Accordingly, that witness embodies a canonical principle; it provides the matrix for a new canon, the emergence of a new body of revelation to stand alongside the covenantal revelation of the Old Testament.[9]

9. For a stimulating development of the thesis that the canon is a function of the covenant, see M. G. Kline, *The Structure of Biblical Authority* (Grand Rapids: Eerdmans, 1972). Pp. 68–75 bear particularly on the New Testament, including the notion of the apostle as covenant witness.

*The apostles and the canon: the canonical dimension.* Plainly, as the apostles die and pass out of the picture, the need is for the preservation of apostolic witness in and by the church. In fact, the New Testament itself gives indications of an apostolic concern for such preservation.

Already at the time of the apostles, their witness is called "tradition" *(paradosis)*. Its authoritative, binding character is seen in the fact that Paul, for instance, commands his readers to hold firmly to it (1 Cor. 11:2; 2 Thess. 2:15; cf. 3:6). Second Thessalonians 2:15 is especially instructive in referring to those traditions passed on "whether by word of mouth or by letter." Notice that here—shortly after 1 Thessalonians, perhaps the earliest New Testament document—written as well as oral apostolic tradition is already in view as authoritative.

Paul instructs Timothy to guard the *parathēkē* (deposit, what has been entrusted; see 1 Tim. 6:20; 2 Tim. 1:14 (12?); cf. 2:2). Here *parathēkē* is similar in meaning to *paradosis* and has the same authoritative ring: Timothy is to preserve and maintain the authoritative deposit of truth.

The New Testament itself, then, anticipates and initiates a trend; it fixes the coordinates of a trajectory. As the apostles die off and their foundational witness is completed, as their oral witness ceases and living apostolic oversight of that witness comes to an end, written apostolic witness becomes increasingly crucial and focal, until it, exclusively, is the foundational Word of God on which the church is being built.

This trend, as just noted, corresponds to the intention of Paul, for instance. Broadly considered, developments in the church concerning the canon during the second through fourth centuries complement that apostolic intention. Those developments involve the increasing awareness in the postapostolic church of its distance from the apostolic past and so an increasing awareness of the foundational, revelatory nature of inscripturated apostolic witness or tradition (note the sense of distance present already in 1 Clement [ca. A.D. 95] and the letters of Ignatius [ca. 110]).

The complement to the apostolic intention, in other words, is postapostolic recognition of the New Testament canon. Furthermore, that process of recognition—because it answers to an apostolic intention—reflects as well, we may say, the intention of Christ. No one less than the exalted Christ himself is the architect of that process.

Notice, however, how little this undeniable, substantial connection between the apostles and the canon provides a criterion of canonicity, even in a looser sense. Most of the New Testament documents with nonapostolic authors do display, either on internal grounds or by reliable tradition, a direct tie to one or other of the apostles. But that is not so clearly the case for Jude and not at all for Hebrews. In Hebrews 2:3, the author seems to separate himself from the apostolic circle while emphatically affirming apostolic tradition. Hebrews is the perennial "loose end" of every effort to provide an airtight rationale for the canon in terms of apostolic provenance.

*The New Testament canon and the history of revelation: the redemptive-historical dimension.* The foundational witness of the apostles to the work of Christ brings to light an important characteristic of all verbal revelation—the correlation between redemptive act and revelatory word; God's Word is given to attest and interpret his saving work. This correlation holds true throughout the entire history of redemption, beginning in the Garden of Eden and reaching its climax in the death, exaltation, and return of Christ. Accordingly, the ongoing history of revelation is a strand within covenant, redemptive history as a whole; the process of verbal revelation conforms to the contours of that larger history.

The history of redemption has an epochal character; it moves forward in decisive steps, not in a uniform or smoothly evolutionary fashion. Consequently, in view of the correlation just noted, high points in redemptive history are accompanied by copious outpourings of verbal revelation. Old-covenant revelation, for instance, tends to cluster around critical junctures like the exodus, key events in the monarchy, the exile, and the return of the remnant.

The negative side of this correlation bears particularly on the issue of the canon and its closing. Times of inactivity in the history of redemption are, correlatively, times of silence in the history of revelation. The rebuilding of the temple and the return of the remnant from exile are the last critical developments before the coming of Christ. After that there is a lull; redemptive history pauses until the final surge forward at Christ's coming. Correspondingly, the ministries of postexilic figures like Haggai, Zechariah, Malachi, Ezra, and Nehemiah and the Old Testament books associated with them focus on those events, and then follows, as intertestamental Judaism in part subsequently recognized, a period of revelatory, prophetic silence, until the time of Christ.

Similarly, after the exaltation of Christ and the founding of the church, there is a pause or delay in the epochal forward movement of redemptive history. Only one event in that history is still future: the return of Christ (with its concomitants). Accordingly, following the contemporaneous outpouring of revelation focused on the first coming of Christ, the history of revelation lapses into silence. Confirming that silence is the disappearance of the apostolate, that prophetic institution established by Christ specifically to provide revelatory attestation and interpretation of the redemption consummated in his person and work.

To say that redemptive history is "on hold" until Christ's return is not to deny the full reality and redemptive significance of what is happening in the church today. Ongoing church history, however, is not an extension of redemption. It is not a prolongation in series with Christ's work but the reflex of that work, the application of its benefits. It is not part of the foundation of the church but the building being erected on the finished, once-for-all redemptive foundation laid by Christ.

As far as the church today is concerned, then, the history of revelation is closed until Christ's return. The expectation of new revelation in whatever form runs counter to the witness of Scripture itself. At issue here is the correlation between redemptive act (in the sense of once-for-all accomplishment) and word revelation; where the former is lacking, there is no place for the latter. The completion or cessation of revelation is a function of the finished work of Christ (see Heb. 1:2, where the work of Christ, along with the corroborating witness of the apostles [or, in 2:3, "those who heard"], is God's final, "last days" revelation-speech).

Recognizing the redemptive-historical character of revelation is crucial to a proper view of the canon. Revelation does not consist of divinely given information and directives *pro me,* just for me. The impact of revelation on the believer ought to be intimate and personal, but it is not individualistic. In its virtually limitless applications to the circumstances of individual believers of whatever time and place, revelation has a corporate, covenantal character; it is for the one people of God as a whole. To the extent we fall into individualistic misunderstandings of revelation, to that extent we will be left with a sense of the insufficiency and incompleteness of the Bible. We will have difficulty in seeing that God's revelation to his people is complete and, so, that the New Testament canon is closed.

## The New Testament Canon Is Closed

Relative to its concrete situation as the postapostolic church waiting for Christ's return—and not by some abstract, historically detached notion of closedness—the church can be confident that its New Testament is complete; there is nothing included that should be excluded, nothing missing that should be included. This conclusion can be focused by reflecting on the proverbial question of what ought to be done should an inspired apostolic writing one day be discovered—say, the previous letter mentioned in 1 Corinthians 5:9.

The sheer improbability of that discovery ought to be appreciated. Such an expectation is detached from a recognition of why God has given Scripture to the church in the first place. It is a matter of tradition which he intends for the church to hold fast and preserve. And the church cannot retain what it does not have.

The church would have to be far less fragmented than it has been for the past thousand years for it to recognize and then reach a consensus that such a writing is indeed canonical. Furthermore, such recognition could hardly claim continuity with what took place in the church during the first four centuries, when it was always a matter of deciding about documents that had all along been known, at least to some degree. But now there would be a new document abruptly introduced after nearly two thousand years.

But suppose, after all, that this hypothetical document were discovered and that it could be decided that it ought to be included in the church's Scriptures. That would still not mean that the present canon is or had been open or incomplete. Rather we ought to conclude that the church, by this addition, has been given a new canon. But just this idea of a new canon—an abrupt expansion, after such a long time, of the church's apostolic foundation—is highly speculative and difficult to square with the trajectories of New Testament teaching.

Granting the existence of inscripturated revelation, then, there are three basic positions on the New Testament canon. Two of these involve some form of the inherently self-contradictory notion of an "open" canon. One view is that *the New Testament is a human anthology of divinely inspired writings.* Strictly speaking, this view denies that God is the author of Scripture (as a whole). The collective entity is the product of fallible human beings, not the infallible construct of God; what we have in Scripture ultimately is the "whole counsel of man," not of God.

Inevitably on this view the meaning of the canon is impaired and its authority rendered defective. Each inspired document of Scripture does not have its authority or its overall intelligibility in isolation but in relation to the others, within the context provided by the Bible as a whole. All the documents of Scripture together constitute the frame in terms of which any one is to be understood finally and comprehensively. Consequently, to say that that frame is not divinely fixed, or is humanly fixed, precludes talking about the unity of the Bible. It casts a shadow of uncertainty on every single document and so undercuts the supreme authority of Scripture.

On another view, *the New Testament is, relatively speaking, a complete entity shaped by God, but is continually supplemented by additional, new word revelation, by living prophetic voices in the church.* This view involves a dualistic misunderstanding of revelation. In one way or other, a distinction is made between a completed, canonical revelation for the whole church and ongoing private revelations for individual believers or particular groups of believers—between a collective, inscripturated revelation of what is necessary for salvation and revelations that go beyond the Bible and specifically address individual life situations, needs, and concerns.

The problem with this view is that it is in tension—even conflict—with what, as we have already intimated, the Bible itself shows to be the covenantal, redemptive-historical character of all revelation. God does not reveal himself along two tracks, one public and one private.

Certainly we may not dictate to God what he can or cannot do, on occasion, in revealing himself today. We must guard against boxing in the Holy Spirit by our theological constructions. At all times the Spirit is sovereign and free, like the wind, as Jesus says, that "blows wherever it pleases" (John 3:8). In his freedom, however, the Spirit orders his activity, and that order, according to Scripture, does not encourage believers today to seek or otherwise expect forms of extrabiblical revelation.[10]

The third view is that *the New Testament is that complete entity in which, along with the Old Testament, God gives his Word and brings his authority to expression, without restriction, in a definitive and absolute way.* This view, as I have tried to show, is most faithful to the apostolic witness of the New Testament itself. Admittedly, this view does not settle all difficulties. For one, the quantitative question remains: Why, of all the inspired apostolic writings, just these twenty-seven? Why not twenty-eight or twenty-six, or some other number?

To this question we must be content to say that just these twenty-seven books are what God has chosen to preserve, and he has not told us why. It seems difficult to improve on the comment of Calvin: "These [books] which the Lord judged to be necessary for his church have been selected by this providence for everlasting remembrance."[11]

In the matter of the New Testament as canon, too, until Jesus comes "we walk by faith, not by sight" (2 Cor. 5:7 RSV). But that faith, grounded in the apostolic tradition of the New Testament, is neither arbitrary nor blind. It has its reasons, its good reasons; it is in conflict only with the autonomy of reason.

## Postscript: The New Testament Canon and Textual Criticism

The questions of canon and of the original text of the New Testament documents are not of the same order. To decide between variant readings is not to be involved, as it were, with the canon issue on its smallest scale.

The key to the categorical difference between these two concerns—text and canon—lies in the historically progressive and differentiated character of revelation. Inscripturated revelation did not come straight down

10. See my *Perspectives on Pentecost* (Phillipsburg, N.J.: Presbyterian and Reformed, 1986), pp. 93–102, esp. pp. 96–99 and 118–20.

11. John Calvin, *Commentaries on the Epistles of Paul to the Galatians and Ephesians*, trans. W. Pringle (1854; reprint, Grand Rapids: Baker, 1979), p. 249.

from heaven into history, already written and all at once. The Bible in this respect differs markedly from the claims made, for instance, for the Book of Mormon (a translation of gold tablets all unearthed at the same time) or for the Koran (dictated to Muhammad in a series of night visions over a relatively short time span). Scripture, instead, originates in history, through the full personal involvement and instrumentality of various human writers, over a long period of time, and with a great variety of literary genres. The Bible is not uniform, a monolithic set of words or sequence of statements. In its unity it is manifold, multiplex (see Eph. 3:10).

The theological importance—even necessity—of this consideration should be appreciated. Its diverse and progressive character is intrinsic to biblical revelation, bound up with the ongoing movement of the history of redemption and the accompanying correlation, already discussed, between revelatory word and redemptive act. To use a figure, inscripturated revelation is not one large gold ingot produced at one point in time but a variety of pure gold nuggets given over an extended period of time.

This figure helps to identify the qualitative rather than the merely quantitative, arithmetic difference between the questions of canon and text. The concern of the former is to identify the collection of gold nuggets—what gold nuggets belong to the collection? The concern of the latter is the transmission of the collection and the removal of the specks of tarnish that have built up on this or that nugget. The difference between the canon question and textual criticism is, in a word, the difference between recognizing the gold and removing the tarnish.

It should not be thought, then, that the logic of an approach to the issue of canon that stresses the a priori of faith, like that adopted above, demands the superiority of either the Received or Majority texts of the Greek New Testament. It is wrong-headed to suppose that, if we admit uncertainty about particular textual variants or recognize that the Majority text is not the best and needs to be corrected, we are then denying God's wise and providential oversight of the transmission of the text and so are pitched into uncertainty about the New Testament canon as a whole.

In this regard, it needs to be remembered that plenary, verbal inspiration (inspiration at the level of words and extending to every word) does not mean that every word in Scripture has the same semantic importance or is equally crucial to its meaning. Nor does verbal inspiration mean that we must have every word of an autograph if we are to understand any word.

The issue of textual criticism needs to be kept in balance. Certainly its principles are not to be canonized and are always open to review and even revision. But as often pointed out, if we adopt any one of the current, mutually conflicting theories of the transmission of the New Testament text and reconstruct, in terms of that particular theory, the best and worst texts, the resulting differences are minimal and do not affect any substantial element of biblical teaching. This observation applies in particular to the differences between the Majority text (or the Received text) and a critically reconstructed text. Giving full, legitimate scope to textual criticism still enables us to continue confessing that God's inscripturated Word, "by His singular care and providence," has been "kept pure in all ages."[12]

---

12. *Westminster Confession of Faith*, chap. 1, sec. 8.

# 11

## Normativity, Relevance, and Relativism

### Harvie M. Conn

*All Scriptural statements must be understood and applied*
*in the light of the conditions and circumstances which*
*they were intended to describe or under which they were*
*originally written. The* truth *of the statements, in the strict*
*sense, is not dependent on those circumstances but the*
meaning *frequently is, and the truth can only be understood*
*if the meaning is understood.*
—Paul Woolley, 1946

Can one believe in the Bible as the only infallible rule of faith and practice and, at the same time, affirm its culturally oriented particularity? Must the evangelical tremble in fear every time he or she hears scholars ask, "How does our understanding of the cultural setting of the Corinthian church affect the way we understand Paul's appeal to women to be silent in the church?" Will our current sensitivity to the New Testament as a word addressed to our century relativize our parallel commitment to it as a word addressed also to the first century?

These are the questions we address in this chapter. We do not intend to lay out particular hermeneutical rules to help us in this inquiry. We will touch on them but only as they aid us in our larger research. Nor will we

185

cover the whole sweep of scholarship. Our concentration will be on the discussions within the evangelical community.

Many of our case studies will come from those texts central to a study of the place of women in culture. Much current evangelical thinking on the Bible's particularity has revolved around these texts. It is not, however, the issue of the Bible's approach to women that we seek to resolve. Our attention is directed to the larger question of the Bible and its culturally related character. We examine these texts (and others) only to the degree they relate to this larger agenda.

## Contemporary Evangelical Discussion

Evangelicals, in a sense, have wrestled with the problems associated with cultural relativity in earlier decades. Linked more with terms like *relevance* and *applicability,* the questions seemed easier then. Is foot washing a continuing ceremony? Must women wear hats or veils in church? Are there times in the official ministry of the church when a woman can teach adult males? What about the use of tobacco and the drinking of alcoholic beverages in moderation?

Then, as now, answers have not always been the same. Evangelicals, in seeking to uphold the infallible authority of Scripture, sought for a variety of ways to account for the diversity of opinion. Some noted that mistakes can occur in applying a scriptural injunction to conditions other than those to which it was truly applicable. Cultural distance between dusty roads and concrete sidewalks translates foot washing into humble Christian service for others. The passage of time transforms the hat from a symbol of modesty to one of fashion.

It was also noted that "there are injunctions which are simultaneously appropriate to certain undertakings and circumstances and not to others."[1] The same Jesus who told his disciples at the Last Supper to buy a sword (Luke 22:36) a few hours later warned the same group, "All they that take the sword shall perish with the sword" (Matt. 26:52). Biblical texts, it was argued, cannot be applied as a universal plaster for any conceivable condition. Their use depends upon their specific applicability.

In many respects, these responses carried a large measure of truth, and still do. But the development of biblical studies has corrected and complicated the situation.

Earlier scholarship carried on these discussions in the name of "hermeneutics," the discipline that taught us skills in exegesis, in determining the meaning of the original author. "Application," an afterthought of

---

1. Paul Woolley, "The Relevance of Scripture," in *The Infallible Word,* ed. N. B. Stonehouse and Paul Woolley (Philadelphia: Presbyterian Guardian, 1946), p. 204.

this, was a homiletical art focusing on the relatively simple extension of exegesis to contemporary faith and life. No guidelines, however, were available to leap the gulf between exegesis and application. No discipline existed to bridge the gap between the two worlds of then and now, there and here.

The awareness of that gap came to the attention of evangelical theology outside its camp, through the work of the early Karl Barth, Rudolf Bultmann, and those who followed them. These scholars, though disagreeing in many areas, had joined in emphasizing the kerygmatic nature of the New Testament, the importance of the interpreting subject and his or her preunderstanding in the act or process of communication. Making use of neoorthodox dependence on existentialism, they saw the New Testament as other than some "objectively perceived" word from God. It did not convey timeless, eternal information unrelated to situations and hearers. The objectivism of liberal (or fundamentalist) scholarship was repudiated; it could not do justice to the biblical text.

Evangelical scholarship could not listen to these men. Their questioning of the authenticity of the New Testament message, their resorting to existentialism to provide a relevant word from Paul or Jesus, were trails down which the evangelical properly did not go. But as a side effect, their hermeneutical call for attention to how to speak the Word of the Lord in the twentieth century was lost.

Only in the last decades of biblical research has the significance of the hermeneutical issue been recognized by the evangelical. Combined with a new sensitivity to what has been called "reader-response" and audience criticism, hermeneutics increasingly has come to be seen "as the operative engagement or interaction between the horizon of the text and the horizon of the reader. The problem of hermeneutics was the problem of two horizons."[2]

The two horizons were those of the biblical text and those of the twentieth-century reader. And the hermeneutical question became not simply, What did the Scripture mean to those to whom it was first given? but rather, What does the Scripture mean to me? The earlier question of relevance has now become an essential part of the quest for biblical meaning. We are called to "grasp first of all what Scripture *meant* as communication from its human writers speaking on God's behalf to their own envisaged readers, and from that what it *means* for us."[3] The question, What do these texts mean *to us*, has given the old question of rele-

2. Roger Lundin, Anthony C. Thiselton, and Clarence Walhout, *The Responsibility of Hermeneutics* (Grand Rapids: Eerdmans, 1985), p. 95.

3. James I. Packer, "Infallible Scripture and the Role of Hermeneutics," in *Scripture and Truth*, ed. D. A. Carson and John D. Woodbridge (Grand Rapids: Zondervan, 1983), p. 337.

vance a new twist. With it we now search for the meaning of *meaning* itself.[4]

In formulating the issue this way, the evangelical has not capitulated to the Barthian formula that Scripture becomes the Word of God to its readers and hearers. The biblical horizon remains the norm of the twentieth-century setting. It is translation we undertake, not transformation. Whether we begin our hermeneutical adventure with problems raised by our world or with a struggle to understand the biblical author's intended meaning, we cannot finish the search without resorting to the final judge of our struggle, the Scriptures themselves. Whether we examine the text or our context, we are always aware that the text is examining us.

In this process, the heart of the hermeneutical task takes on a significance it did not have forty years ago. That heart does not lie simply in the effort to find the biblical "principles" that emerge out of the historical meaning of each passage. The Bible does not passively lie there while we search it for theories that we later fit realistically into our setting. The Word is a divine instrument of action. And our hermeneutical task is to see how it applies to each of us in the cultural context and social setting we occupy in God's redemptive history. We are involved in looking for the place where the horizons of the text and the interpreter intersect or engage.

Drawn into this search for fusion, then, has come a new sensitivity to human cultures and their role in the process of understanding. Both horizons are embedded in different cultures, sometimes comparable, sometimes not. How is meaning found when what is common sense in one culture is not common sense in another? The exhortation of Paul to obey one's master in everything (Col. 3:22) is addressed to a world of silent, involuntary slaves. But what does it mean in a culture where employers are to some extent partners in work with their employees? "If we say that the biblical command means today that we should give appropriate respect and loyalty to employers rather than unconditional obedience, are we watering it down, or are we rather expressing the nub of the matter in terms appropriate to modern working conditions?"[5]

A linguist asks a group made up of Africans and missionaries to tell

4. For an overview of evangelical participation in these discussions, consult J. Julius Scott, Jr., "Some Problems in Hermeneutics for Contemporary Evangelicals," *Journal of the Evangelical Theological Society* 22 (1979): 67–77. See also Grant R. Osborne, "Preaching the Gospels: Methodology and Contextualization," ibid. 27, no. 1 (1984): 27–42; Gordon D. Fee, "Hermeneutics and Common Sense: An Exploratory Essay on the Hermeneutics of the Epistles," in *Inerrancy and Common Sense,* ed. Roger R. Nicole and J. Ramsey Michaels (Grand Rapids: Baker, 1980), pp. 161–86.

5. I. Howard Marshall, *Biblical Inspiration* (Grand Rapids: Eerdmans, 1983), p. 105.

him the main point of the story of Joseph in the Old Testament. The Europeans speak of Joseph as a man who remained faithful to God no matter what happened to him. The Africans, on the other hand, point to Joseph as a man who, no matter how far he traveled, never forgot his family. Differing cultural backgrounds prompted each of the two answers. Which is legitimate understanding? Are both?

In the U.S. hippie culture of the 1960s, long hair on boys had become the symbol of a new era, for some a sign of rebellion against the status quo.

For Christians to wear that symbol, especially in light of I Corinthians 11:14, "Does not nature itself teach you that for a man to wear long hair is degrading to him" (RSV), seemed like an open defiance of God Himself. Yet most of those who quoted that text against youth culture allowed for Christian women to cut their hair short (despite verse 15), did not insist on women's heads being covered in worship, and never considered that "nature" came about by a very *un*natural means—a haircut.[6]

Have our cultural, social meanings been read back into the author's intended meanings?

## A New Agenda of Problems

From this discussion has emerged a new set of questions or, at least, an old set with new emphases. What are some of them?

First, given the historical/cultural nature of divine revelation, how can we better understand the process? And how do we relate this process to the inerrancy of the written revelation?

Until recently evangelicals have been able to keep separate the questions of inerrancy and hermeneutics. The affirmation of biblical veracity was seen as the foundation for understanding the record, a given presupposition isolated enough from exegetical study to stand on its own as a touchstone for truth. The touchstone still stands. But its isolation is questioned. The issue of inerrancy has become for many "essentially the question of *how* the evangelical is going to *do* theology while holding to Biblical authority."[7]

This closer link between norm and the interpretation of norm has come as scholarship has paid more attention to the occasional character of Scripture. This is more obvious in dealing with the letters of Paul, for example. It is less obvious, but also equally true, of historical narratives

---

6. Gordon D. Fee and Douglas Stuart, *How to Read the Bible for All Its Worth* (Grand Rapids: Zondervan, 1982), p. 59.
7. Robert K. Johnston, *Evangelicals at an Impasse* (Atlanta: John Knox, 1979), p. 2.

like the Books of Chronicles or Luke–Acts. They are not first of all systematic, theological treatises, compendia collections of Paul's theology or Luke's. The theology they present has been called by some "task theology," theology oriented to pastoral issues, born out of the struggles of the church as it seeks to understand its task in God's history and our world.

To understand their theological intention, then, the reader or hearer must understand the original intent of the text. The cultural particularity of the biblical message must be acknowledged in our search for its message for all people of all cultures. Whether we speak of the "culture-bound" character of Scripture or of its "culture relatedness," we are recognizing that "the eternal message of God's salvation was incarnated in a specific, cultural language of an ancient, historical people."[8]

But given this reality, can we ever find permanent, culturally universal, normative teaching in Scripture? If cultural factors constantly interact to shape the message of Scripture, does not the authority of the text die the death of a thousand qualifications?

The second set of questions asks, Given the cultural, social, and worldview dispositions of the interpreter, how can we ever penetrate to a true understanding either of the text or of its significance in the here and now? How do we keep our private meanings from constantly intruding into the text as the final word?

In the past, evangelicals have shared with liberal scholarship a deep appreciation for the merits and necessity of historical-grammatical exegesis in the exposition of Scripture. Often characterizing it as "objective" research, the evangelical has properly defined the rules for this research in terms of grammatical interpretation, formal analysis, and sensitivity to the redemptive history that surrounds and defines the text.

Yet there have also been warnings against the ease with which the goal of objectivity can be reached. The work of Cornelius Van Til in the area of apologetics has called attention repeatedly to the myth of objectivity. The translator engaged in eavesdropping on the Scripture in the world comes with what Van Til has called presuppositions that affect the process of listening. Van Til's warning has not been well heeded in the evangelical community. The popularity of a view of human reason as a hermeneutical instrument relatively untouched by sin or culture has helped to create an evangelical malaise.

Post-Bultmannian scholarship has, however, reinforced the warning against a self-projection of the interpreter's consciousness on the text.

---

8. Alan Johnson, "History and Culture in New Testament Interpretation," in *Interpreting the Word of God*, ed. Samuel Schultz and Morris Inch (Chicago: Moody, 1976), p. 131.

The interpreter brings his or her own built-in limitations to the process of understanding. Meanings are grounded in prejudgments or pre-understanding and become part of the hermeneutical search.[9] These warnings have also been underlined by a growing sensitivity on the part of the evangelical toward cultural anthropology and its awareness of the place of cultural settings in creating meaning and significance.[10] Thus,

> if the social context we move in tends to be politically conservative, it is surprising how, when we read the Bible, it seems to support separation of church and state, decentralized government, a "no work–no food" concept, strong military, separation of the races, etc. On the other hand, others find it easy to see how concerned the Bible is with social problems, activism, poverty programs, integration of the races, demilitarism, and the general criticism of middle-America, especially when they live within a context of political leftism or liberalism.[11]

In short, we are all biased already in our thinking and knowing, bringing assumptions structured by our cultural perceptions, even by the language symbols we use to interpret reality. "We are, that is, 'interested' before we begin to read a text and remain active as we read it. We belong, to a great extent through language, to the theological, social, and psychological traditions that have moulded us as subjects and without whose mediation we could understand nothing."[12] D. A. Carson puts it bluntly: "No human being living in time and speaking any language can ever be entirely culture-free about anything."[13]

In sum, the idea that the interpreter is a neutral observer of biblical data is a myth. How then do we avoid hermeneutical discoveries based largely on what we have assumed? If what we hear from the text, and how we act upon what we have heard, is so heavily influenced by the baggage we carry with us in the process, how do we avoid the relativism of selective listening and selective obedience?

Third, given the hermeneutical gap separating the biblical world from ours, what interpretive clues will help us cross legitimately from what is culturally specific in the Bible to what is culturally specific in our world?

---

9. A careful survey of the development of the idea of preunderstanding will be found in Anthony C. Thiselton, *The Two Horizons* (Grand Rapids: Eerdmans, 1980), pp. 103–14, 133–39, 303–10.

10. The volume that has created this awareness, more than any other, is Charles Kraft, *Christianity in Culture* (Maryknoll: Orbis, 1979).

11. Johnson, "History and Culture," p. 133.

12. Lundin, Thiselton, and Walhout, *Responsibility of Hermeneutics*, p. 27.

13. D. A. Carson, ed., *Biblical Interpretation and the Church: The Problem of Contextualization* (Nashville: Nelson, 1984), p. 19.

What are the limitations of "application"? How do we measure the comparable contexts of at least two cultural horizons?

How, for example, do we judge the wisdom of President Ronald Reagan's 1985 usage of Luke 14:31–32 in his support of administrative proposals for a continued military buildup? Reagan listens to Jesus asking, "What king, going to encounter another king in war, will not sit down first and take counsel whether he is able with ten thousand to meet him who comes against him with twenty thousand?" (RSV). And then the president crosses the hermeneutical gap by commenting, "I don't think the Lord that blessed this country as no other country has ever been blessed intends for us to some day negotiate because of our weakness."[14] Did Reagan stumble in the gap?

In the past, evangelicals have dealt with such insecurities by appealing to a "plain meaning" in Scripture, a meaning that is clear and unambiguous. Cultural factors may "clarify" that plain meaning, but they may not challenge it. A recent restatement warns, "If an understanding of some biblical cultural context or some contemporary cultural form is used to contravene the plain meaning of the text, Scripture itself is no longer the authority."[15]

Increasingly, however, this appeal to "plain meaning" is being questioned by scholars within the evangelical community. It is said to be oriented basically to only one of the two horizons under discussion, that of the text itself. And it therefore assumes that our interpretation can fairly safely correspond with that of the authors of Scripture. But it makes it very easy for those interpreters or communicators unaware of the pervasive influence of their own culture on their own interpretations to slip unconsciously into the assumption that our interpretational reflexes will give us the meaning that the original author intended.

For example, when Jesus refers to Herod as a fox (Luke 13:32), our contemporary cultural reflex can interpret the plain meaning to be sly. But in the biblical world, the reference may be intended to signify treachery (see v. 31). When a well-off, white North American pastor or scholar reads, "Blessed are you who are poor" (Luke 6:20), hermeneutical reflexes tend to interpret the poor as the pious, the humble, those who do not seek their wealth and life in earthly things. An American black believer, reflecting on years of racism and oppression, will identify more quickly with what are perceived to be the political and economic implications of the term. But against the background of the culture of the Old

14. Quoted in "Reading the Bible Ecumenically," *One World* 8, no. 4 (March–April 1985): 11.
15. J. Robertson McQuilkin, "Problems of Normativeness in Scripture: Cultural Versus Permanent," in *Hermeneutics, Inerrancy, and the Bible*, ed. Earl D. Radmacher and Robert D. Preuss (Grand Rapids: Zondervan, 1984), p. 222.

Testament, the category may take on significance different from both readings.[16]

When Paul speaks of the husband as the head of the wife (Eph. 5:23), our hermeneutical reflexes think of a boss or general manager in a corporation. The dominant image becomes authority as lawful power to act, to control or use. And while something resembling this idea is argued as its exclusive sense in the New Testament,[17] the term is also said to be used as that which nourishes the rest of the body, the fountain of life which feeds the body (Eph. 4:15–16; Col. 2:19). Which meaning is appropriate in Ephesians 5:23 cannot be determined by the cultural connotations we give it now, but by its usage in the passage. The plain meaning is not so plain.

A call for the plain meaning of Scripture assumes too easily a larger measure of cultural agreement between our two horizons than is sometimes there. And where the Scriptures use cultural, verbal symbols that are familiar to us (foxes, the poor, head), the danger of hermeneutical error becomes even larger. We may assume a number of cultural agreements on meaning which are not intended in the text. It is exegesis of the text and of our own culturally intended meanings that will provide a way out, not the plain meaning of only one partner in the understanding process.[18] With these assertions, we return to our earlier observation concerning evangelical hermeneutics: mistakes can occur in applying a scriptural injunction to conditions other than those to which it was truly applicable.

Given this obligation for a bicultural approach to hermeneutics (complicated by the presence of a third cultural set of perceptions when we begin communicating to others), does not the biblical message to our world lose its timelessness? Does not the normativity of Scripture disappear in placing undue emphasis on the meaning the text has for the people who read it? Are cultural universals dislocated in our study of the culturally specific?

The three questions we have cited (and there are more) raise legitimate questions about relativism. And they cannot be ignored.

16. A helpful approach to this text will be found in Herman Ridderbos, *The Coming of the Kingdom* (Philadelphia: Presbyterian and Reformed, 1962), p. 188. For another, and more debatable, perspective on these same perceptions, using the discipline of cultural anthropology, consult Bruce J. Malina, "Interpreting the Bible with Anthropology: The Case of the Poor and the Rich," *Listening* 21, no. 2 (1986): 148–59.

17. A lengthy essay by Wayne Grudem examines this question of the meaning of *head* in Greek literature and argues that the connotation of "source, origin" is nowhere clearly attested. See "Does *kephale* ('head') Mean 'Source' or 'Authority Over' in Greek Literature? A Survey of 2,336 Examples," in *The Role Relationship of Men and Women*, ed. George W. Knight III (Chicago: Moody, 1985), pp. 49–80.

18. A rich discussion of "plain meaning and interpretational reflexes" is found in Kraft, *Christianity in Culture*, pp. 131–34.

What constitutes a valid interpretation if we loosen up the link between text and meaning? How is the Scripture our authority if its meaning for us is different from what the text actually says? What is to prevent this kind of two-sided hermeneutics from becoming a cloak for Scripture twisting and subversion? Have we not landed ourselves in the liberal camp by a circuitous route? Is it not fatal to give up total continuity between what the text says and what it means for us? Is not the door wide open to private revelations in interpretative guise?[19]

## Living in the Hermeneutical Spiral

Following the lead of Hans-Georg Gadamer, scholars associated with what has been called the New Hermeneutic have described this process of understanding as a hermeneutical circle. But the model has its problems. Evangelicals have feared that to bind text and exegete into a circle is to create a relationship of mutuality where "what is true for me" becomes the criterion of "what is true."[20] Instead, it has become more popular among evangelicals to speak of a hermeneutical spiral.

Behind the idea of the spiral is the idea of progress in understanding; it is closer to the biblical image of sanctification, of growth in grace. Within the spiral, two complementary processes are taking place. As our cultural setting is matched with the text and the text with our setting, the text progressively reshapes the questions we bring to it, and in turn, our questions force us to look at the text in a fresh way. As J. I. Packer puts it, "Within the circle of presuppositionally conditioned interpretation it is always possible for dialogue and critical questioning to develop between what in the text does not easily or naturally fit in with our presupposition and those presuppositions themselves, and for both our interpretation and our presuppositions to be modified as a result."[21]

The interpreter or communicator comes to the text with an awareness of concerns stemming from his or her cultural background or personal situation.

These concerns will influence the questions which are put to the Scriptures. What is received back, however, will not be answers only, but more questions. As we address Scripture, Scripture addresses us. We find that our culturally conditioned presuppositions are being challenged and our questions corrected. In fact, we are compelled to reformulate our previous

19. Clark Pinnock, *The Scripture Principle* (San Francisco: Harper and Row, 1984), p. 215.
20. For evangelical criticisms of the circle model, consult Anthony C. Thiselton, "The New Hermeneutic," in *New Testament Interpretation: Essays on Principles and Methods,* ed. I. Howard Marshall (Grand Rapids: Eerdmans, 1977), pp. 323–29.
21. Packer, "Infallible Scripture," p. 348.

questions and to ask fresh ones. . . . In this process of interaction our knowledge of God and our response to his will are continuously being deepened. The more we come to know him, the greater our responsibility becomes to obey him in our own situation, and the more we respond obediently, the more he makes himself known.[22]

The process is a kind of upward spiral. And in the spiral the Bible always remains central and normative.

How does one avoid overstepping boundary limitations within the spiral? Are there guidelines that will help us?

### False Leads

Previously formulated evangelical norms in this search for guidelines and hermeneutical clues can, we believe, lead astray. Much of it was formulated in earlier discussions and still reflects the background of that agenda. The battles fought with these verbal symbols were significant and still are. But in the contemporary search, they can sometimes mislead.

One problematic reference is the term *principles,* usually linked with adjectives like *eternal, abiding, timeless,* or *normative.* Often the term is associated properly with a desire to defend the integrity and canonicity of the biblical record. It continues to find use in responding to those practitioners of the New Hermeneutic who move toward subjectivity in their tendency to relegate the quest for the original author's meaning to a secondary place in the spiral. Behind the term *principles* lies a commitment to the ultimate authority of Scripture and to the certainty of hermeneutical answers in seeking understanding. None of these concerns can be laid aside.

At the same time, the term can also carry into the debate meanings that do not aid in the discussion. If associated with the concept of the plain meaning of Scripture and an appeal to the clarity and sufficiency of Scripture, it can minimize the complexity of the Bible. Too often the word can be used to convey the implication (intended or not) that minimal modification of these "principles" will help us move with relative safety from our world to the biblical world and back again.

Linked to this usage is often a sharp distinction made between what are regarded as normative commands in Scripture and culturally conditioned injunctions. The interpreter's task is then seen as determining in which category a particular imperative or admonition belongs. The assumption is that the normative command yields a cultural universal,

---

22. John R. W. Stott and Robert Coote, eds., *Down to Earth: Studies in Christianity and Culture* (Grand Rapids: Eerdmans, 1980), p. 317.

whereas the culturally conditioned injunctions are limited in their movement from then to now.

Again, there is much value in this distinction. Behind it is most assuredly the desire to maintain the authority of the Word in the face of some sort of cultural relativizing of the commands of Scripture. And flowing out of it can come related guidelines of much use for hermeneutics. At the same time, this distinction can easily encourage polarization. It appears to assume that historical and cultural particularity is essentially a limitation, making all knowledge tentative and conditioned. Finding cultural universals then demands a search for those commands of Scripture with no, or as few as possible, cultural qualifications.

But all reading is necessarily culture dependent, both in the text and in its translation by the reader. Even our human commonality as image of God (Gen. 1:27–28) does not eliminate that dependency. There is a "preunderstanding" written into the Bible as a partner in the hermeneutical dialogue that must be recognized. The Scriptures were not written only for our culture or for all cultures, but also for the ancient culture. And they assume, even in what to us are perceivable universals, a number of cultural givens that surround and amplify the text itself. Even such cultural universals as the Ten Commandments come in a wrapper of cultural conditioning. The prohibition of idolatry assumes a cultural world of polytheistic orientation. The forbidding of taking the name of the Lord in vain is structured in an animistic world where it was felt that word magic, the manipulation of the world and the gods through some divine name, could be used for blessing or curse.[23]

And there is a further complication to the distinction between cultural universals and culturally conditioned injunctions. It is provided by the second partner in the hermeneutical dialogue, our own cultural understanding. Assuming we accurately assess the Bible's universals, how do we transpose them into our cultural settings with their own cultural ideals? What actions display kindness or self-control (Gal. 5:22–23) in a given setting? Comments a missionary, "An executive in an industrial country is being patient if he waits for someone ten minutes. A Bahinemo of Papua New Guinea would think nothing of waiting two hours. In one village of southern Midanao, my daughter and I were given gifts equal to a month's wages, as a demonstration of their hospitality. In the U.S. the most lavish hospitality to a stranger seldom adds up to a day's wages."[24]

Perhaps, however, the largest problem with the distinction is that it can possibly lead to a rift between the reader and the text as that reader

23. Geerhardus Vos, *Biblical Theology* (Grand Rapids: Eerdmans, 1948), pp. 154–55.
24. Quoted in Kraft, *Christianity in Culture,* pp. 248–49.

searches for cultural universals to which he or she feels committed to obey and culturally conditioned injunctions that one believes, in the nature of the case, are less normative. The distinction can have the effect of creating a "canon within the canon." And some evangelical discussions already hint at some danger in this precise area. Plans are made for distinguishing between the "central core" of the biblical message and what is dependent upon or peripheral to it, between what is "inherently moral" and what is not. The motivations behind the distinctions, as we have noted already, are laudable ones. No evangelical wants to twist the Scripture deliberately into any conceivable cultural wax nose. But there may be other distinctions to be made that will safeguard the gospel in a more useful way. If "all the Scriptures" could be utilized by Jesus to explain his ministry (Luke 24:27), surely we, as "witnesses of these things" cannot be restricted in doing any less. Cultural conditioning, maximal or minimal, does not stand in the way of the scribes of Christ seeking to bring forth things new and old from the treasury of their illumined understanding.

### Some Clues from the Godward Side of Hermeneutics

Hermeneutics, on the one hand, is a human vocation to handle rightly the message of truth (2 Tim. 2:15). In our struggles with Isaiah 53 and Revelation 20, it is still proper to ask, "How can I understand unless someone guides me?" (Acts 8:31).

At the same time, our object of study is the Word of God, and the goal of the process is sanctification (2 Tim. 3:16–17). And in this sense, hermeneutics also has a Godward side, a divine participation in the spiral that we cannot forget. The Lord, in the Scriptures, has accommodated himself to the limits and needs of the human condition. As Father, he baby-talks to his creation in the Bible (Heb. 1:1–2), describing himself in human languages and human images. As Teacher, he fits his infinity to our small measure, bridging the great hermeneutical gap between himself and the creation by descending to meet the limitations of human nature. He is tutor, not tyrant, fitting the instruction to where the pupil is. As Physician, he stoops to heal the diseased creature. We do not wander through the hermeneutical spiral alone. God has accommodated even his ways of revelation to our condition.[25] And in that Godward accommodation in Scripture, there are guidelines to aid in our human search for meaning and significance.

25. Ford Lewis Battles, "God Was Accommodating Himself to Human Capacity," *Interpretation* 31 (1977): 34–36; Clinton M. Ashley, "John Calvin's Utilization of the Principle of Accommodation and Its Continuing Significance for an Understanding of Biblical Language" (Th.D. diss., Southwestern Baptist Theological Seminary, 1972), pp. 91–121.

1. The most obvious is our recourse to Scripture for hermeneutical stability. Wherever we begin in the spiral, the only proper control for our judgments remains the original intent of the biblical text. "In the Protestant tradition since the Reformation, a central concern of biblical hermeneutics has been that the interpreter allows the text of Scripture to control and mold his or her own judgments and does not subordinate the text to the interpretative tradition to which the interpreter belongs."[26] The parameters of meaning, the outer limits beyond which our search for contemporary significance cannot go, are always defined by the biblical text.

This is easily said but often not as easily done. "Although everyone employs exegesis at times, and although quite often such exegesis is well done, it nonetheless tends to be *only* when there is an obvious problem between the biblical texts and modern culture."[27] Witness the massive volume of biblical studies in the last decade centering on women and their roles in home, church, and society. These can be directly traced to the stimulation provided by the issues revolving around women's liberation in the world's cultures. The rise of the gay movement has played a similar role in our intense study of those texts dealing with homosexuality.

None of this is meant to say that learning to think exegetically is the only task in hermeneutics. But it is a basic task. A powerful safeguard against relativism and a barrier to inappropriate "application" remains the priority of exegesis in looking for meaning and significance.

Suppose, for example, in our congregation in Chicago there existed an absolute prohibition against women speaking or preaching in public worship. How would we judge its hermeneutical propriety? One key textual control would be the words of Paul, "Women should remain silent in the churches" (1 Cor. 14:34). And our question would be, What did that text mean to the original readers at Corinth? Is it a prohibition "precise, absolute and all-inclusive"? Are its grounds universal, turning "on the difference in sex, and particularly on the relative places given to the sexes in creation and in the fundamental history of the race (the fall)"?[28]

The solution to the question must come from a close examination of the text. What does Paul mean by "speaking" (v. 34)? Is its meaning "simple and natural," an obvious contrast to the silence or not speaking mentioned in the same verse? What of the probable parallel to "speaking" in verse 35, Paul's admonition to the wives "to ask their own hus-

26. Lundin, Thiselton, and Walhout, *Responsibility of Hermeneutics*, p. 80.

27. Fee and Stuart, *How to Read the Bible*, p. 21.

28. B. B. Warfield, "Paul on Women Speaking in Church," *Outlook* (March 1981): 23–24.

bands at home"? Does this indicate that Paul is not dealing with just any speaking of the women at all but rather with the kind of speaking that can be silenced by the women asking their husbands at home? Is the easiest way to understand the talking, in the light of verse 35, as that of "asking questions," not to preaching, teaching, or prophesying?

How are we to understand words like "they are not allowed to speak, but must be in submission, as the Law says"? Is this an appeal to a general law apart from Paul's personal command? Perhaps to the Old Testament, as the term *law* frequently does? Or to Genesis 3:16? Is not Paul, with this kind of language, stressing the universality of the prohibition?

Exegesis must wrestle with these difficult issues. Is the submission of the women, for example, submission to the husbands or to the law? If the latter, could "the law" be a reference to the order of worship, the women being thus exhorted to avoid whatever unseemly behavior had been disturbing the order of worship at Corinth? Or could it be that verses 34 and 35 are not in fact expressing Paul's own opinion but are quoting perhaps directly from a previous letter to the apostle, the views of one group within the church? The reference to "the law" then could be a reference to "some type of legalistic bondage newly raised by the Jewish community." And verse 36 is Paul's strong repudiation of these views. Or, again, are these verses a commentary on verse 29, "Let two or three prophets speak, and let the others weigh what is said"? (RSV). Women were then, on this view, taking part in judgment of the prophets, in the culturally shameful act of participation in public debate.

None of these alternatives, some more plausible than others, are meant to deny what has been called the universality of the prohibition. Nor would our choices render the universal culturally relative. Most assuredly the choice would define the nature of the universal prohibition. Is Paul prohibiting all speaking by women in public worship? Or is he perhaps prohibiting the boisterous flaunting of a woman's newfound freedom in Christ and in his worship? Is he prohibiting women from passing judgment on the prophets and leaving themselves and the church open to misunderstanding from "those who are outside"? Or is it simply a judgment against culturally perceived immodest behavior?

Whatever we answer, only one of these alternatives could be used in support of that Chicago church's decision to bar women from teaching in public worship. But whatever our choice, the universalism of the prohibition is not lost in the text's cultural setting. A better understanding of the situation addressed makes more likely the possibility of a better understanding of the "universal" embedded in the text.

2. Another Godward side to hermeneutics aids in our search for what has been called universals. We speak of the dynamic process of the self-revelation of God recorded in Scripture. There is a history of redemption

that sweeps us in unity from the first promise of the gospel in the garden to its fulfilment in the New Jerusalem. God leads history to its redemptive consummation in cultural epochs determined by God's saving acts. And revelation follows that epochal structure, amplifying the unitary message of salvation as redemptive history progresses.

In this history of special revelation, cultural particulars are recognized through their links with God's redemptive epochs. But their significance is kept in place when the interpreter, a participant in the history of redemption, grasps the organic relation of these successive eras. They become part of the God-centered stage of one God-centered design.

Time and place, then and there, are points in the whole line or continuum of God's progressing work throughout the ages. They do not cloud God's self-disclosure. They are the setting which God gives it and out of which he shapes it. The promise of covenant faithfulness comes to childless Abraham in terms of children numberless as stars; to an enslaved race in Egypt it takes the form of divine deliverance from oppression (Exod. 3:12). To a David anxious to build a house for God, it comes with the return assurance that God will build a house for David (2 Sam. 7:11–14). At a meal, cultural eating habits become kingdom designations of the new covenant in the broken body and shed blood of Christ (Luke 22:19–20). God not only gives his transcultural Word in culture; he uses the cultural moment and historical time to deliver that Word to culture-bound people.

Culture does not simply provide the Lord with sermon illustrations and examples for spiritualizing fodder. It becomes the providentially controlled matrix out of which his revelation comes to us. Part of the task of the discipline called biblical theology becomes the searching of that cultural particularity for those "universals" that link Rahab's act of faith to ours.

This redemptive history also fuses the horizon of the biblical text to ours. To quote Geerhardus Vos, "We ourselves live just as much in the New Testament as did Peter and Paul and John."[29] We share a common hermeneutical task, those of us "on whom the fulfillment of the ages has come" (1 Cor. 10:11). We are part of the eschatological history of redemption.

Viewed in this light, the traditional sermonic distinctions between explication and application become highly suspect. Scripture presents no truth divorced from reality—no theory, information, or doctrine which must be bent toward and applied to genuine life by the effort of preacher or teacher. Every hermeneutical struggle with the Word in our cultural setting is, by the nature of redemptive history, "a link in the chain of

29. Vos, *Biblical Theology,* p. 326.

God's acts" in history; the sermon links the completed work of God's redemptive history to our contemporary benefiting from it.[30]

How does one determine what is culturally restricted to the biblical time period and not also to ours? In view of the progressive nature of Scripture, one looks at subsequent revelation and the light it throws on earlier texts. The goal of the development is never the correction of previous errors, for God does not lie. The goal is the consummation of all things, the restoration of creation to what it was intended to be.

Again, the biblical materials on women supply a useful sample. In keeping with the divine accommodation to the Word, the Lord allows polygamy, even laying down rules for its regulation (Deut. 21:15–17). He permits divorce because of the hardness of our cultural hearts (Matt. 19:8), in spite of his divine creation intent for lasting monogamy (Gen. 2:24; Mark 10:4–9). Even in the New Testament, the pattern continues. Culturally perceived improprieties prompt Paul to warn against married women's appearing in worship service with hair uncovered (1 Cor. 11:4–7). Our liberty in Christ must not be curtailed, but always it must be exercised with a view to possible cultural misunderstandings by "outsiders" (1 Cor. 11:5, 13–14).

And yet, this accommodation is always accompanied by a divine eschatological polemic against the culture, pointing to Christ as the transformer, the repossessor, of our social settings. Even within the old order, there is an "intrusion ethic," an intrusion into the present of the consummation order of Christ's final judgment. Divorce, though permitted in the old order, is thus reexamined by Christ in the new day of the kingdom of God (Matt. 5:32; 19:9). In the new age of the Spirit, daughters as well as sons, servants both male and female, will be filled by the Spirit and be participants in the prophethood of all believers (Acts 2:16–18). Over against those forms of Judaistic chauvinism of the first century that prohibited women from being legal witnesses in law courts or studying the law of God, women will testify before men of the resurrection of Christ (Luke 24:1–10). They will be exhorted by Paul to study the covenant word, to "learn in silence" (1 Tim. 2:11 RSV). Mary will be commended for staying out of the kitchen (a culturally defined role responsibility) and "listening to what he said" (Luke 10:38–42). It is not simply the context that "limits the recipient or application." It is the place of that context in the history of unfolding special revelation.

3. The Holy Spirit is an active participant in the hermeneutical spiral. He brings into being the first horizon of the text (2 Peter 1:20–21). He opens our understanding (John 14:16–17, 26) and, through what in

---

30. Sidney Greidanus, *Sola Scriptura: Problems and Principles in Preaching Historical Texts* (Toronto: Wedge, 1970), pp. 91–93, 232.

the past has been called illumination, "causes the letter of the Bible to become charged with life and to become the living voice of God to us."[31] The closed canon is opened to our world through the ministry of that Spirit.

All this means an activity of the Spirit in connection with both horizons. How can we bring the text over the hermeneutical gap of the centuries and watch it address our situation? Here too the Spirit leads us into all the truth and takes the things of Christ and declares them to us (John 16:13–15).

The Word of the Spirit sets up parameters within which people of God are to move. We ought to love our neighbor. We ought to do justice. We ought to help the poor. The Spirit of the Word gives guidance in our search for when and how. How can we love our neighbor in Russia or Honduras? How is justice done on our block when homeowners join in denying access to a black family to purchase a house? What does our commitment to the poor mean in a society where black salaries are sometimes 20 percent of whites' in comparable jobs? The same Spirit who communicates the meaning of the text communicates also its significance for our setting.

This is not intended to make the Spirit into some kind of magical answering service floating somewhere between God and humanity in the spiral. The Spirit does not play the role of some "God out of a box," a deus ex machina, undertaking some mechanical, hermeneutical homework assignment. The Holy Spirit is the God who addresses us, not an intermediary between God and us.

And when he does address us, it is through the human perception of those to whom he speaks. "When the biblical writers or Christian theologians speak of the testimony of the Spirit, this is not to invoke some *additional means* of communicating the word of God, but is to claim that a message which is communicated in human language to human understanding addresses man *as* the word of God."[32]

Here is another reason why we can trust the reliability of our perceptions of God's culture-related truth. The Holy Spirit's blessing makes the Bible a mirror in which the common people look and can cry, "We are pilgrims like Abraham; we are in bondage in Egypt, and Jesus liberates us also." Without benefit of theologian or erudite language, Spirit-filled people can say, "God speaks my language."

Here is also why we sometimes see in a clouded and misguided way. The Spirit does not bypass our cultural and experiential conditioning, our finiteness and sinfulness. The Spirit works through all these condi-

31. Pinnock, *Scripture Principle*, p. 163.
32. Thiselton, *Two Horizons*, p. 90.

tioning factors, enabling us to see adequately. But all these things may hinder us from receiving the message of the Spirit more adequately.

## Some Clues from the Human Side of Hermeneutics

Looking at the hermeneutical spiral from the human side is not as awesome and frightening when we remember that the process begins with, is participated in, and is consummated by the Lord. Cultural particularities, in spite of their complexities, are not barriers to a sovereign God but merely part of his providential design. His Word, set loose in his creation, does not return empty (Isa. 55:11).

At the same time, our participation in hermeneutics is real also. And as we have noted, that is not a neutral participation without theological, cultural, or psychological presuppositions. We cannot escape the influence of our preunderstandings in looking for meaning and significance. How, then, does my specific sociocultural and psychological background aid or distort my reading of Scripture? That is a basic question.[33] Limitations of space allow us only a few suggestions.

1. Before a proper "fusing" of the two or three horizons can take place, there must also take place a "distancing." That is, "we must become aware of the differences between the culture and thought-background out of which the words of the text come and that of our own thought and speech. Only so can we be saved from the particular naivete that H. J. Cadbury pinpointed when he wrote *The Peril of Modernizing Jesus.*"[34] We can and must bring our preunderstandings to a level of self-consciousness. In the light of day, we then evaluate their appropriateness in relation to the cultural setting and to the text. Borrowing language from some liberation theologians, we must cultivate a "hermeneutics of suspicion."

Strange though it may seem, overfamiliarity with the Bible can sometimes inhibit that process.

By a very young age most people with a Christian upbringing know the parable of the prodigal son so well that it loses all force for them. They *know* right from the beginning that the father will welcome the wayward son back home and that the father typifies God. The father's forgiving love is taken for granted, and so the original force of the parable gets lost. But the first hearers, who had never heard the story before, probably expected that

33. This is only one of several questions asked by Alan Johnson in his extremely helpful essay "A Response to Problems of Normativeness in Scripture: Cultural Versus Permanent," in *Hermeneutics, Inerrancy, and the Bible,* ed. Earl D. Radmacher and Robert D. Preuss (Grand Rapids: Zondervan, 1984), pp. 257–82.

34. Packer, "Infallible Scripture," pp. 339–40.

the son would suffer some kind of chastisement from his father—just as the son himself expected. They would listen with bated breath to see just what would happen when he came near his home again. They were in for a surprise when Jesus reached the climax of his story, a surprise that we may fail to experience, with the result that the story loses its intended emotional impact.[35]

The same process of familiarity breeding misunderstanding takes place as we study the parable of the Pharisee and the publican (Luke 18:9–14). Our familiarity with the text gives its surprise ending the wrong meaning and reduces its shock value for us. We know that Pharisees are hypocrites, understood by us in terms of insincerity. We have already identified them as stereotyped villains. In the same way, the publican is not the greedy robber familiar to its first listeners; he has become the humble hero. The parable then, shaped by our cultural understanding, becomes "a reassuring moral tale which condemns the kind of Pharisaism that everyone already wishes to avoid."[36]

But to the first hearers, the Pharisee was an example of godliness and piety, themes underlined by Jesus with no irony or tongue-in-cheek intended. The shock, then, was over Jesus' affirmation of the justification of the wrong person, the ungodly. The double-take ending has been lost in the changed attitudes between now and then over Pharisaism.

These parable studies are more than samples of misunderstanding; they are also demonstrations of the technique of "distancing" we are commending at this point. The cultural, social expectations of the hearer are suddenly jolted by the surprising meaning of the speaker. And a reassessment of meaning is demanded. Using technical language, the horizon of the communicator (speaker) and the horizon of the receptor (hearer) suddenly intersect in a way that demands that the receptor look again. The receptor must reevaluate what before seemed clear, familiar, and firm. Like humor, the punch line works with our assumptions by questioning them.

There are many ways in which that may take place. Sometimes it will be a Bible verse, long nestled securely amid our preunderstanding, suddenly erupting into our consciousness to shake past assumptions. For Martin Luther it was a word from the past first addressed to the Romans, "The just shall live by faith." The encounter with Romans totally rearranged Luther's hermeneutics.

Or again it may be a set of circumstances in which the providence of God places one. The situation may be new enough to make one look again at the Scriptures, and new light breaks forth. My own Bible studies held

35. Marshall, *Biblical Inspiration*, p. 99.
36. Thiselton, *Two Horizons*, p. 15.

with beggar boys in Seoul, Korea, began to open my eyes to seeing the biblical category of the poor in a new light. And out of that experience my understanding of the Bible and my ministry were changed.

Or again cultural value changes on a larger, social scale may create an atmosphere, planned by God's design, that shakes our equilibrium long enough and hard enough to distance us from our long-held assumptions. The countercultural movement in the United States in the 1960s touched the ministry of a traditional church in California. And out of the influx of hippies and their conversion into "Jesus people" came a new understanding of body life in the church, an understanding that has since affected the hermeneutics of the wider church. In the same way, missionaries have testified to the new meaning they have found in Scripture, and its significance for life, that has come from immersion into a culture foreign to them. Old cultural ways of perception have been jolted by the blockbuster of culture shock. And out of the shock has come a rearranged hermeneutics.

Extrabiblical disciplines have also initiated the irritation process that leads to distancing. The behavioral sciences—psychology, cultural anthropology, linguistics, sociology, communications—are more and more shaking the cloistered world of the theologian and the church member. And out of this engagement, this intersection, new reexaminations are taking place in the hermeneutical spiral.[37]

For some evangelicals today, this interaction is viewed with special concern. Negative pictures of these disciplines fear the relativism they may bring. And sometimes this concern is related to what is called the "independent authority" of Scripture.

One of the dangers in this kind of response is that it can split apart the Word of God in the Bible (special revelation) from the Word of God in creation (general revelation). Is not creation also a continual source of God's truth (Ps. 19:1; Rom. 1:20)? Cannot wise men and women, touched by the Spirit, also unlock divine truth through disciplined study of the creation? The hermeneutical task, after all, does not allow us to isolate the world we live in from the world of the Bible.

2. Most of our discussion has concentrated on the distortions that our presuppositions bring to understanding. We also need to recognize that there are times when those same assumptions may aid us in the task.

In our turning to God, we are increasingly drawn by the Holy Spirit into a new cultural world. Our way of perceiving the cosmos, our world view, begins to undergo reshaping. We are given a spiritual pre-

37. For samples of this interaction, consult Charles Kraft, "Can Anthropological Insight Assist Evangelical Theology?" *Christian Scholar's Review* 7 (1977): 165–202; Harvie M. Conn, *Eternal Word and Changing Worlds: Theology, Anthropology, and Mission in Trialogue* (Grand Rapids: Zondervan, 1984), pp. 330–38.

disposition to understand the things of the Spirit (1 Cor. 2:14). He makes over our values and perspectives. We become, in this process called conversion, increasingly familiar with the structure of biblical narrative. What seemed like nonsense before now becomes the only sense we can make of things. We see more and more the world as God wants us to see it, from creation to fall to redemption to consummation.[38]

In short, we find ourselves more and more operating in a context increasingly comparable to the design of God. Our predispositions to understand what God says and does become more closely proximate to his vision of reality. God has not changed, but we have. Two horizons are fusing in our "heart" level, the control box that touches also our pursuit for meaning significance.

Now, a sentence like "All have sinned and come short of the glory of God" (Rom. 3:23 KJV) matches our new predispositions. We no longer tie it solely to our next-door neighbor's children but to ourselves. Axheads that float, fish that swallow men, and city walls that collapse with the blowing of trumpets are no longer answered with a scientific smirk and a wink. One man's death and resurrection for others was foolishness; now it becomes the wisdom of God (1 Cor. 1:23–24). The biblical context remains the same. But ours has been changed by faith.

On still another level our presuppositions can aid us. This occurs when there are comparable particulars and comparable contexts in the two horizons. "Whenever we share comparable particulars (i.e., similar specific life situations) with the first-century setting, God's Word to us is the same as His Word to them."[39]

If the culture of the first horizon is at any given point very similar to ours, our interpretational reflexes are going to serve us fairly well. At this point the element of truth in the idea of "plain meaning" becomes visible. No matter, then, how we understand the image of the husband as the head of the wife, the call for a husband to love his wife as his own body, to love her to the point of self-sacrifice on her behalf (Eph. 5:28–29), conveys meaning fairly easy to transpose to twentieth-century Philadelphia or Buenos Aires. We may struggle with Peter's judgments against "braiding of hair, decoration of gold and wearing of robes" (1 Peter 3:3). Is he condemning ostentation and extravagance? Or does it cover eye makeup and hair coloring also? But his description of the "unfading beauty of a gentle and quiet spirit" (v. 4) is much easier to grasp.

Such cultural universals as the Ten Commandments also intersect

38. For a full treatment of this fourfold structure of biblical narrative, consult Henry Vander Goot, *Interpreting the Bible in Theology and the Church* (New York: Edwin Mellen, 1984), pp. 67–78.

39. Fee and Stuart, *How to Read the Bible,* p. 60.

with our interpretational horizons fairly easily. "Creation mandates," so called because they were given by God before the fall, by their very nature, may be extrapolated into our world with a minimum of struggle. The call to marry, to cultivate the earth and rule over it, and to work defines the duties of Adam and Eve and of Harvie and Dorothy Conn. And it defines them without a heavy measure of complications. "Similarly, if a Scriptural statement relates to experiences that are common to all mankind our culturally-conditioned interpretational reflexes can be of considerable help. When the Scriptures say 'go,' 'come,' 'trust,' 'be patient,' and the like, they are dealing with experiences that are common to all human beings and therefore readily interpretable. Likewise with respect to illness and death, childbirth and rearing, obtaining and preparing food, and the like."[40]

Again, though, we must be wary. Identifying comparable contexts requires careful judgment of both the biblical setting and our own. And we may go astray in either or both of these areas.

3. It will also help and not simply hinder us to acknowledge that there are levels of cultural particularity in both horizons and therefore levels of particularity in interpretation. Much of the biblical material, for example, is presented in cultural forms that are very specific to cultural practices quite different from ours. In fact, because of their specificity to the cultural agreements of the first readers, these materials communicated with maximum impact. But they have minimum impact on us.

Generally, evangelical writers today see cultural-bound perceptions as a handicap. They spin off guidelines for hermeneutics that discard the peripheral for the core, or divide the theological from the moral, in their search for the usable. More general rules can also be brought into play. The priority of didactic passages over the record of historical events, of more systematic passages over those less so, is used.

With modifications, many of these standard arguments can be very useful. We do not speak against them per se. But they are often negative in their attitude toward culture's specificity. What we are concerned to underline here is the value, not simply the danger, of cultural particularity. Cultural perceptions are not to be obliterated in our search for the significance of the Bible for us. They aided first-century readers in better grasping the significance of revelation for them. And they do for us also.

Paul's sensitivity to cultural perceptions in his day was acute. In 1 Corinthians 11:14 he writes, "Does not even nature *(phusis)* itself teach you that if a man has long hair, it is a dishonor to him?" (NASB). And in speaking of women without some sort of hair covering in worship, he

40. Charles Kraft, "Interpreting in Cultural Context," *Journal of the Evangelical Theological Society* 21 (1978): 362.

calls it "shameful" (v. 6), not "proper" (v. 13). The same word, "shameful," appears in his evaluation of "women speaking in the church" (14:35) or his sensitivity to "even mentioning what the disobedient do in secret" (Eph. 5:12).

What does Paul have in mind in these passages? Is he concerned over violation of some kind of Stoic "natural order"? We think not. He seems most naturally to be referring to the general order of human culture and social custom, those cultural values that designate a practice as seemly and becoming, unseemly and unbecoming. And he is arguing for the inappropriateness of a Christian's practice in the light of cultural mores.

His goal in this instruction is not the obliteration of cultural perceptions as a hindrance to hermeneutics. Nor is he promoting the rule of cultural perceptions over hermeneutics. It is an understanding of cultural particularities as an aid to the application of the law in our day. There is what Herman Ridderbos calls a relativizing element in such appeals to custom,[41] a positive concern for the judgment of people that we must seek, not to expunge or ignore, but to listen to and find.

This cultural relativism is not the kind that allows a person to do anything that conforms to his or her own culture, anything that party pleases, as it were. Paul's ultimate motivation here and elsewhere is his concern that the church not give unnecessary offense to the world. He remains apprehensive in so many of the texts we have cited that the church will be perceived by the world's cultures as licentious in its consciousness of our new freedom in Christ. We are to have a good reputation with outsiders.

As an exhibition of our calling to love "those who are without" (1 Cor. 5:12–13; Col. 4:5; 1 Thess. 4:12), we are obliged "to respect that which is right in the sight of all men" (Rom. 12:17). Paul's focus here is on the need for maintaining a deportment that approves itself to all people (cf. 2 Cor. 8:21).[42] The cultural norms of behavior governing Christian conduct are norms that even unbelievers recognize as worthy of approval. When Christians violate these cultural proprieties, they bring reproach upon the name of Christ and upon their own profession. This does not mean that the unbelieving world prescribes cultural norms of conduct for the Christian in, for example, his or her attitude to women. But it certainly means that the Christian in determining the will of God for here and now must have regard to what can be vindicated as honorable in the forum of men's and women's judgment. Again, Paul is nodding to the insights of

41. Herman Ridderbos, *Paul: An Outline of His Theology* (Grand Rapids: Eerdmans, 1975), p. 463.
42. John Murray, *The Epistle to the Romans,* New International Commentary on the New Testament, 2 vols. (Grand Rapids: Eerdmans, 1959, 1965), 2:138.

human culture as a proper partner in the hermeneutical process. Stamped on those things honorable and just is the effect of the work of the Law written on the hearts of all people (Rom. 2:15).

Cultural perceptions are not only problems for hermeneutics; they are also aids. And again, as always, it is the task of exegesis of the Scripture to make the final determination.

## Conclusions

Obviously this chapter leaves many questions unanswered. In deference to other authors in this volume, we have left out a study of the nature of language as it touches the question of culture and relativism. We have done very little to define specifically the levels of cultural particularity. And still waiting is the massive question of what might be called extrapolation. That is, what legitimate procedures allow us such an extended application of the text as to cover nineteenth-century slavery practices or twentieth-century biomedical ethics? What are the ground rules for "a developmental hermeneutics"?

But we trust we have reaffirmed one conviction on the part of the reader: Scripture stands, its veracity untainted by either the cultures in which it comes to us or the cultures to which it goes. God's revelation can make use of our cultures but always stands in judgment over them. The hermeneutical spiral should not leave us dizzy in confusion but always moving ahead. The Bible still shines "forth as a great, many-faceted jewel, sparkling with an internal divine fire and giving a clear and adequate light to every pilgrim upon his pathway to the Celestial City."[43]

43. Woolley, "Relevancy of Scripture," p. 207.

# 12

# The Use of the Bible in Ethics

## David Clowney

*Such then is the ethical ideal of the Scriptures. It presents to us an absolute ideal such as no other ethical literature presents. This ethical ideal is a gift of God to man, and the power to set out upon the way to that ethical ideal is also a gift of God to man. It is this that assures us that the ideal will be reached without a doubt. Then this ethical ideal, just because it is absolute, demands that all evil be destroyed. Hence both in the Old Testament and in the New it is a part of the task of the people of God to destroy evil. Finally, because this ethical ideal is an absolute ideal and demands the complete destruction of evil, its full realization lies in the life hereafter; Biblical ethics is an ethics of hope.*
*—Cornelius Van Til, 1955*

To say that the Bible is God's inerrant Word must mean, among other things, that it is an utterly reliable guide for living. "Your word is a lamp to my feet and a light for my path." That is the promise claimed by the author of Psalm 119:105, and by modern believers as well. It is a promise of great comfort.

The practical inerrancy of the Bible is irrelevant, however, unless we know how to use the Bible. And it is not always so easy to know this, even if the main outlines are clear. Believers use the Bible very differently.

Henry, for example, is sure that women should wear hats in church: 1 Corinthians 11:3–16 says so. To Susan it is equally clear that the hat rule is a foolish and unbiblical oppression of women. Each might accuse the other of abusing Scripture.

In the ensuing discussion, Susan might tell Henry that the hat rule was a mistake on Paul's part. In that case she would be denying the inerrancy of Paul's apostolic judgment, and both she and the Corinthians would need some way of culling Christ's wheat from Paul's chaff. This would be no trivial matter. But I will not pay it much attention here. The moral perfection of Scripture has been well defended elsewhere. My goal is rather to understand how the Scriptures function to perfect us.

Susan and Henry might also differ as to what Paul meant by "a head covering." This disagreement could be settled in the same way as could any other question of interpretation, by attention to the text, to dictionaries, to studies of first-century customs, and so on (with issues of hermeneutical method lurking in the background, of course). I will not pay direct attention to this sort of disagreement, either.

But suppose what Henry and Susan disagree about is the modern relevance of Paul's instructions. Both think them relevant, but in different ways. Susan thinks that Galatians 3:28 ("There is neither . . . male nor female, for you are all one in Christ Jesus") expresses an abiding principle that governs all Christian existence. The instructions about head coverings, on the other hand, she sees as applications of principle, appropriate for the Corinthians but not for us. When she reads Paul's instructions to the churches, she looks for principles like the one in Galatians 3:28. She will pay attention to the head-covering rule only as it illustrates such a principle. Susan sees Henry's approach to the Bible as legalistic, obscurantist, and lacking in perspective—like that of the Pharisees, who tithed even the herbs from the borders of their gardens but did not understand about mercy, justice, and love. Henry, on the other hand, is looking for explicit rules when he reads the same passages. So he sees Susan's focus on the Galatians passage as a perversely arbitrary preference for one verse over another. He thinks that, by ignoring the particular applications of principle with which the Bible is filled, Susan often gets the principles wrong, too.

In this third case, Susan and Henry are disagreeing about how the Bible should guide our lives. That is the kind of disagreement that I want to help resolve. My hopes are modest ones. I am not proposing a doctrine which I think believers must understand before they can live biblically. If I were, what I say would be wrong or superfluous, since believers have been living biblically for centuries without its aid.[1] And while I hope

1. Being able to explain how the Bible guides one's behavior is neither necessary nor sufficient for biblical living, because knowing how to live biblically is a form of wisdom. It is

what I say is correct, I am not foolish enough to suppose that understanding or believing it will produce biblical living. But when God's people face puzzling choices about which we disagree, and when appeals to scriptural authority produce accusations that Scripture is being misused, then it is worth trying to explain more exactly what we already know implicitly. A clear explanation can resolve some disagreements, expose others as conflicts between faith and unbelief, and help us to apply Scripture better.

I try to express here some part of the Bible's own teaching about its life-guiding function and to show how the Bible is both relevant and sufficient to guide our lives now. I have found it helpful to organize this chapter around three common biblical themes: law, history, and personal relationship. The Bible, I maintain, guides us in the following ways: By giving us God's will, it serves as a *law* for life in Christ. By telling the *true story* of Christ our Redeemer, t gives us meaning and direction and shows us our own lives and times as part of the continuing history of salvation. Finally, by the power of the Holy Spirit, Scripture *brings us face-to-face* with our God, ourselves, and our neighbors in such a way as to call forth from us the response of Christ's love.[2]

## Commands for Grown-ups: The Bible as God's Law for Life

I have borrowed the title of this section from an excellent essay by Richard Mouw,[3] because in my opinion the title of Mouw's essay precisely captures the way in which the Bible provides rules for life. The commands of God contained in Scripture are often very general (e.g., "Love your neighbor as yourself"). Even when they are quite specific, we are

---

a practical skill (like knowing how to counsel); it is communal (like knowledge of the past); and it depends (like knowledge of one's sins) on the state of one's heart before God. Like other forms of wisdom, it is quite possible to have it without being able to explain it very well. (In fact, that is probably the rule.)

2. Texts on ethics sometimes discuss the norms, goals, and motives of conduct, or distinguish deontological, teleogical, and agent-centered approaches to morality. Those familiar with John Frame's work will recognize the influence of his developed version of this distinction on my outline. Frame has used these three categories to produce a powerful multiperspectival description of Christian ethics which I have found enormously helpful. Until he publishes some of it, those interested can find it in his syllabus for "Doctrine of the Christian Life," a course he teaches at Westminster Seminary in California. The same trinocular vision is expressed in his *Doctrine of the Knowledge of God* (Phillipsburg, N.J.: Presbyterian and Reformed, 1987) and in Vern Poythress's *Symphonic Theology* (Grand Rapids: Zondervan, 1987).

3. R. Mouw, "Commands for Grownups," in C. Curran and R. McCormick, eds., *The Use of Scripture in Moral Theology* (New York: Paulist, 1984), pp. 66–77; reprinted from *Worldview* 1972.

expected to show a spiritually creative maturity in carrying them out. Perhaps we could take as a model for such mature obedience the leper who returned to thank Jesus for healing him (Luke 17:11–19). Mechanical rule-following would have kept the grateful leper on the road to Jerusalem, where Christ had sent him with the other nine. But like many who are new to the community of faith, this Samaritan grasped the point of Jesus' presence more clearly than did the old-timers. Jesus not only commended his spontaneous action but condemned the ungratefulness of the nine.

The "grown-ups" part of Mouw's title has biblical antecedents in such verses as Ephesians 4:11–16, John 15:15, and Galatians 3:26–4:7. There new-covenant believers are described as adult heirs, responsible for mature, God-glorifying behavior. In this respect we are contrasted with old-covenant believers, who are called "children" and "slaves." In keeping with our status as adults, Paul's letter to the Ephesians emphasizes the need for wisdom to understand what is pleasing to the Lord. Similarly, Jesus in John 14–16 teaches the disciples about the coming Holy Spirit, who will lead them into all truth. He emphasizes that, as friends rather than slaves, the disciples have been told what he is doing. The implication is that they will be able to obey his commands in a creative rather than a mechanical fashion.

In sum, one way in which the Bible is meant to guide conduct is this: it contains exemplary divine commands, together with some of the reasons for those commands. Although these commands were first given to others, they were "written down for our instruction" (1 Cor. 10:11); from them we learn the will of God in the somewhat different circumstances of our own lives. In this way the Bible is God's law for his people.

Three common objections to taking the Bible as law deserve an answer. One is that we are not under law but under grace. A second is that the Bible could not contain a legal code sufficiently detailed to guide our conduct. A third objection is that, whatever life instructions the Bible may contain, they are not relevant now, because their ancient contexts are simply too different from our own. None of these three objections can survive criticism. However, each of them is based on an important truth about the normative function of Scripture. I will try to bring out these truths in my response.

### Law Versus Grace

The Reformers, as they battled legalism and works righteousness, insisted that Christian believers are free from the Law as a means of salvation, free from the condemnation of the Law, and free from all those ceremonial types and shadows which Christ has brought to an end (e.g., blood sacrifices and dietary regulations). But they never said that the

Law is irrelevant to the Christian. The Law, especially "the moral law," continues to have its uses, they said. It is useful in showing sinners our need for Christ and useful for maintaining an outward, civic righteousness among the unsaved. About a "third use" for the Law there was some discussion. The Reformed community in particular insisted that the Law is useful as a guide for life in Christ. Thus the Reformation creeds and catechisms continue to use the Decalogue as an outline for Christian ethics and to seek normative instructions for Christian life in both Testaments.[4]

The Reformers were surely correct about the so-called third use of the Law. Whatever changes take place from old to new covenant, the same God who spoke from Sinai has now spoken to us in his Son and "warns us from heaven" (Heb. 12:25). The new-covenant revelation, in other words, comes with the force of a command. If the heart of the command is that we abandon the rags of our own righteousness and run to Christ for cover, that does not make it any less a command. Jesus, in John 15, says that his friends are those who do what he commands, and he gives them "a new commandment." Matthew portrays him as the second Moses, speaking from the mount. Other examples will readily come to mind.

It will not do, either, to think of these passages as mentioning "law" and "commands" in a kind of metaphorical fashion. Many of them indeed speak of the "law of love" or "the perfect law of liberty", and love and liberty are not qualities which can be achieved or practiced by rule.[5] Nevertheless they are commanded, and indeed they already were commanded in the old covenant (the love commandment is a quotation from Lev. 19:8 and Deut. 6:5). God continues to require of us the same things (e.g., justice, mercy, love, and worship of him only) that he always did require. He still hates and will avenge the same things (murder, hatred, deception, adultery, idolatry, and the like) that he always did hate and avenge. In the presence of the Redeemer, these requirements are not canceled but intensified; the righteousness of those who enter the kingdom must exceed that of the scribes and Pharisees (Matt. 5:17–20). It there-

4. For a clear and simple biblical defense of this traditional position on the uses of the Law, see John Murray, *Principles of Conduct* (Grand Rapids: Eerdmans, 1957), pp. 181–201.

5. Ernst Fuchs, in "Glaube und Geschichte im Blick auf die Frage nach dem historischen Jesus" (cited in J. T. Sanders, "The Question of the Relevance of Jesus for Ethics Today," in C. Curran and R. McCormick, eds., *The Use of Scripture in Moral Theology* [New York: Paulist, 1984], pp. 54–56), argues that the love command is not really a command but a call into a new existence, since it cannot be fulfilled except by one who already loves. Fuchs is right about what the love command calls for but wrong in thinking that this requirement differentiates it from any other commandment of the law. It only says more explicitly what all of the commandments require. It is, in fact, part of all of them—in some cases rather explicitly so (as in the first and last of the Ten Commandments). Jesus was only quoting the Old Testament when he gave it as a summary of the Law.

fore seems specious to deny that God's Word still comes to us in Scripture as Law and important to affirm the traditional Reformed emphasis on the third use of the Law as a guide for Christian conduct.

Objections to the third use of the Law come from a proper fear of legalism. The true antidote to legalism is not to forget about Law, however, but to remember that the righteousness Jesus requires is also the righteousness Jesus gives. He expects new-covenant obedience as the one who has kept the Law for us and who now, having written it on our hearts, will keep it in us.

Unless we are related to the Law through Jesus, we will certainly get it wrong. We will get the motivation wrong and wind up back with the legalistic Pharisees. In fact, we will even get the content wrong; for we will not be able to tell what to do about the Sabbath, or about divorce and remarriage. Nor in general will we be able to understand how the apostles used the Old Testament as a manual for Christian conduct, without being arbitrary or legalistic. (How *does* Paul get "Pay the preacher" from "Do not muzzle the ox while he treads the corn"?) There is no mechanical way of sorting temporary ceremonial law, exemplary theocratic civil law, and permanently binding moral law from one another. It is roughly true that the Decalogue summarizes the moral law (what does not change with the coming of Christ). But when a question about a particular commandment arises, it cannot be solved simply by appealing to its presence in the Decalogue. It is only by seeing the relation of Christ to the Law that we get a clear solution.

Two illustrations should suffice to establish this point about Christ and the content of the Law. The first is that of the Sabbath commandment. Nearly all Christians agree that something happened to the Sabbath commandment in the new covenant. The apostolic communities obviously met for worship on the first day of the week, not the seventh. As far as observance of the Jewish Sabbath is concerned, Paul told the Colossians not to let anyone hold them to account with respect to a feast, new moon, or Sabbath. These things, he said, are part of the shadow cast (in the past, typologically) by Christ. We no longer need them (Col. 2:16–17).

Christians are divided about what has happened to the Sabbath commandment in the new covenant. While I believe this is a resolvable dispute, it is not my intention to resolve it here. My point is simply that the presence of the Sabbath commandment in the Decalogue is insufficient to resolve the dispute—which everyone who is concerned with the status of the first rather than the seventh day of the week has implicitly admitted. Furthermore, there is no decisive New Testament text that directly states the relation of the Sabbath day to the first day of the week, or that explicitly says how the Sabbath command is or is not binding on Christians. The Sabbath question can be resolved only by understanding the relation of the Sabbath to Christ, as Colossians 2:16–17 and Hebrews 3–4 teach us to do.

A second illustration of the way that the Law belongs to us in Christ is provided by a segment of Paul's teaching on divorce. One can see Paul's Christocentric vision in operation by comparing 1 Corinthians 7:12 with Ezra 10:11. The severe will of the Lord for the religious protection of the postexilic community was that those who had married foreign wives should send them away with their children. But Paul tells a Christian whose unbelieving spouse is willing to stay married not to seek a divorce. Under the dispensation of shadows, the unbeliever contaminated the believer. But in the presence of Christ, the influence works in the other direction: "For the unbelieving husband has been sanctified through his wife, and the unbelieving wife has been sanctified through her believing husband. Otherwise your children would be unclean, but as it is, they are holy" (1 Cor. 7:14). The coming of Christ has transformed the application of the Law; the missionary dynamic of the Spirit's fulness affects marriages as well as ministries. And Paul very obviously wants his readers not only to understand a rule but to follow and be able to imitate the Christian moral reasoning by which he arrives at it.[6]

The whole Law must now be understood in this same way, in Christ. The need for this focus may not be immediately apparent in every case, since, because of the unchanging character of God which it reflects, there is much of the Law that does not change. Murder, theft, and adultery were out under the old covenant, and they are out under the new. But the point may be put positively, and then its truth is more obvious. To be "inlawed to Christ," as Paul puts it (1 Cor. 9:21), is to please God in the power of Spirit of Christ. So the ethical passages in the Epistles urge us to put on Christ, to imitate Christ, or to be conformed to him. We are to give to one another as Christ has given to us, speak truth to one another in love and for Christian edification (because we belong to his body), speak truth to our neighbors as Christ's witnesses, and so on.

To see the Law in Christ is to see its point. It is also to move away from a merely legal understanding of Christian obedience, toward a vision of

6. The two situations may not be perfectly parallel. (One presumes that Paul is speaking primarily to converts with unbelieving spouses, not to Christians who have deliberately married non-Christians.) But they are alike enough to make it obvious that the coming of Christ has transformed the application of the Law. Besides, while Paul does forbid believers to marry unbelievers, it is obvious what he would say to someone who wanted to use a violation of this instruction as an excuse to seek a divorce. He would go through the same reasoning ("seek to please your neighbor for his good, to edify him"; "let this mind be in you which was also in Christ Jesus"; "I complete in my body what remains to be completed of the sufferings of Christ for the sake of his body, the church"; "your children are holy"; etc.) and obtain the same result ("abide in the calling in which you were called"; "who knows whether you will save your spouse"; etc.).

the goals of the kingdom and the spontaneous response of a loving heart to the Redeemer. It is to see how Christian love for God and for neighbor fulfils the Law. How, for example, do I keep the sixth commandment? By loving my neighbor's life, because he is God's image, thus by wanting him to be the best image of God he can be, and therefore partly by giving him the gospel.

The old-covenant Law, then, understood in Christ, serves as a positive guide for Christian conduct. That is how the apostles used it to instruct the Christian community. And that, when they explain themselves, is how they understand their use of it (see, e.g., 2 Tim. 3:14–17). The examples of their use of it are the best lessons in how, concretely, we may use it as such a guide without coming back under its bondage. Having trusted Christ, who fulfilled the Law for us, the same Law now shapes our gratitude as Christ keeps the spirit of it in us.

### Letter Versus Spirit

Are the Scriptures, applied by the Spirit, sufficient to guide the conduct of regenerate persons? Yes, because of the kind of guide that they are. Return for a moment to the hypothetical discussion between Susan and Henry with which I began. Susan is right in thinking that some passages (e.g., Gal. 3:26–29) express basic principles, while others apply such principles to particular situations different from ours, and that it is the principles we are meant to grasp.

This distinction is clear from the New Testament itself. The instructions of the Jerusalem council, for example, are best explained as wise applications to a particular situation of more general principles about not offending fellow Christians. Taken this way, they express a consistent apostolic ethic, the same ethic Paul is communicating when he tells people they are free to eat meat offered to idols but should abstain if eating would tempt another to sin. If the instructions of the council were taken as universally binding, they would conflict with the instructions Paul gives his churches in Romans, 1 Corinthians, and elsewhere (cf. Acts 15:28–29 with Rom. 14 and 1 Cor. 10:23–33). But this would be a foolish way to take them. The principle is what matters. The application will differ from case to case, and absolutizing the application is a bad mistake. I believe this is part of what Paul means when he contrasts letter and spirit (2 Cor. 3:6), since to have the Holy Spirit is also to have the Law written on one's heart and to understand its spirit (one might say, to have the Spirit of the Law).

This is really quite a critical point about the normative function of Scripture. A great deal of damage has resulted when Christians have expected specific instructions from the Bible which it does not provide, rather than seeking to act on the principles of life in Christ which it teaches. One distressing example of such damage is the series of decisions made by church mission boards at the turn of the century about polygamy (or rather, to be strictly correct, about *polygyny,* the practice of having more than one wife). These decisions continue in force until the present day in all but a few of the African churches begun by missionaries. Since God cares so much about marriage, missionaries from a monogamous culture sought a rule in the New Testament that would address polygyny. First Timothy 3:2, 12 was read as disallowing polygynous elders and deacons and as implying that polygyny was improper for any church member (of course, other passages were appealed to as well). Most churches have refused to baptize polygynous converts for this reason. Some have urged the men to send away all but their first wives. Nearly all have refused to ordain a polygynist as an elder or deacon.[7] By now this policy has been adopted almost as a test of orthodoxy by most evangelical African churches, often against the counsel of modern missionaries who have begun to think differently.

As a matter of fact, it is most unlikely that the 1 Timothy passage and its parallel in Titus 1:6 have anything to do with polygyny. Paul would not have been warning his readers against a practice that was not found in their culture; and polygyny was rare among those who would have read the Pastorals, if indeed it was to be found at all.[8] The best interpretation of these verses, in my judgment, is that Paul wanted elders, deacons, and enrolled widows to be people who were sexually beyond reproach, faithful to their partners.[9]

7. An exception is the Lutheran church in Liberia, which in 1951 began admitting to baptism and communion polygamists who were married previous to their conversion. See E. Hillman, *Polygamy Reconsidered,* (Maryknoll, N.Y.: Orbis, 1975), pp. 192–95, for a description of this decision and its results, with citations of primary sources. Other recent changes of policy in African churches on this matter are noted in L. A. Foullah, "A Socio-Theological Evaluation of Polygamy," *Evangelical Ministries,* January–April 1985.

8. It appears that polygyny was occasionally practiced among the Jews in the first century, but only infrequently and among the wealthy. In the Roman world it was illegal; that it would be found in Ephesus among the readers of 1 Timothy is most unlikely. See J. Jeremias, *Jerusalem in the Time of Jesus,* trans. F. H. Cave and C. H. Cave (London: SCM, 1969), pp. 93–94, 369–70; and Hillman, *Polygamy Reconsidered,* pp. 139–78). As decisive as the social background of the epistle's first readers, and more accessible to modern exegetes, is the evidence of the parallel language in the list of qualifications for an enrolled widow in 1 Tim. 5:9. If an elder or deacon is to be *mias gunaikos andra* (lit., "of one woman the man"), so must an enrolled widow be *henos andros gunē* (lit., "of one man the woman"). The phraseology is so obviously parallel that Paul must be making the same kind of stipulation in both cases: in other words, if he is disallowing polygynous deacons and elders in the first two cases, in the third case he is disallowing *polyandrous* enrolled widows (those married to more than one man at a time). But this is impossible: there were no polyandrous widows among Paul's readers, for polyandry was unknown in that society.

9. A variety of interpretations has been defended for these verses. A. T. Hanson (*The Pastoral Epistles* [London: Marshall, Morgan, and Scott; Grand Rapids: Eerdmans, 1982]), gives a list of the standard options and cites defenders of each on pp. 77–78. Hanson himself

If this understanding is correct, then Paul has nothing directly to say about polygamously married candidates for church office. Neither does any other New Testament writer. But the urge to find some relevant instruction was irresistible to the mission boards. And the expectation that Scripture would speak to their concerns through step-by-step instructions led them to disastrous conclusions. Through this decision the church has been deprived of the leadership of godly men who refused to send any of their wives away. Through it, extended families have been deeply alienated from one another, and women have been sent away from homes where they had a right to stay.[10] Missionaries and native pastors have reported cases to me in which these women were not received back into their fathers' houses either and turned to prostitution to support themselves.

I do not mean to suggest that the Bible has nothing to say about polygamy. Nor would I suggest that polygamy is condoned for New Testament believers by its presence in Old Testament Israel. The creation model for marriage is monogamous, and Jesus and the apostles regularly appeal to this creation model as the norm for marriage. Furthermore, polygyny as an institution is oppressive to women and treats them more as property than as "joint heirs of the grace of life." Monogamous marriage is the Christian norm, and upholding it as a norm is part of gospel proclamation.

This is quite a different sort of conclusion, however, from that drawn by the African missionary boards and churches. As an expression of basic

takes the verses as barring divorced persons from the offices in question. J. N. D. Kelly (*A Commentary on the Pastoral Epistles* [New York: Harper and Row, 1963], pp. 75–76) thinks Paul's "plain meaning" excludes persons who have married more than once. Like the interpretation I prefer, these suggestions give a consistent reading to the same phrase as it appears in the various lists for overseers, deacons, and widows. It must also be admitted, in their favor, that "partner of one spouse" is an odd way to say "faithful to one's spouse," so that one cannot help wondering if that was all Paul meant to say. But these interpretations have their own difficulties, the chief of which is that they seem to go against what Paul elsewhere permits (remarriage after divorce, in some circumstances) or even recommends (remarriage for a young widow, in this same letter [5:14]). The interpretation I have recommended still seems to me the most plausible. It has been adopted by many commentators, among them Herman Ridderbos (*De Pastorale Brieven* [Kampen: J. H. Kok, 1967], pp. 90–91) and J. H. Houlder (*The Pastoral Epistles* [Harmondsworth: Penguin Books, 1976], pp. 77–78).

10. For the history of the dealings of the church with polygamy in Africa, see Hillman, *Polygamy Reconsidered*, and (for the particular case of the AIM churches in Kenya) J. Gration, "The Africa Inland Mission and Its National Church in Kenya Between 1985 and 1971" (Ph.D. diss., New York University, 1974), pp. 124–30. For anecdotal testimony of some of the painful consequences of the churches' policies toward existing polygamous marriages, see Foullah, "Social-Theological Evaluation of Polygamy."

principle, it does not automatically bar polygamous converts from serving as elders and deacons, let alone from baptism and communion. And the reasons which ground it speak forcefully against the practice of "putting away" second and subsequent wives. Instead of generating all the answers by application of a rule, it requires the church to grapple with the heart of a polygynous culture, to understand the role played by polygyny within the culture, and to see how the love and holiness of Christ may come to expression in that cultural context. A monogamous church would ultimately emerge from this struggle; but perhaps this result would come in the second and third generations, and among younger converts. Where the new monagamous pattern gave offense, it would then be the offense of the cross that was offered, not that of human coldness and legalism.[11] For the expectation that Scripture must speak to us step-by-step, where in fact it does not, is a form of legalism.

Rather than providing us with step-by-step instructions (like those found in Exodus and Leviticus), in the Scriptures the Holy Spirit has for the most part taught us by example. Particular biblical stories or instructions are like paradigms in language study. They are samples of principles in action, and by writing the law on our hearts the Spirit provides us with the wisdom to "go and do likewise." That does not mean that we will never find in the Scriptures specific rules that apply to us directly. When our circumstances match the key circumstances of a scriptural paradigm, then any instructions God gives there bind us as firmly as they bound their first recipients. But it is the principles, the basic or central commands, that the Lord wants us to get hold of. It is these on which we can live, as well in the twentieth century as in the first; by paying attention to these, we will be able to discern how specific New Testament instructions are relevant to us. If we do not grasp the basics, we will have the same trouble recognizing God's will for us that folks of Jesus' day had in recognizing him. Flesh and blood were not able to prove his messiahship; too many of the details appeared to be wrong. Only a spiritually illuminated understanding of the point of the old covenant would prepare one to see who Jesus was. The Lord said that Pe er had to be taught it by the Father.

Given the need for prayer and for a regenerate heart as conditions of the right sort of discernment, can we say more about how to tell which biblical specific apply to us and which do not, or how to know what is most basic? Certainly we can. Here, as elsewhere, Scripture itself must

11. See Charles Kraft, *Christianity and Culture* (Maryknoll, N.Y.: Orbis, 1975), pp. 362–64, for a discussion of this problem and for a painful description of the messages actually sent to a polygamous society by confronting polygamy before one deals with the heart of the culture and the hearts of its members.

be our guide. We must ask what the scriptural writers take as of fundamental importance and see how they justify the particular instructions that they give. Then we can follow their model.

The example of Christ is one basic source of appeal for the apostles. Some others are the law of love, the order of creation, our holiness as children of our holy God, our oneness in Christ, our freedom in the Spirit, the Great Commission, and God's intention to sum up all things in Christ. These basic sources of appeal take us to the heart of Christian ethics.

In the dispute about head coverings, then, Susan is in the right when she looks for basic principles rather than for specific instructions. Yet she may need Henry's correction. We may not simply conclude, as some Christian ethicists have done, that the principles in Scripture bind us, but the applications never do.[12] Whether or not they apply to us depends on the relevant similarity of our circumstances to those to whom the Word first came.

12. Alan Verhey appears to make this mistake in his recent book on New Testament ethics, *The Great Reversal* (Grand Rapids: Eerdmans, 1984), pp. 169–97. He suggests (pp. 176–77) that there are three levels of moral reasoning: the "moral-rule" level (which directly guides conduct), the "ethical-principle" level (which gives principles that guide conduct but does not provide specific rules), and the "post-ethical" level (giving answers to questions like "Why be moral?"). The Scriptures function normatively for us at the last two of these three levels, he says, but not at the first. "We should refuse to license the movement in argument from the New Testament to . . . a moral rule. We should rather license the movement from the New Testament to claims about the reality within which we must respond, to claims about our identity as people loyal to God, and to claims about the dispositions and intentions that mark truthfulness to that reality and integrity with that identity" (p. 179). Verhey's emphasis on the "ethical-principle" and "post-ethical" levels of Scriptural guidance is salutary. But he is wrong to deny Scripture any action-guiding role at the "moral-rule" level. His position implies, if I have understood him, that the specific instructions of Jesus and Paul about divorce, simply because they are moral rules and not "ethical principles," do not bind us (172–73). This conclusion compromises the moral authority of Scripture. If those rules bound their first-century readers, they bind us just as firmly; for they are grounded in creation and redemption, and it is implausible to suppose that they are only germane to specific first-century contexts.

Of course, the instructions of Jesus and Paul about divorce are paradigmatic rather than exhaustive, and for that reason it is not enough for us only to take them as rules. That this is so is obvious from the relation between them: Paul takes the principles Jesus works from and applies them creatively to a situation (mixed marriages in the church) that Jesus was not addressing. Both Jesus and Paul must be seen as commanding Christians to stay married, not as providing specific excuses for divorce. On the other hand, the paradigmatic character of their teaching means that we should not expect every possible exception to be listed and that difficult cases should be decided on principle, rather than by seeking to stretch the vocabulary of the available texts until it "fits" cases that the author was not talking about. Example: is persistent physical abuse grounds for divorce? The question may not be dismissed by saying "that's not on the list of exceptions." Neither (in the face of Peter's and Paul's remarks about sharing Christ's sufferings) may it simply be answered by saying "God wants us to be happy," though his care for the victimized and his anger at the victim-

## New Rules for New Times?

But what about those circumstances? Do modern times call for modern rules? Is the Bible an outdated guide for living? The reasons usually given for thinking so are like Bultmann's claim that no one can use radios and electric lights while believing in the spirit-and-miracle world of the New Testament. They miss the point. A few obstacles to Christian faith and practice (secularity, for instance) are indeed unique to modernity. But the main stumbling blocks (the lust of the flesh, the lust of the eyes, the pride of life, the deceitfulness of riches, the foolishness of the thing preached) are just what they always were. The normativity of the Bible cannot be dismissed by calling the appeal to Scripture a return to the Dark Ages.

Nevertheless, the objection that "times have changed" deserves attention. One answer to it has already been given. Where it does not speak directly, Scripture guides our lives in much the same way as where it does speak directly—namely, by principle and example. To apply scriptural teaching about marriage, divorce, and remarriage requires spiritual wisdom and Christian love. Solutions are not mechanically obvious, even though there is a great deal of very direct teaching on this subject throughout the Bible. To apply scriptural teaching to questions of modern medical ethics likewise requires wisdom and love. It is harder to see how things should go in the second sort of case, since there are fewer relevant scriptural paradigms. But the essential process is not different. Discerning the will of the Lord is not automatic in the first case; and it is not impossible in the second. The Bible can provide norms for situations that it does not directly address.

But might the norms the Bible gives us themselves undergo development as times change? For lack of a better term, I will call this the question of progressive moral revelation. It cannot be answered simply by saying "God doesn't change; the moral law reflects his character; so it doesn't change either." There is indeed a deep truth in this statement. It is certainly the same God of whose unchanging character we learn progressively more as revelation unfolds. Nevertheless, progressive moral revelation is what we are faced with in the change from old covenant to new. While the ethics of Jesus are based in the old covenant, they fulfill,

---

izer will certainly bear on discerning what should be done. The relevant principles to ask about are (1) why Jesus and Paul indicate that marriages are to be preserved and (2) why they allow adultery and desertion by an unbeliever as grounds for divorce. A partial answer seems to be that adultery betrays the marriage covenant in such a basic way as to dissolve it. Arguably, the inveterate abuser is violating the marriage covenant in the same basic way, and a Christian woman not only should not continue as his victim but could rightly choose to divorce him.

intensify, and go beyond what Moses and the prophets taught. His presence calls for a heart righteousness that exceeds that of the scribes and Pharisees: for turning the other cheek, for example, and for placing the emergency needs of the kingdom above other concerns.

As the apostles understood what Christ had accomplished, they began to see that substantial ethical changes must result (no more kosher, no more holy wars, stay married to your unbelieving spouse if you can, etc.). The Book of Acts records this realization as a process, not an instantaneous event. May we expect this process of realization to continue from apostolic times to the present? Might there be a development of the Christian moral consciousness, recognizably based on principles laid down by the apostles, but going beyond anything that they explicitly taught? Should we say, for example, that Peter and Paul permitted slaveholding for the hardness of first-century believers' hearts (though it was not so from the beginning) but that we have now progressed past that hardhearted time to one in which we clearly recognize the sinfulness of slaveholding? And if we are inclined to say this about slavery, has not the women's movement shown us other issues of justice about which we should say the same thing?

These are not presumptuous questions. They deserve an answer. They also show why, in a volume on biblical inerrancy and hermeneutics, I have chosen to write about how the Bible should be used. Answer these questions in one way, and it does not matter whether we say the Bible is inerrant. We will have reduced the normativity of the biblical canon (the word means "rule") to an empty formality and conceded the real guiding function to the spirit of the age. Nearly anything could be rationalized as a "development of basic New Testament moral principles." Yet answer them in another, and we will be mere legalists, preferring the letter to the Spirit, and missing the gospel.

These questions bring us to the limits of the legal approach to Christian ethics. To answer them we must consider not only norms, principles, commands, and rules but also our place in salvation history and our existence before the face of God and others. I will take the historical or situational viewpoint first and ask what progress of moral revelation Scripture actually records, and how the Bible defines our situation in relation to that of New Testament believers.

## "On Whom the Ends of the Ages Have Come": Ethics and Redemptive History

### Why Law Is Not Enough

While various sections of the Bible have the form of law codes or of ethical instructions, most of the Bible does not have that form. Hence to see its action-guiding role as primarily legal must be to miss something important about it. And indeed it is. The Lord shows us how to please him by telling us stories as much as by giving us instructions. Some of these stories are parables; the bulk of them, however, compose the true history of redemption which fills half of both Testaments.

Here, as always, God's revelation in Word matches his creation; for stories control our lives. I cannot really be said to do something unless I do it intentionally. But another way of putting this truth is to say that, whenever I have acted, I have lived out a story I have told myself. Usually it is part of a story which one of the groups I am part of is also telling. The story has elements of plot (the action with its expected consequences), character (my motives for acting), and setting (the environment in which this action will have these consequences). If Sharon sees her life as meaningless, she will at best tell fragmented stories about pieces of her life; or perhaps she will tell a coherent story with an end she does not care for, or one with no point. Conversely, she will find her life meaningful if the story she tells and believes hangs together and if she can see it heading toward satisfying conclusions.[13] Persons who literally have no idea what they are doing are not, in fact, doing anything.

I may be Hamlet in my own story, and Polonius in yours; and we may both be right. Nevertheless there is a truth of the matter about our various stories, and a way in which they fit together. If I am only fantasizing, I will butt heads with reality sooner or later and be forced, perhaps painfully, to revise my notions of what my life is about. So it is essential to the success of what I do that the story I tell myself be for the most part true.

There is one whole true story, of which yours and mine are part. In the words of the Sunday school pun, history is His Story. You and I are authors of our own histories only because we are characters within God's. And God has given us the outline of that history in the Bible.

The biblical story guides Christian living in several ways. It motivates us by holding before us the goal to which we are headed. A marvelous example of this is 1 Corinthians 15, where Paul tells us that the sting of death, the great destroyer of life's meaning, has been drawn. In Christ we may expect the resurrection; and therefore we are to "be steadfast,

---

13. Alasdair MacIntyre, in his fascinating book *After Virtue* (Notre Dame, Ind.: University of Notre Dame Press, 1981; 2d ed., 1984), has reconstructed Aristotle's ethics of the virtues along historicist lines, concluding (roughly) that the virtues are those qualities of the will which humans need to live out together a true story we can believe and which will lead us to a conclusion we can find satisfying. Stanley Hauerwas has undertaken a Christian development of the same themes in his *Community of Character* (Notre Dame, Ind.: University of Notre Dame Press, 1981), as well as in his other writings. I am deeply indebted to both these men for helping me see how the biblical story essentially forms Christian behavior.

immoveable, always abounding in the work of the Lord, because you know that your labor in the Lord is not in vain" (v. 58).

Like the Old Testament case law and the ethical instruction of the Epistles, the various stories within biblical history also serve as moral paradigms, examples which we may follow (or avoid) when in similar circumstances. An example of this function is the story of the temptation of Christ. I choose this example deliberately because it is so obviously a worthless and damning paradigm for anyone who has not fled to Christ for the covering of his righteousness (all the moral paradigms in the Bible share this trait; this one is just more obvious). But to the redeemed, Christ's responses to Satan's temptations are an example we may follow, as our temptations resemble his and his Spirit works in us. Of course it takes wisdom—the mind of Christ, in fact—to tell good examples from bad ones. The case of Jesus is obvious, but some others are not; the biblical writers do not always grade their protagonists!

Besides giving us motives and examples, the biblical story defines our reality by placing us within the flow of redemptive history. Perhaps this is its most important action-guiding function. The Bible tells us who we are, the nature of our world and our times, our final destination, what goals God will be using us to achieve, what we should seek, and what we may expect and hope for. We act to achieve the goals which God says he is using us to achieve. In this way we can compare our situation with that of the biblical characters, and their applications of biblical norms can be a model for ours. This historical consciousness is very evident in all Paul's epistles. It lies behind the exhortation in Ephesians 5:15–16. There he tells us, "Be very careful, then, how you live—not as unwise but as wise, making the most of every opportunity, because the days are evil." Historical consciousness guided Paul's own conduct—for example, in the case of the collection for the Jerusalem church. He was so convinced that his collection for the Jerusalem saints brought a movement of redemptive history to its climax (see Rom. 15:15–16, 25–29; cf. Isa. 60:11) that he insisted on delivering it personally, even when the Holy Spirit warned him through Agabus that his plans would get him jailed. He expects his Ephesian readers to exercise a similar spiritual wisdom, so that, understanding God's saving purposes, they may recognize and seize the seasons of redemptive opportunity God places before them.

As with law, so with history: the key is Christ. It is to the Christ-centered biblical history, then, that we must look to get an answer to the questions left unanswered a few paragraphs back; to those questions I now return.

## Is Our Situation the Same as That of New Testament Believers?

According to the New Testament, the basic answer to this question is yes. Time is structured, from the biblical perspective, by the history of salvation, which has climaxed in the advent, death, resurrection, and ascension of Christ and in the coming of the Holy Spirit. Those who live between the first and second comings of Christ are those "on whom the fulfillment of the ages has come" (1 Cor. 10:11); and that is our situation as much as it was that of the first-century Christians. Like them, we are charged to make disciples of all nations. Like them, we will experience resistance and persecution from the world because we will be in the world but not of it. Like them, we await the return of our Lord from heaven and the transformation of all things at that time. Like them, we have the word of prophecy made more sure in the ministry of Jesus and in the foundational testimony of the apostolic canon. For us, as for them, center stage in world history is occupied by God the Redeemer, who is glorifying himself in the church and in Christ Jesus before the human, angelic, and demonic audience. What the world counts important is, from this point of view, merely supporting action, props, and stage setting for God's drama. We therefore should not expect to see fundamental changes in the goals of God's people akin to those that characterized the change from old covenant to new. On the other hand, we should expect to see new or fuller applications of what is foundationally given in Christ through the apostles.

The New Testament itself does provide examples of situationally adjusted applications of principle within the context I have described. I have already mentioned the most obvious one, namely, the Jerusalem council's directives. They are obviously specific to one situation. Paul's somewhat different behavior and his instructions to his churches do not indicate conflict among the apostles; rather, they show that times change, and kingdom goals are pursued differently in different situations.

The case of the Jerusalem council is fairly straightforward because we can see what becomes of it within the history that is recorded in the New Testament. But what of the other cases I have mentioned? Could there be cases in which the time for change is now?

I think we must say, "Yes, certainly there could be and have been such cases." To recognize them and to get them right, we will need to be guided once again by the Bible. While the Bible does not give us a formula, relevant biblical modes of argument are very definitely available. The case of slavery provides an instructive example. Its abolition should be seen as a development of New Testament principle, and thus the Bible may accurately be said to condemn it as immoral. This conclusion is not simply the rationalization of twentieth-century Christians, who have grown up thinking slavery to be vile and immoral and who therefore do not wish to believe that the New Testament sanctions it.[14]

To see this condemnation of slavery we may look first at the Pentateuch, where Jews were strictly forbidden to hold fellow Jews as slaves, although foreign slaves were allowed (Exod. 21:2–11; Lev. 25:39–55). Indentured servanthood was permitted but would be ended at the Jubilee. The exception to these instructions proves the rule, since it involves a deliberate choice by the slave and still does not affect his descendents. In Leviticus, Jews may not hold Jewish slaves, because the people have been liberated from slavery by God, who now owns them (25:42, 54–55); hence they may not enslave each other nor "rule harshly over one another" (25:42).

Now the Jews expected the Messiah to bring in the Jubilee; and the New Testament writers certainly present Jesus as the fulfilment of these liberation passages. From this fact alone, as well as from attention to the verses I have quoted, one would expect that the church would be the home of freedom and that no Christian would be permitted to hold another in slavery. Additional support for this expectation comes from the polemic in Revelation against Babylon (Rome?) for her vile crime of slave trading. Notice the vicious irony of the inclusion of human lives on the list of Babylon's wares in 18:10–13; and compare 1 Timothy 1:10. It is almost shocking, then, to find the apostles commanding slaves to obey their masters, while not telling masters to free their slaves. In this instance the move from old- to new-covenant ethics looks, on its own terms, like a move backward.

What should we make of this? It helps to see how the apostles ground their instructions to slaves and masters. To begin with, they never use the creation-order appeal in talking about slavery. They do not believe that slavery is "natural," as Aristotle did (*Politics* 1.3–7). Second, Paul in 1 Corinthians 7:21–33 urges slaves to take their freedom if they can get it, because living free is most appropriate to freedom in Christ. He appears to have Leviticus 25 in mind, and to be translating it into the new-covenant context, when he speaks of freedmen being Christ's slaves and says, "You were bought at a price; do not become slaves of men." So Paul recognizes legitimate arguments from the new life in Christ against the propriety of slavery and bases them in a christological interpretation of

14. John Murray came to the latter conclusion in his *Principles of Conduct* (Grand Rapids: Eerdmans, 1957), pp. 92–106. We are well rid of slavery, he said; it is far preferable not to have it. But abolitionists were wrong to argue that slaveholding was a sin; the Bible does not support this conclusion.

the old covenant. Third, the exhortations to slaves to obey their masters are phrased as obligations to render service to the Lord and are justified by references to the way Christ suffered on our behalf, as well as by the need to live a blameless life before everyone.

For a modern person there are certainly puzzles here. But the theme of 1 Corinthians 7, "abide in the calling in which you were called" (v. 20), may provide the most helpful key. The gospel works gradually, like leaven. It appears that the apostles were interested in the transformation of life within existing social structures by the love and power of Christ, rather than in focusing on the structural social changes which the application of Christian principle would eventually bring. In fact, the principles which the apostles laid down for life in the church are fundamentally incompatible with a system of slavery. Sociologically, it would not work for one's slave to be one's church elder; yet by the distribution of Christ's gifts, a slave might have this calling. This incompatibility, together with the way Paul deals with it, is already evident in the case of Onesimus. Not only does Paul refrain from sending him back to Philemon until Onesimus is ready to go, but he pleads with Philemon to recognize the way in which the old wineskins of the slaveholding economy will not hold the new wine of the demands of kingdom service. Onesimus is needed in the ministry of the gospel, and Paul asks Philemon to free him for that purpose.

It is not a far-fetched rationalization, then, to say that the leaven of freedom was set to work in the New Testament by the apostles and that the full expression of it, when the dough had risen, was the abolition of slavery. Abolition was a consistent outworking of New Testament principle in a society in which the gospel had been at work. It was right to expect nineteenth-century slaveholders to keep in step with this movement of the Spirit and not to rationalize attempts to preserve slavery by appeal to what was acceptable in the first century.[15]

What about current issues of justice for women? Are they parallel? In some ways, yes. In others, apparently not. On the one hand, redemption moves in the direction of equality, against the restrictions of the surrounding culture. Christ's treatment of women; his appearance to faithful women as the first witnesses of his resurrection; the significant role of women on Paul's ministry team; the mutual obligations of husbands and wives in the apostolic instructions, so unlike the one-sided secular household-duty lists of the day[16]—all of these flesh out the gospel procla-

15. See Hillman, *Polygamy Reconsidered,* pp. 195–96, for a comparison between this case and that of polygamy.

16. For a discussion of this contrast, with references to the relevant literature, see A. Verhey, *Great Reversal,* pp. 67–69 and passim.

mation of Galatians 3:28 (cf. Eph. 2:14). In the church, there is no court of the women, any more than there is a court of the Gentiles. The middle wall of partition has been broken down, and there is neither male nor female, for we are all one in Christ Jesus. In the light of this clear New Testament message, modern Christians should give thanks for the breaking of false stereotypes, the new legal protections, and the new opportunities that women have won in recent decades. Indeed we should be ashamed that we have played so small a role in this charge. Women who would not have stumbled over Christ have very often stumbled over us.

On the other hand, it is hard to miss the grounds on which Paul argues at least for male-female role differences, if not for a hierarchy of authority. In Ephesians 5, the husband's headship (a nurturing role, but apparently also one of primary accountability) is grounded by Paul simultaneously in creation and redemption, by his claim that the mystery of marriage, quoted from Genesis, means Christ and the church. Again, when Paul in 1 Timothy 2:11–15 forbids a woman to "teach or have authority over a man," his grounds are in the orders of creation and redemption. The same is true for 1 Corinthians 11:3–16.

In these passages, Paul argues for his conclusions by appeal to the order of creation, transformed in Christ. In other words, he appeals to the structure of a situation which is as much ours as his.[17] To that extent, he cannot be seen as prescribing a course of action expedient for the first century to avoid offense, but no longer necessary now. Nor, I believe, can he and the other apostles be read as pointing to a kind of development which is now in process from the order of creation (in which Adam was Eve's head) to the situation in heaven (in which we neither marry nor are given in marriage but are like the angels).[18] It is not that either one of these suggestions can be ruled out in advance as incompatible with biblical authority. Rather, because of the way the apostles argue for their conclusions, I believe we must take them as stating norms for male-female relations in marriage and church life that apply equally to the first century and to our own day: Those norms have often been misconstrued in a way that has wronged women. Nevertheless it seems to be apostolic teaching that, from the creation to the consummation, men and women

17. See Harvie Conn's chapter in this volume for further remarks on these passages. Just how and why the apostles are arguing from these grounds and how their conclusions apply to us must be decided by the interpretation of these somewhat obscure and difficult passages. I am not here advancing any such interpretations, nor am I satisfied that I can yet provide them.

18. For a defense of a developmental hermeneutic for Christian ethics, see Richard Longenecker, New Testament Social Ethics for Today (Grand Rapids: Eerdmans, 1984), pp. 16–28, 70–93. Longenecker argues that the order of redemption is transforming that of creation and that this transformation includes male-female relations in the church.

have differing roles to play with regard to authority and responsibility in family and church life. In contrast to the abolition of slavery, an abolition of those differences cannot be a fuller expression of basic principles laid down in the New Testament.

Does there appear to be a practical conflict between these two basic norms of equality and difference? Perhaps this appearance should not trouble us so much. Perhaps we have created it ourselves. For a long time, men in authority in the church have paid much attention to one norm, but little to the other, and thus it is likely that we have not understood either very well. We have fallen away from the apostolic example rather than developed it, and God has had to use the world to confront us with the truth. The evangelical church, in effect or explicitly, has forbidden women to develop and exercise the full range of God's gifts to the body through them. It has taken the changes brought by the largely secular feminist movement to show us (men) that women can do most anything (including study and communicate scriptural truth) just as well as men. In the resulting time of adjustment, confusions and tensions should hardly surprise us. Nor should we rush to abandon one norm in favor of the other, nor feel that we have run past the place where Scripture is an adequate guide. If we trust God's provision for us in the Scriptures, we will rather assume that there will be room for us as Christian sisters and brothers to work out the relation of our created differences and our unity in Christ more fully than we have so far done. As with other "difficult questions," so with this one: we may well find that, even if we only do what we can all agree on but are not now doing, we will learn what comes next.

It may be that the illustrations have overwhelmed the main point of this section, so let me repeat it: Scripture functions to define our situation, to tell us the story of redemption in which we are living, so that we may know how to keep on living it. It tells us who we are in Christ and how Christ works out his redemption in our lives, giving us specific examples of God's work in the lives of first-century Christians as regards slavery, male-female identity in Christ, and the like, so that we can get the point. In this way the illumination the Spirit gives us through the Scriptures enables us to see and seize the *kairoi*, the seasons of redemptive opportunity that God places before us (Eph. 5:16). The history of God's redeeming work goes on unfolding, as the gospel goes into all the world. But the finished work of Christ also defines the time in which we live as fundamentally the same as that of the New Testament, and the basic principles by which we live are given to us there. There is room for a fuller development of these principles, but not for the introduction of new ones or for outgrowing the ones with which we started. And if we want to know what counts as a development of biblical principle, a continuation of the story, and what is a departure, it is to the Bible that we must turn once again for an answer. The Bible is rich with answers to such questions. I have tried to show some ways in which those answers may be found.

## "I Am Your God; You Are My People": Covenantal Ethics

### Why Goals and Commandments Are Not Enough

One of the most devastating passages in the Bible is the letter from the glorified Christ to the Laodicean church (Rev. 3:14–22). When I read it, I hear the Lord asking what he will find when he comes to drink from me. Will he be warmed by the zeal of a heart aglow with the Spirit? Will he be refreshed by the coolness that comes when the passions of sin have been put to death? Or will he taste only the worldly lukewarmness of half-controlled sin and half-hearted religiosity? I know the answer; and I know that, without the living water of the Holy Spirit, he will spit me out.

Unpleasant as it is to face, this is surely the experience of any honest Christian. It shows more clearly than anything I can think of why pleasing God is more than rules, goals, and programs. "Man looks at the outward appearance; but the LORD looks at the heart" (1 Sam. 16:7). What God wants of us is ourselves. Like a lover, he is jealous for our hearts and not just our actions. Likewise what he gives us is himself, so that from him we can have something worth offering back to him. "To glorify God and to enjoy him forever," in the well-chosen words of the Westminster Shorter Catechism, is the point of human life, created and redeemed: that God should be our God, and we his people. And therefore it is also the point of the Bible to bring us into face-to-face communion with our God in an eternal bond of mutual love and allegiance. Changed by this bond of communion, our hearts open to one another as well. We will not merely do right by one another and help one another, but we will "love one another deeply, from the heart" (1 Peter 1:22).

The Bible is full of rich images which convey its personal point. God is the Father, from whom the whole family on heaven and earth is named. He is the husband of his people; he is our king, our shepherd, our nursing mother, our counselor, our kinsman-redeemer. Many of these relationships are implied in the covenant relationship which God establishes with his people. The facts about ancient Near Eastern covenants will be familiar to most readers of this essay. Covenants were relationships of absolute obligation to loyalty and service on the part of the subject people, and of (theoretically) absolute obligations to loyalty and protection on the part of the sovereign. They assumed a history (usually conquest by the sovereign) and included laws (payment of taxes, military service, and no fealty to other sovereigns). But in their essential nature they were oath-bound relationships of allegiance.

God's continuing covenant with his people both resembles and differs from its ancient Near Eastern counterparts. Whereas the Near Eastern suzerains gained a great deal more than they gave in their covenant relationships, the reverse obviously obtains in our case. God's oath to us is one of love, sealed to us in the blood of his only Son. But like those ancient covenants, God's covenant with us is also a relationship of oath-bound allegiance. When the Bible is considered as law or as history, a cold heart can take it abstractly as mere rules for conduct or another plan for action. But when we face its divine author, it is obvious that only a personal relationship of total love and allegiance will satisfy God's call.

### What Ethics of the Person Contributes

What does attention to this intensely personal character of Christianity and of the Bible contribute to our understanding of Christian ethics? The most obvious thing, perhaps, is motivation. Only by knowing and responding in love to Jesus Christ will we want to please God; and wanting that is the most important thing. Only by loving our neighbors with the love we have received from Jesus will we please them for their good, to build them up.

The personal perspective also illumines the functions of the Bible as law and as instructive history. Scripture is law because it comes as *God's* commands. If it were not from him, it would have no force. But that means we will not view the Bible as a bare legal code. Rather, we will ask how the divine requirements it records reveal God's character, how they point us to ways of loving God, and how by keeping them the character of Christ will be formed in us. Likewise a relationship of love with God leads us to love our neighbors. For as James says, how can we love God and hate his likeness? So we will also be asking how God's expressed will for us is for our own and our neighbor's good, and how it points us to love and to seek that good. Again, standing before God's face we will recognize the goal of salvation history as a fellowship of the redeemed with God and one another. If the results of our supposed law keeping and kingdom seeking are bitterness, strife, coldness, and alienation, we can know from that fact alone that something is drastically wrong, however right and orthodox we may otherwise appear to ourselves to be.

If God intends to form Christ in us and to draw us individually and corporately into the fellowship of the Trinity, some other things follow as well. Among other results, we will begin to see many relationships between ethics and psychology. Standing before the face of God and before one another, our actual character and motives are a mixture of guilt and forgiveness, crushed spirits and freed hearts, deep wounds, outrageous follies, confidences, joys and depressions, shame, pride, fear and courage, love and selfishness, self-concepts false and true, attitudes, commitments, beliefs, and a great deal more. The mixture unique to each of us has formed in us from our earliest days, through our family relationships, our social interactions, and the sins and sanctification of ourselves and of others. Only the Spirit of God can move over the face of these turbulent waters and make a new creation. It is that new creation, not a few outward actions or temporary intentions, that will truly please God; and as we seek to obey him, we are totally dependent on him to complete it in us. We cannot do it. But we can look to Jesus and can help others do the same. As we do so, we will sometimes find ourselves in the position of the apostle Paul, who spoke of being "in the pains of childbirth" until Christ was formed in the Galatians (Gal. 4:19). Whether the labor pains are for ourselves or for others, we will want to know what is coming to birth so we can assist at the delivery. In other words, we will be driven to ask how the work of Christ formation is proceeding in a particular person or group. And this question may give us a very different point of view from that produced by thinking about laws or goals. It generates a proper Christian realism, especially about others, and even about ourselves. No one grows all at once in every area of life. There are many areas in which growth and direction are needed in a person's life at any given time. The personal point of view will force us to ask what God's current agenda is for a person, whether for oneself or for another, and to set other matters aside for another day. Of course you and I can never know the whole answer to this question. But sometimes we can get a pretty good idea.

Being able to ask and, at least partially, to answer this question about priorities in personal spiritual growth is a key ingredient in the gift of counseling. Furthermore, whether we then proceed to encourage, rebuke, comfort, instruct, or simply pray, our main task may not be to apply a principle or hold forth a goal (essential though these activities are) but to display Christ the Redeemer for the allaying of fears, the healing of wounds, the uprooting of perennial lusts, and the provision of the mantle of praise in exchange for a faint spirit. It seems to me that the Beatitudes point primarily in this direction. They can hardly be seen as rules. They say more about how to be than about what to do: more about character, that is, than about action. There is a great richness to them. In various ways Christ himself exemplifies them. They solicit conversion to Christ, hold forth the comfort and reward of Christ, and promise the character of Christ, to hearts that see their need because they have met Christ. From meeting Christ, a changed life flows.

Scripture brings us face to face with our God, our neighbors, and ourselves. In this role its principal function is not to show us what to do but to make us into people who will do it. Nevertheless, besides convicting, transforming, assuring, and motivating us, the personal character of Scripture does also guide us. As the legal point of view leads us to seek in Scripture God's principles of conduct, as as the situational/historical view leads us to pursue the goals of the kingdom, so this point of view also helps us see how to please the Lord. Here the action-guiding questions are the following: who is the Lord, how has he loved us, to what does his presence call us, what sorts of persons are we and should we be because we are in Christ, and how, in that light, should we live?

A concrete example of the discussion of a moral issue from this point of view is provided by Stanley Hauerwas's excellent chapter on abortion in his recent book *A Community of Character*.[19] Hauerwas asks what kind of people we as Christians are, that we find abortion intolerable; he concludes that we are those who receive life as a gift from God and therefore cherish it. Rather than laws about the sanctity of life or reflections on kingdom purposes, Hauerwas is here arguing from communal Christian identity before the face of God to an understanding of the traditional Christian stand on abortion. I do not think Hauerwas would want to substitute this approach for the others I have just mentioned. But his chapter brings out in a fresh way how attitudes of love toward the fetus and the mother and God, the giver of life, are inseparable and thus shows the personal grounds for a Christian position on abortion.

## Conclusion

All the treasures of wisdom and knowledge are hidden in Christ. Naturally, the Word of Christ is rich beyond our understanding of it. I have tried in this chapter to show some of the diverse ways in which the Spirit uses Scripture to guide our lives.

I do not see the three ethical uses of the Bible which I have discussed as mutually exclusive, nor do I view them as alternatives to be chosen among on particular occasions. A Spirit-filled use of the Scriptures always involves all three of them to some extent, and emphasizing any of them at the expense of the others is a sure route to the abuse of Scripture (e.g., to legalism, "situation ethics," or subjectivism). I thus hope this essay will not lead readers to "pick and choose" but rather will encourage an enriched understanding of the Spirit's multifaceted use of the Bible in our lives.[20]

I have tried to indicate some common abuses of Scripture in ethics,

19. S. Hauerwas, *Community of Character*, pp. 196–229.
20. My colleagues John Frame and Vern Poythress provide helpful discussions of the interrelation of these three perspectives in the works referred to in n. 2 above.

thereby to fend off slurs on its sufficiency or moral perfection. I hope I have conveyed some sense of the clarity and power of Scripture to teach us to please God, and some of its continuing character as "alive and powerful, and sharper than any two-edged sword" (Heb. 4:12). To me these attributes of God's Word do not mean that all our questions about Christian living are immediately answerable from the Bible. Rather, as history progresses under the lordship of Christ and as we stand together before God's face, depending on his Spirit, the Bible is God's complete, sufficient, wise, and perfect provision of the principles, direction, and knowledge of him we need in order to learn how to please him now.

# 13

## Bible Authority
### When Christians Do Not Agree

### George C. Fuller and Samuel T. Logan, Jr.

*It is evident that we find it extremely difficult to carry on in
love discussions of matters on which we differ. That ought
not to be. Gossip, evil-speaking, backbiting, and slander
should not be heard among us. Let us firmly resolve to
desist once and for all from the cruel pastime of
caricaturing each other and from the vicious practice of
setting up a straw man, knocking him down, tearing him to
shreds, and withal leaving the impression that he who was
demolished is some flesh-and-blood member of our church.
And let us beware of lightly accusing of lovelessness those of
our number who vigorously oppose error and earnestly
contend for the faith once for all delivered to the saints. Such
judging is itself loveless in the extreme.*
                                                    —R. B. Kuiper, 1959

As Christians we should define biblical authority carefully. The
Bible of course stands without our defense, but part of our continuing
witness is a vigorous challenge to those who seek to invalidate its claims.
We have never believed, and do not now hold, that one's understanding of
biblical authority is a matter of indifference. The whole of one's under-

237

standing of the gospel and the response it demands are directly related to the nature of scriptural authority.

## Biblical Authority Affirmed

While Christians seek a proper understanding of the Bible's view of its own nature and authority, the church and the theological school must recognize and confront the views of those who come to different conclusions. Some of them may not agree with us concerning the Bible's own position on this critical matter. Westminster never has regarded lightly differences and distinctions in this matter, and our commitment is that we never shall. We mention below some of the specific reasons for this commitment, but it is obviously implicit in all of the other chapters in this volume.

This chapter does not specifically seek to define or defend biblical authority—the subject of other, and important, writing. It does seek some understanding of how we should respond to Christians whose views of biblical authority differ from ours. A Christian's position with regard to biblical authority is not determinative of his or her Christian identity, which is based on a relationship with God through his Son. And certainly Christians, here and elsewhere, are called to experience fellowship with all others for whom Jesus prayed and died.

Never, however, is the quest for full expression of our mutual faith to obscure the importance of this issue. Misunderstanding and misjudgment in this area can undermine Christian witness and ministry. Where that danger seems apparent, we must speak carefully and clearly, and on the basis of a considered position, which we respectfully believe to be the biblical teaching on the matter. Commitments to basic Christian fellowship do not preclude the possibility, even the importance, of pointing out important error, as seen from our perspective, and indeed demonstrating the logical and practical implications of such erroneous posture. A father can continue to love a son, while calling him from dangerous error. To maintain casual, detached apathy under such circumstances is in fact evidence not of love but of nonlove, a mindset that can allow that child professedly loved to destroy all that is important to his father and to himself, while observing in warm, smiling silence.

The first chapter of the *Westminster Confession of Faith* says, "The authority of the Holy Scripture . . . dependeth . . . upon God (who is truth itself) the author thereof." Those who are charged to stand for that pivotal proposition must therefore speak clearly against its denial. To do otherwise is to act contrary to nature; it is to deny our reason for being; it repudiates our own heritage, our linage.

One cannot logically claim to be a Christian and, at the same time, deny the authority of the Bible. Whatever one believes about Jesus is derived from the Bible, and at least to that extent, he or she must rely on it as an authoritative source of information. Even those who may deny or question some affirmations of the Bible (e.g., the virgin birth) must find it authoritative in regard to the remaining information on which their faith is based.

And yet some seek both to affirm their faith in Jesus Christ and to deny the inerrancy of the one written source of information about him whom God has given us. How is this position even possible? Westminster has historically suggested at least two ways. Both emerge from the inconsistency that seems so frequently to bedevil both Christians and non-Christians.

The first form this inconsistency takes, at least in the life of the non-Christian, has to do with the highly complex but deeply significant doctrine of common grace. Without seeking to resolve the intricacies of the various Reformed debates over the nature of common grace, we note here only that common grace is *at least* God's restraining activity whereby he keeps sinful men and women from being as wicked and as wrong as their own presuppositions would lead them to be.[1]

The second form this inconsistency takes is closely related to the first. In seeking to make sense of a world which one's contingency-oriented presuppositions render chaotic, the non-Christian, according to Cornelius Van Til, will often "borrow capital" from the Christian world view.[2] The point is that, in both cases, inconsistency results and individuals may therefore affirm the deity of Christ while denying the inerrancy of the Scriptures which describe him.

But non-Christians are not the only ones who are inconsistent. As John Murray points out in his discussion of Romans 7, there is nothing short of contradiction (Murray's term) within believers themselves.[3] Those who have actually trusted Jesus as Savior and Lord may inconsistently deny the authority of the Scriptures from which their knowledge of him is derived.

Francis Schaeffer has sought to explain more fully the point that both Van Til and Murray are making. In the following quotation, Schaeffer is discussing Christianity and the arts, but his point may be applied to a wide variety of circumstances, including the one before us:

1. Cornelius Van Til, *The Defense of the Faith* (Philadelphia: Presbyterian and Reformed, 1955), pp. 165–69; see also Henry Van Til, *The Calvinistic Concept of Culture* (Grand Rapids: Baker, 1959), pp. 232–37.

2. Van Til, *Defense of the Faith.*

3. John Murray, *The Epistle to the Romans,* 2 vols. (Grand Rapids: Eerdmans, 1959), 1:256–73.

There are, therefore, four kinds of people in the realm of art. The first is the born-again man who writes or paints within the Christian total world view. The second is the non-Christian who expresses his own non-Christian world view. The third is the man who is personally a non-Christian but nevertheless writes or paints on the basis of the Christian consensus by which he has been influenced. . . . The fourth person is the born-again Christian who does not understand what the total Christian world view should be and therefore produces art which embodies a non-Christian world view.[4]

The point is that there are consistent Christians and consistent non-Christians, but there are also inconsistent Christians and inconsistent non-Christians. We believe that consistent Christianity requires us to affirm the inerrancy of the Scriptures. But we also believe that there are many inconsistent Christians and many inconsistent non-Christians writing and speaking about the Bible in our world today. In this chapter, we emphasize the need to resist energetically two prime temptations: (1) to regard as non-Christian anyone who differs from us on the doctrine of Scripture, and (2) to gloss over the fundamental inconsistency of affirming the incarnate Word while denying the written Word.

Specifically, in the first part of this chapter, we argue that, in light of the inconsistency which plagues all of us, we must respond with care and grace when we meet others who differ from us over the nature of biblical authority—and we will meet many such. People who profess faith in Jesus define the Bible's authority in widely diverse manners. Organizing those definitions onto a spectrum may be helpful, if not too simplistic. Code words on the spectrum might be *inerrant* (often used on the right quarter of the spectrum, *infallible* (more popular in the middle half), and *normative* (a favorite of the left quarter), although such terms are rapidly becoming less useful. It is also clear that these terms overlap and are sometimes used interchangeably.

At the far right end might be those for whom the only statement of relevance is "The Bible is inerrant; no need exists to discuss or to define this article of faith." That affirmation is made in a space that contains no other statements and surely no questions. It is a self-contained statement. Its domain is not cluttered with questions of parallel passages, culture and context, semantics and symbolism, sources and style. Perhaps those who hold to such a nonanalytic view might even pick a certain Bible to be regarded as inerrant—for example, the original (non-existent) autographs, or the Textus Receptus, or the King James translation, or for that matter, the Vulgate. Those at the right extreme of the hypothesized spectrum would see it as presumptuous for any lesser authority (such as

4. Francis Schaeffer, *Art and the Bible* (Downers Grove, Ill.: Inter-Varsity, 1973), p. 46.

a seminary professor) to seek to qualify the affirmation about the Bible with a question such that simply asking it might be thought to undermine the Bible's ultimate authority.

At the left end of the spectrum are those who find the Bible to be authoritative as a somewhat reliable source for faith in Jesus, but for them it does not differ in nature from similar books. It is narrative and myth, religious reflection and social comment. While helpful in describing events of religious importance, especially Jesus, it may reveal more about its authors than about the history it sets forth. Its value (and whatever authority it may be said to possess) is as a source book in history, which in some instances betrays the thought processes that created the events it reports (either out of nothing or from some kernel of fact), in most cases revealing the patterns of thought that grow out of the events.

For such people, the Bible does have a role of critical importance, in that it is the only significant primary source on the life of Jesus and the development of the early church. But for them to speak of the Bible as "inerrant," "infallible," or in some concrete way "the Word of God" is only to make a religious affirmation that is without basis in the world of tangible objects and verifiable statements.

## The View from the Extremes

How do people on one end of the spectrum relate to those at the other end? Often a kind of branding occurs, using the terms *liberal/radical* or *conservative/fundamentalist*. Those at the left see their counterparts as "naive," "uninformed," "unenlightened," "obscurantist." In the other direction move words like *compromiser* and *rationalist,* and with them much concern that the authority of God's Word is being replaced by the authority of human words.

Each group suspects that the other may be sacrificing the gospel through its deficient view of biblical authority. Those on the right are accused of allowing a pharisaic literalism to undermine the spirit and intent of a gospel of all-pervasive love. The "liberals" are charged with throwing out the baby with the bath water; reducing the authority of the Bible, they inevitably give away crucial elements in the gospel message.

This spectrum came into focus only a century and a half ago. Before that time, the issue of biblical authority was not widely debated within Christendom. Of course, it did compete with other authorities (e.g., the church) for the allegiance of Christians. But except among a few detractors, it was assumed to be a fully accurate and authoritative basis for Christian faith.

At first, attackers and defenders were lined up at the extreme ends of the spectrum. Like seesaw riders, they reacted against the postures of those on the other end. But not much was happening in the middle of the game.

Gradually the spectrum has become a continuum of views, particularly in recent years. Some on the left have discovered that the Bible must be and is more than "just another book." God is at least involved in the events it uniquely reports. And some on the right recognize that issues raised by their detractors demand reasonable response; and those answers sometimes lead to more careful definition with regard to inerrancy. It is possible to create one's own simple spectrum. List the first ten seminaries that come to mind, and then arrange them according to their views on scriptural authority, right to left. Obviously your arrangements asks for generalizations and value judgments, and your arrangement may not agree with mine, but it will demonstrate that a continuum exists. And on that line, incidentally, there seems to be an infinite number of points, as statements and positions are balanced with counterassertions and denials, all shaded with increasingly complex nuances and qualifications.

In regard to another issue a Westminster professor once commented, "There is always someone on your right." On our spectrum, the only way to avoid that possibility is to be at the right extreme, a position (as described above) that may be theoretically attractive but not actually palatable for many Christians. The Westminster Seminary community (or, for that matter, the Dallas Seminary community) should expect to see people on the spectrum as it glances to the right. And concerns from the right will likely be expressed in predictable ways: attacks based on partial or imperfect perceptions, charges of infidelity to our shared heritage, withheld support, and the founding of a new seminary, the latter to serve a real or imagined disenfranchised constituency. But it is at least a healthy corrective to remember, "There is always someone on your right."

Since this spectrum has only two endpoints, most positions have potential critics both to their left and to their right. It would not be surprising, for example, for Westminster to be criticized as being "too conservative" (by its more liberal detractors) and "too liberal" (by its more conservative detractors) at the same time. Some might understand Westminster as hopelessly naive, while others would understand it as capitulating to the falsely assumed autonomy of this world.

## Discontinuity in the Spectrum

A major question focuses on a potential gap in the spectrum. As one moves from right to left across the spectrum, is there some point at which one relinquishes any proper understanding of biblical authority? Is there a point, to the left of which the critical elements of the gospel are no longer necessarily derived from the Bible, because its authority has been too weakened and damaged?

If we were reflecting basic Christian faith, we might structure a continuum from belief to unbelief, or to antibelief. On that display it might be quite proper to recognize a chasm between views that reflect basic biblical and Christian understanding and those which do not. While we recognize, for example, that Christians may act and even believe inconsistently with their own most fundamental presuppositions, we do affirm most vigorously that there is an eternity of difference between the Christian, no matter how inconsistent, and the non-Christian. But the question we are now asking is not about a gulf on the spectrum between belief and unbelief. Our subject is not basic Christian faith but is rather biblical authority, which, as we have noted, is not always consistently related to one's actual faith in Christ. Furthermore, as we have been trying to suggest, it is not necessarily the position on the furthest possible right edge of our theoretical spectrum which is most consistent with Christian faith or with what Scripture teaches about itself.

But the question we now ask is also critical. As one moves leftward across the spectrum, does one enter a portion of the spectrum where the nature of the biblical authority that is affirmed is simply too shallow to support gospel foundations? Is there a critical dividing line between adequate and inadequate views?

No doubt there is such a point, since, at the extreme left end, all that is supernatural is removed from the Bible and quite possibly all that is miraculous (e.g., Jesus' birth, atoning death, and resurrection) is reduced to humanistic explanation. Somewhere on the trip to the far left, biblical content has been decimated critically, as biblical authority becomes less demanding. If at the end of the journey we find a view of Biblical authority that is not sufficient to maintain basic gospel truth, then we have crossed that gap in the spectrum and moved into a region populated with views at best dangerously inconsistent, if not clearly hostile toward the gospel and its proclamation.

But where is this critical point? Most people on the conservative portion of the spectrum tend, so we think, to place that critical point just slightly to their left. They tend to see any weakening of their position as fraught with most serious consequences. Is it perhaps true that most conservatives have already made whatever adjustments to the doctrine of inerrancy they feel to be necessary and acceptable? Whatever their specific position on the spectrum, they have moved to the left about as far as they can go. Further movement will put the gospel itself in jeopardy. And movement beyond the gap, and further toward the left extreme, is through a marshland where footing is totally insecure and where the gospel—if it is to be found at all—is without foundation. Ultimately the Bible is seen as "just another book," one which happens to deal with important religious material.

Those on the left, we can add, may also have a "gap theory." As they look to the right, they may feel that those on the other side of the gap have a view of the Bible that distorts the gospel toward sterility and pharisaic impotence. To observe their feelings is not, of course, to admit their validity. But warning about potential danger should always be gratefully received.

## Life on the Spectrum

Most Christians hold views on biblical authority that place them somewhere between the extremes. As their views become known and discussed, they are sometimes denigrated by those to their left and right, the most vehement attacks deriving from those who occupy the most proximate points on the spectrum.

If one is at the left end of the spectrum, how would one like to be regarded by those at the far right? And what impact should such Christian principles as love and concern for truth have on the approach made toward such a person?

First of all, a person on the left would want his or her profession of Christian faith to be accepted by others. Presumably it would focus on Jesus as Savior and Lord and on salvation as God's gift through grace. It would include a clear declaration of God's love made specific in the cross of Jesus. One's profession of faith is not an incidental matter; it is the basis for fellowship with those to one's right, even at the extreme right, on the spectrum. One expects that one's view of biblical authority should not be regarded as prima facie evidence that a profession of Christian faith be ignored or regarded as incredible. One on the left may ask, "Before we discuss the nature of biblical authority, can we first establish our fellowship in Christ? Though you regard my view of Scripture as deficient, and I understand your concern, the Bible itself establishes Christian fellowship on the basis of profession of faith in Jesus. Though one or both of us may be inconsistent Christians, can't we recognize that fellowship, before we discuss biblical authority?"

Such a person should also hope that others to the right will seek to understand his or her presuppositions and the system built upon them. As a person of integrity and as a Christian, one comes to one's view of biblical authority not out of malicious intent but on the basis of influences and information that are felt to be determinative.

One on the left should also expect and indeed welcome challenge and criticism as evidence of Christian concern—all the more so, since others feel that that one is on the wrong side of a gap that separates views of biblical authority that properly undergird the gospel and those that either directly or indirectly, either now or later, undermine the gospel and its cause. One's response to such challenge should be not a fusillade of epithets hurled rightward but rather a willingness always to reexamine one's position to see if indeed the case for it may have been overstated. Perhaps one has made a genuine profession of faith in Christ without developing an adequate view of scriptural authority. Perhaps, in a word, one's view of God's Word is inconsistent in some way. It is possible that one's present understanding of the nature of the Bible is not really sufficient to incite or sustain true Christian faith, either personally or in the next generation of potential believers. One ought not to allow pride in one's perspective to prevent a sensitive hearing of voices from the right.

Suppose, by contrast, a Christian is on the right extreme. Such a one would hope that those to the left would recognize the possibility that he or she has good and sufficient reasons for holding a certain view of the Bible. One would also want them to recognize that one's view of the Bible is closely linked to faith in Jesus; it is in fact likely that the Christian on the right sees them standing or falling together.

From those to the left, a believer on the right end of the spectrum should also expect challenge and criticism. Such a one can expect to be asked, "Have you really looked at the evidence in the Bible itself? What do you mean by authority (inerrancy), in light of the varied nature of the language of poetry and prophecy? How does your view of inerrancy, for example, approach the parallel accounts of Jesus' statements?"

## Proper Response to Challenge

The proper response to such challenges from the left is not to hurl epithets leftward, for their proponents may feel that one's view of Scripture is so naive and so inconsistent with the biblical evidence itself that one's advocacy lacks integrity. Of course, no one must yield to criticism (from left or right), however well intended it may be. But only to the eventual undermining of one's cherished position can one totally ignore the reasoned attacks of others. It is fitting therefore to analyze and to respond to attacks from the left. Such attacks can be welcomed as opportunities to defend the gospel account (see 1 Cor. 16:9).

That task is not easy. It calls for study in philosophy and apologetics, semantics and linguistics, hermeneutics and epistemology. As some to one's right see one communicating with those on the left, they may interpret that activity as actual and harmful movement to the left and may verbalize their concerns.

Most views on biblical authority are somewhere between the extremes. From the majority of fortresses, one can see others to the left and to the right. By interpolating from life at the extreme positions, we can learn something about life at any point in the spectrum.

Wherever one's posture on the spectrum, one can expect those to the right to communicate in terms that question one's fidelity to the gospel or the integrity of one's "compromising spirit." Those to one's left will whisper that one is hopelessly naive and ill informed; if necessary, they will use the term *obscurantist*.

How would one on the left hope to be regarded by those to the right, assuming that the whole spectrum represents people who profess to be Christian? One would want them to accept a profession of faith in Christ first and at face value; one would like conversation to begin at that level. One would further hope that some fair hearing would be available for one's presuppositions and system, not simply accusations of intentional malicious motivation.

At the same time, someone on the left should expect—even welcome—a challenge to his or her posture, especially from those who believe one is to the left of the critical gap. They will point out that such a view of biblical authority is in no way consonant with the gospel of grace and in fact that one's posture with regard to the Bible undermines true Christian ministry. That danger surely exists, and such affirmation should be received and analyzed carefully.

How, then, would one want to be regarded by those on one's left? It would be hoped that they too regarded one in the context of Christian fellowship. One's presuppositions relating to a supernatural gospel and book are important, and one would ask critics to evaluate them with care. Also, challenges should be expected and welcomed, especially those that ask one to give more meticulous attention to the evidence. Although one may not now or later be able to respond adequately to some criticisms, one surely has nothing to fear in looking at evaluations graciously offered.

## Issuing Challenges Properly

Much has been implied in this discussion about "walking in the shoes" of those with whom one disagrees so that one can treat them as one would want to be treated. But there is another aspect of the topic "When Christians Do Not Agree" which, as has been intimated above, must not be ignored. When danger is apparent, warnings must be issued—in love but firmly. An irenic, tender spirit should not—must not—preclude vigorous protestations against that which would compromise the authority of God's Word. When others inconsistently separate incarnate Word from written Word, the voice of protest must be raised.

Specifically, the recognition that different Christians will locate the gap on the spectrum in different places does not mean that where it is located is a matter of indifference. We at Westminster have historically sought to identify the gap as precisely as possible, and that is our continuing effort today. In this context, it is crucial to provide a bit of perspective to the present discussion.

In his various works, Cornelius Van Til commented often and at length about the danger of "passing the gap." For example, in his unpublished classroom syllabus "An Introduction to Systematic Theology," he made these statements:

> If an authoritative interpretation were not given to the redemptive facts, if the interpretation were left to men, it is certain that the redemptive revelation of God would not be able to reach the ends of the earth and maintain itself to the end of time.[5]

> Only the Spirit could give the correct interpretation of the facts of redemption. Now, since authoritative interpretation of thought can come through expression in language only, it follows that this expression itself must be completely accurate. If it were not, there would be no authoritative communication of the thought or meaning of special revelation.[6]

Van Til's point is clear: without an absolutely dependable, inerrant Scripture, we have no sure source of knowledge about the great works of God in our salvation. The Christian simply cannot do without a Bible that can be implicitly and explicitly trusted.

But, of course, Van Til's concern was also directed outward. Not only is an inerrant Scripture necessary for the Christian's own life before God, but it is also necessary for any apologetic contact the Christian may have with non-Christians.

> It follows that on the question of Scripture, as on every other question, the only possible way for the Christian to reason with the non-believer is by way of presupposition. He must say to the unbeliever that unless he will accept the presuppositions and with them the interpretations of Christianity there is no coherence in human experience. That is to say, the argument must be such as to show that unless one accept the Bible for what true Protestantism says it is, the authoritative interpretation of human life and experience as a whole, it will be impossible to find meaning in anything. It is only when this presupposition is constantly kept in mind that a fruitful discussion of problems pertaining to the phenomena of Scripture and what it teaches about God in his relation to man can be discussed.[7]

5. Cornelius Van Til, "An Introduction to Systematic Theology" (unpublished classroom syllabus, Westminster Theological Seminary), p. 134.

6. Ibid., p. 152.

7. Van Til, *Defense of the Faith,* p. 150.

For some of these reasons, Westminster has always been convinced institutionally that there is a chasm, a gap, the far side of which represents critical danger to the gospel of Jesus Christ. Our suggestion that those whom we see on the far side of the gap be treated graciously in no way entails compromise with the position they represent. We warn those in danger as we would want to be warned from our right—graciously, lovingly, out of a genuine desire that they see their error and return to the full blessing of God. A properly issued challenge comes not in the spirit of Jonah, who actually desired destruction for the Ninevites, but in the spirit of Jesus, who actually desires repentance and blessing for sinners.

Can anything more be said about the nature of the gap, as we have called it? Is it possible to specify the kinds of mindsets which lead individuals to adopt positions regarding Scripture which we at Westminster consider positively dangerous? Perhaps a few suggestions, which actually arise out of the statements by Van Til quoted above, will help to identify those positions to which we must issue challenges.

First, it should be recognized that two basic and quite different perspectives seem prominent among those whom we would argue are on the far side of the gap: we might call these perspectives *pietism* and *humanism*. While the first sort of outlook seems much less dangerous than the second, it in fact emanates from the same location—practical abandonment of trust in the authority of the Word of God written.

When well-meaning Christians so exalt their personal relationship with God, their personal fellowship with his Spirit, that they begin to build their doctrines on their experiences, they are, in fact, abandoning the authority of Scripture as Scripture itself defines that authority. We must challenge such pietism; we must remind such Christians, in the words of Jonathan Edwards, that "God has not given us his providence, but his word, to be our governing rule."[8] To build our beliefs on what we have felt or on what we have experienced is to build on the most tenuous of foundations. These sands can shift in a moment's time.

As we challenge such compromises of biblical authority, we must do so not by dismissing as irrelevant the concerns of pietists but by inviting them to embrace even greater concerns. That is, the foundation of biblical authority is the very character of the God whose Word it is. Thus to trust Scripture fully is to focus the attention of our hearts and minds on him rather than on our own experience of him.[9] Such a distinction, which

---

8. Jonathan Edwards, *An Humble Inquiry into the Rules of the Word of God Concerning the Qualifications Requisite to a Complete Standing and Full Communion in the Visible Christian Church*, in *The Works of Jonathan Edwards*, ed. Sereno Dwight and Edward Hickman, 2 vols. (Edinburgh: Banner of Truth Trust, 1974), 1:477.

9. The most thoroughly biblical and the most pastorally astute analysis of such focusing is offered by Jonathan Edwards in *A Treatise Concerning Religious Affects*, in *Works* 1:274–78.

sounds a bit technical, in fact has the most profound consequences in faith and in life. To what source shall we look, as Van Til put it, for knowledge of God and for knowledge of the salvation God has accomplished for his people? The challenge to the pietist is thus a firm one because it involves the fundamentals of the faith. But it is a challenge expressed without the inflammatory language of personal attack. It is a challenge that seeks to build upon the pietist's professed love for God and that invites him or her to an even more consistent expression of that love.

The challenge to the humanist has similar ingredients, even though the humanist is often seen as the antithesis of the pietist. In fact, historically the humanist perspective on biblical authority has remarkable structural similarities to the pietist perspective. If the pietist tends to substitute human experience for biblical authority, the humanist tends to substitute human reason or human welfare for biblical authority.[10]

The humanist tends to argue either that what the Bible says cannot be true because human reason says otherwise[11] or that what the Bible says cannot be true because that would simply be unfair to human beings.[12] In either case, the problem is similar to that of the pietist—God is replaced by humankind as the ultimate authority; in the language of Paul, the Creator is replaced by the creature as the object of worship.

For this reason, the errors of the pietist and the humanist are so deadly, and we must not hesitate to challenge them. They both involve some form of idolatry. And this matter of ultimate authority is one possible guideline for determining when differences of interpretation identify an individual as being across the gap and in the area of rejection of biblical authority. In conversations with others with whom one does not agree, watch for the signs of worship-substitution. Is the person manifestly eager to hear God speaking and to obey what he or she hears? If so, then differences of interpretation of Scripture are on the proper side of the crucial gap. Or is this person reluctant to accept the full authority of God, no matter where that authority may lead, preferring instead to in-

10. For an analysis of the rise of the humanist attitude toward biblical authority, see Henning Graf Reventlow, *The Authority of the Bible and the Rise of the Modern World* (Philadelphia: Fortress, 1985). See also Samuel T. Logan, Jr., "The Origins of Modern Attacks on Biblical Authority," *Westminster Theological Journal* 49, no. 1 (Spring 1987): 119–42.

11. See, for example, Rudolph Bultmann's rejection of biblical miracles in his essay "New Testament and Mythology," in *Kerygma and Myth*, ed. Hans Werner Bartsch (New York: Harper and Row, 1961), pp. 1–44.

12. See the discussion of the reasons why the doctrine of the imputation of Adam's sin came to be rejected in eighteenth-century America in Conrad Wright, *The Beginnings of Unitarianism in America* (Hamden, Conn.: Shoe String, 1976), pp. 59–90. See also C. Samuel Storms, *Tragedy in Eden: Original Sin in the Theology of Jonathan Edwards* (Lanham, Md.: University Press of America, 1985), pp. 31–70.

sist that God conform to human image? If so, the spiritual danger is critical, and discussion must become challenge.

A specific example might help. Few modern questions provoke more vitriolic debate than those focusing on the biblical teaching about the proper role of women in the church. Westminster's faculty and board of trustees believe that Scripture prohibits the ordination of women to the office of elder (ruling or teaching). But we also believe that the Scripture commands the church to make use of the spiritual gifts of women in ministry that does not require ordination.

As we talk with those who believe that women can be ordained, our most important task is to listen, to see whether their position reflects a genuine attempt to hear exactly what Scripture is saying about such difficult topics as headship or whether they are insisting that Scripture conform to what they regard are the "rights" of women. We must be open to the possibility that those who disagree with us have not crossed the crucial gap but simply interpret the biblical data differently. Yet we must also be willing to challenge, tenderly but vigorously, any suggestion that God's Word be judged by human standards.

Likewise, in our response to challenges from those who believe that any form of female ministry, ordained or unordained, is unbiblical, we will seek the same courtesy. We will ask them to see that we genuinely want to hear the voice of God as clearly in Joel 2 and Acts 2 as we do in 1 Timothy 2. And we will listen to them as they challenge us—to be sure that we are not substituting human authority for that of our sovereign Lord. At all costs, we must indeed avoid the kind of worship-substitution which results when the creature or the creature's experience or reason replaces the Creator in our spiritual perspective.

Disagreement about the meaning of a biblical passage is one thing; rejection of divine authority in favor of human authority is quite another. The gap is there, and while in practice it often appears to be just to the theological left of the one speaking, it in fact has objective characteristics. Proper response to challenges as well as the proper issuing of challenges must take that objectivity into account.

## Proper Outlook Toward Others

The last question, and perhaps the most important one, is How should we treat others on the spectrum, those to our left and those to our right? Part of the answer has been suggested above. We should treat those to our left just as we would wish and expect to be treated by those to our right: with recognition of their Christian profession, with some openness toward understanding their presuppositions and thought system, and with a readiness to challenge graciously, but firmly, those views which appear to us to be on the other side of the gap of biblical authority.

Some would say that we should treat those who appear to us to be on the other side of the gap as non-Christians, but we must demur. Because of the fact of inconsistency as outlined above, we can never be sure whether those whom we regard as being on the dangerous side of the gap are non-Christians or inconsistent Christians. And we believe that biblical charity requires us to give them the benefit of the doubt (1 Cor. 13:1–7). This requirement takes on specific weight in light of our conviction that pietists as well as humanists may actually be "beyond the gap."

Those on our right should also be regarded as Christians. Part of our obligation will be to challenge them to look again and more carefully at biblical information so that their formulations will include reflection on the full range of evidence. While the gap will not be in our range of view when we look to the right, full consistent obedience to the intentions of Scripture probably will be. But again our discussions must be conducted in grace, without even a hint of condescension, believing the best about those who join us in professing allegiance to Jesus Christ.

Whether looking to the right or to the left, we must, for Christ's sake, avoid the acrimony and denigration that has often moved along the spectrum. In the light of history, however, we can anticipate hostile and sometimes unreasonable attacks from detractors on both sides. It will always be in order to isolate potentially justified criticisms from irrelevant and unfair chaff in order to deal with issues that matter.

And we must always deal graciously in our hearts and in our responses with those who may unfairly and maliciously attack us. The spirit of the gospel should be manifest, especially in those who claim proper understanding of the source book for that gospel.

# 14

## Evangelicals and the Bible
### *A Bibliographic Postscript*

#### John R. Muether

The chapters in this volume were not written in an intellectual vacuum. The authors have wrestled with issues that have engaged the wider world of evangelical biblical scholarship, and their work must be understood in that larger context. In order to familiarize readers with that context, we conclude with a bibliographic essay. It cannot claim to be even remotely comprehensive. Its more modest goal is to guide readers to the major figures and the significant developments of recent evangelical scholarship.

### Historical Background

It is helpful to place current issues in historical perspective. Several recent works shed important light on twentieth-century evangelical biblical interpretation. Mark Noll's *Between Faith and Criticism* is required reading for anyone who desires to learn this history. Noll reminds us that there are important shared assumptions when evangelicals encounter the Bible: "Whatever else one may say about the Word of God . . . the Word of God always involves the truth-telling Bible" (p. 6). When evangelicals entered the critical environment of the university, a clash of two cultures—the culture of faith and the culture of criticism—ensued.

Noll goes on to analyze five stages of that encounter within the last century. Noll's work is especially helpful in showing how evangelical commitments have shaped evangelical biblical scholarship.

Another book that serves that same purpose is by Kenneth Hagen, Daniel Harrington, Grant Osborne, and Joseph Burgess: *The Bible in the Churches: How Different Christians Interpret the Scriptures*. The hermeneutical approaches of three major traditions (Catholic, evangelical, and Lutheran) are compared. Grant Osborne's analysis of evangelical hermeneutics notes the development in this century from an emphasis on private interpretation that rejected critical methods to a dialogue within a broader community of scholarship (and with it, greater comfort with critical methods). Daniel Harrington concludes the symposium with an analysis of points of agreement and disagreement between the traditions.

Current evangelical discussions on the Bible should also be understood in relation to broader themes of American culture. The essays in *The Bible in America* (ed. Nathan O. Hatch and Mark A. Noll) serve that end admirably. The writers demonstrate how biblical authority has been defined and shaped in part by forces and events in American history. Richard Mouw's "The Bible in Twentieth-Century Protestantism: A Preliminary Taxonomy" isolates four mindsets among contemporary Protestantism: doctrinalist, pietist, moralist, and culturalist. Mouw shows how each mindset brings different presuppositions to the Bible, and he suggests how these differences can explain some of the current conflicts and tensions within evangelical biblical scholarship.

The complex ways in which the Bible has influenced American culture was the subject of a six-volume series, "The Bible and American Culture," produced by the Society of Biblical Literature. Titles in the series have explored themes such as popular culture, literature, law, education, and social reform.[1]

George Marsden's *Reforming Fundamentalism* is ostensibly a history of Fuller Theological Seminary. But this institutional history is also a window on a larger history, that of the evangelical movement, and therefore, a perspective on recent debates on biblical interpretation. The struggles that Fuller encountered in defining biblical inspiration in a critical environment reflect the broader evangelical struggles. In some ways Marsden's book is a sequel to his earlier history on fundamentalism. That work, *Fundamentalism and American Culture*, is widely ac-

---

1. *The Bible and Bibles in America* (ed. Ernest S. Frerichs), *The Bible and Popular Culture in America* (ed. Allene S. Phy), *The Bible and American Arts and Letters* (ed. Giles Gunn), *The Bible in American Law, Politics, and Political Rhetoric* (ed. James T. Johnson), *The Bible in American Education* (ed. David Barr and Nicholas Piediscalzi), and *The Bible and Social Reform* (ed. Ernest R. Sandeen).

claimed as the best resource on the debate on the Bible of the turn of the century, out of which evangelicalism arose.

## The Seventies: Focus on Inerrancy

In the 1970s, evangelical debates about the Bible focused on inerrancy. Two books, by their provocative and controversial nature, did more than anything else to shape the discussion: Harold Lindsell's *Battle for the Bible* and Jack Rogers and Donald K. McKim's *The Authority and Interpretation of the Bible*. Lindsell's book defined inerrancy as "the most important theological topic of this age." But critics (even those partial to inerrancy) noted that the book contained little exegetical defense of the doctrine and that it concentrated on overstatements against the doctrine's critics. For example, Lindsell withheld the term *evangelical* from all who did not affirm inerrancy.[2]

A symposium by the faculty at Gordon-Conwell Theological Seminary was one of the responses to Lindsell's book. *Inerrancy and Common Sense* (ed. Roger Nicole and J. Ramsey Michaels) affirmed inerrancy but denied that it violated the canons of common sense. So, for example, John Jefferson Davis argued in his essay that inerrancy did not directly impact issues such as the age of human beings and the earth; J. Ramsey Michaels suggested that *inerrancy* as a term may not deal with the phenomena of Scripture as well as *verbal inspiration;* and Richard F. Lovelace contended that history does not support Lindsell's slippery-slope argument about noninerrantist institutions.

Other responses to Lindsell sought the hermeneutical high ground in going above and beyond the battle. In *Beyond the Battle for the Bible,* J. I. Packer reminded us that inerrancy is not the only battle: "It is not enough to fight and win the battle for biblical inerrancy if we are then going to lose the battle for understanding the Bible and so for living under its authority" (p. 36).

Less convincing was Harry R. Boer's *Above the Battle? The Bible and Its Critics,* which claimed that the reliability of the Bible did not require inerrancy. Boer cited alleged disparities in the Gospels that discredited inerrancy, and he distinguished infallibility and inerrancy in an argument similar to that of Stephen T. Davis in his *Debate About the Bible.* Both Boer and Davis confused "error" and "imprecision," in insisting that inerrancy required scientific precision, an idea supported by few inerrantists.

Historical support for the distinction between infallibility and iner-

---

2. Lindsell's thesis was supplemented and updated in the sequel he published three years later, *The Bible in the Balance.*

rancy was offered in the other major work of the 1970s, *The Authority and Interpretation of the Bible*, by Rogers and McKim. The thesis of this massive study was that biblical inerrancy was not the position of historical Protestantism. The church, it argued, has in the past confessed to the complete reliability of the Bible for faith and conduct while allowing for errors on matters of scientific and historical detail. A key to the Rogers and McKim proposal was its reliance on the historiography of Ernest Sandeen *(Origins of Fundamentalism)*, who stressed that Warfield and Hodge of Old Princeton had developed a unique definition of inerrancy. The debate that Rogers and McKim prompted seemed to focus as much on the interpretation of Warfield as on the interpretation of Scripture.

Two books by William J. Abraham, *The Divine Inspiration of Scripture* and *Divine Revelation and the Limits of Historical Criticism*, attacked the traditional view of inerrancy in arguments similar to those presented by Rogers and McKim. The Warfield approach was said to be overly deductive, emphasizing the divine role in inspiration at the expense of the Bible's truly human quality. Instead Abraham argued for a view of biblical inspiration that maintained confidence in it as God's Word while recognizing the imperfections of its human authorship.

Rogers and McKim were not without their critics. Most prominent was John D. Woodbridge of Trinity Evangelical Divinity School. What began as a book review eventually became a book-length response, *Biblical Authority: A Critique of the Rogers/McKim Proposal*. In the doctrine of Scripture of Augustine, Luther, Calvin, and others, Woodbridge found no evidence for a dichotomy between matters of faith and scientific detail. In blaming Warfield for the current evangelical mindset, Woodbridge concluded, Rogers and McKim actually reveal how captive they themselves are to higher-critical commitments.

As this debate developed, both sides further staked out their views in symposiums. In *The Authoritative Word* (ed. Donald McKim), advocates of limited inerrancy addressed, in tones sometimes hostile to conservative views, issues of biblical authority under three main headings: sources and canon, doctrine and its development, and current views. Among the twelve essays in *Scripture and Truth* (ed. D. A. Carson and John D. Woodbridge) were several historical studies, exploring the doctrine of Scripture of the church fathers (G. Bromiley), the Reformers (W. R. Godfrey), and Old Princeton (Woodbridge and R. H. Balmer).[3] The cause of inerrancy was also advanced by several works sponsored by the International Council on Biblical Inerrancy.[4]

---

3. Many of the contributors also participated in a companion volume, *Hermeneutics, Authority, and Canon* (ed. D. A. Carson and John D. Woodbridge).

4. Among them: *The Foundation of Biblical Authority* (ed. James M. Boice), *Inerrancy* (ed. Norman Geisler), *Biblical Errancy* (ed. Norman Geisler), *Challenges to Inerrancy* (ed.

While the inerrancy debate dominated discussions during this decade, it did not exhaust the interests of evangelical scholarship. At least two other studies were of such significance that they warrant mention here. Meredith G. Kline's *Structure of Biblical Authority* (1972) explored the relationship between covenant and canon. The Bible's covenantal structure, Kline argued, was the key to its canonical status. The conclusions of this seminal work gave new support to conservative views on the dating and authorship of the biblical books.

No less important was Carl. F. H. Henry's massive, six-volume *God, Revelation, and Authority*. Interacting fluently with a great variety of theological and philosophical viewpoints, Henry used revelation as a starting point to explore other loci of systematic theology.

## The Eighties: Focus on Hermeneutics

While Lindsell and Rogers/McKim principally dealt with biblical inerrancy, both books, and the reaction they generated, caused evangelicals to consider the relation between biblical inerrancy and biblical hermeneutics. Walter Kaiser summarized this connection in 1979: "Much of the current debate over the Scriptures among believing Christians is, at its core, a result of the failure on the part of evangelicals to come to terms with the issue of hermeneutics."[5] In the same year J. Julius Scott, Jr., noted how new this field was to evangelicals: "For many evangelical Christians, hermeneutics is an area whose importance is granted but whose nature and content is little understood."[6]

As attention turned to hermeneutics, two biblical scholars tested the boundaries of evangelical hermeneutical understanding. In his controversial 1982 commentary on Matthew, Robert Gundry employed the tools of redaction criticism to assert that Matthew embellished historical events to achieve his theological purposes. Evangelical response to Gundry's work varied from those who insisted that redaction criticism, in principle, was incompatible with biblical inerrancy to others who saw Gundry's particular application to be excessive. The result was

---

Gordon Lewis and Bruce Demarest), *Inerrancy and the Church* (ed. John D. Hannah), and *Hermeneutics, Inerrancy, and the Bible* (ed. Earl D. Radmacher and Robert D. Preus).

5. Walter Kaiser, "Legitimate Hermeneutics," in *Inerrancy* (ed. Norman Geisler), p. 117.

6. "Some Problems in Hermeneutics for Contemporary Evangelicals," p. 67. Scott's article itself was evidence of this new evangelical engagement; less than twenty years earlier, J. Barton Payne, a predecessor of Scott at Wheaton Graduate School, expressed a different attitude toward hermeneutics in an article with the provocative title "Hermeneutics as a Cloak for the Denial of Scripture."

Gundry's forced resignation from the Evangelical Theological Society.[7] About the same time, J. Ramsey Michaels published his redaction study of the Gospels, *Servant and Son: Jesus in Parable and Gospel.* Michaels's exegetical conclusions about the messianic self-consciousness of Jesus raised questions both about the inerrancy of Scripture and the sinlessness of Jesus; these questions were serious enough to force his resignation from his teaching post at Gordon-Conwell Theological Seminary.

The evangelical reaction to Gundry and Michaels demonstrated great uncertainty about the compatibility of a high view of Scripture and the application of critical methods. Yet at the very least, these episodes may have served as reminders about the importance of literary form in biblical interpretation. Evangelical scholarship of late seems to have reawakened to the pursuit of literary and genre criticism. New popular works have introduced the art of interpreting literary genres. Gordon Fee and Douglas Stuart's *How to Read the Bible for All Its Worth* was a useful introduction to the different types of literature that make up the Bible. Recently Inter-Varsity Press has introduced a new "How to Read" series, designed to facilitate understanding of the unique features of the different types of biblical literature. When completed, the series will include works on interpreting prophecy, Gospels and Acts, the Epistles, the Pentateuch, Old Testament history, and the psalms.[8]

The current scene in hermeneutics presents several other new approaches. A fine summary of the current state is found in *A Guide to Contemporary Hermeneutics: Major Trends in Biblical Interpretation,* (ed. Donald K. McKim). McKim collected a diverse group of twenty essays to explore recent developments such as literary approaches, structuralism, contextualization, and liberation and feminist theologies.

Among the current issues is the question of where meaning lies in interpretation. Carl Henry and Walter Kaiser are among the many evangelicals who have adopted the distinction that E. D. Hirsch, Jr., makes in *Validity in Interpretation* between meaning and significance.[9] Hirsch argues that meaning lies in the text but that significance describes the relationship between meaning and reader. While his field is the broad realm of literary criticism, Hirsch's championing the cause of authorial intent has implications for biblical hermeneutics: "If the meaning of a text is not to be the author's, then no interpretation can possibly correspond to the meaning of the text" (p. 5).

7. For a discussion of the Gundry case and the evangelical reaction, see two articles by David A. Turner: "Evangelicals, Redaction Criticism, and the Current Inerrancy Crisis" and "Evangelicals, Redaction Criticism, and Inerrancy: The Debate Continues."
8. Published thus far: *How to Read the Bible* (A. J. Conyers), *How to Read Prophecy* (Joel B. Green), and *How to Read the Psalms* (Tremper Longman III).
9. Carl Henry, "The Interpretation of Scriptures: Are We Doomed to Hermeneutical Nihilism?"; Kaiser, "Legitimate Hermeneutics."

While evangelical scholarship carefully guards authorial intent, there is of late increasing appreciation for the role of the interpreter in biblical interpretation. Anthony C. Thiselton's *Two Horizons* asserts that there are two cultural and historical horizons to consider: those of the author and the reader. The reader cannot ignore his or her own historical context in the interests of objectivism. Thiselton borrows from Hans-Georg Gadamer *(Truth and Method)* the denial of the possibility of pure objectivism in interpretation, tracing the idea to the Enlightenment "prejudice against prejudice."[10] According to Thiselton, when we come to the text acknowledging our prejudices, preunderstandings, and presuppositions, and when we "fuse the two horizons," we will arrive at a fresher and deeper understanding of the Bible.

## New Challenges: The Hermeneutics of Liberation

A significant feature of contemporary evangelical scholarship is its greater willingness to listen to other voices. Vatican II has unleashed a great renewal in Catholic biblical criticism. Raymond E. Brown's *Critical Meaning of the Bible* exemplifies this new trend. Appropriating modern critical methods, Brown contends, is critical for moving the church toward reform and establishing ecumenical relationships between churches. Evangelicals are also hearing the calls for hermeneutics of liberation from three different sources: feminism, black theology, and liberation theology.

A considerable diversity of viewpoints is found in contemporary feminist hermeneutics.[11] The concerns of feminist theologians are summarized well by Elisabeth Schüssler Fiorenza in *Bread, Not Stone: The Challenge of Feminist Biblical Interpretation*. Fiorenza describes the feminist approach as the "hermeneutics of suspicion," approaching the Bible dialectically as a patriarchal document and yet a source of a liberating vision. This dialectic renders the Bible not a timeless archetype but an open-ended paradigm for emancipation. Her litmus test for adapting the words of men as the Word of God are whether or not the text seeks to end domination and exploitation. An anthology edited by Letty Russell, *Feminist Interpretation of the Bible,* is another valuable introduction to feminist concerns. Twelve essays address feminist hermeneu-

10. A helpful summary of Gadamer's influence on contemporary biblical hermeneutics is found in Robert Grant and David Tracy, *A Short History of the Interpretation of the Bible.*

11. "'Feminist theology' is not a single systematic device. . . . Feminist thought exhibits the same variety as other forms of theological thought," according to Donald K. McKim in his 1983 article "Hearkening to the Voices: What Women Theologians Are Saying." McKim makes a distinction between "reformists" and "revolutionists" in feminist theology.

tical issues under three sections: "Feminist Critical Consciousness," "Feminists at Work," and "Feminist Critical Principles."

By far the most prominent representative of black theology is James Cone. In his provocative writings Cone has located the meaning of the gospel in liberation from various forms of oppression, especially focusing on the American black experience in a racist white culture. *Black Theology and Black Power* is an attempt to relate theology to the radical Black Power movement of the late 1960s. A more systematic development of his oppressor/oppressed metaphor is offered in *A Black Theology of Liberation*. In one of his most recent works, *For My People*, Cone reflects on the development of black theology, reevaluates his own early work, and interacts more with liberation and feminist theology.

Standing in tension with Cone's single-minded stress on liberation is J. Deotis Roberts's *Liberation and Reconciliation: A Black Theology*. As the title suggests, Roberts argues that black theology must also be a theology of reconciliation: "Black theology must speak of liberation. . . . But at the same time, it must speak of reconciliation that brings black men together and of reconciliation that brings black and white men together" (p. 152). Unless one speaks of reconciliation, black theology reduces to "the religion of Black power."

Liberation theology provides another hermeneutic of liberation. Robert McAfee Brown summarizes some of these hermeneutical concerns in *Unexpected News: Reading the Bible with Third World Eyes*. Brown laments that the "unexpected good news" of the Bible has been missed by affluent Christians who read the Bible from privilege and comfort. A third-world hermeneutic reveals a Bible concerned with the poor and the victims of oppression.

One of the most profound articulations of the hermeneutics of liberation theology is *Liberation of Theology*, by Juan Luis Segundo. Segundo sets forth a hermeneutical circle for freeing one from established, deductive, academic-style methodologies. The circle raises questions about the preconditions to commitment and leads to radical reinterpretations of the biblical message. One essential precommitment for Segundo is a political commitment to revolution: there is "no such thing as Christian theology or a Christian interpretation of the gospel message in the absence of a prior political commitment" (p. 94).

## Evangelicals, the Bible, and the Future

What can this recent history tell us about the future? Can evangelicals continue to survive in both the world of faith and the world of criticism? Sociologist James Davison Hunter does not think so. In his *Evangelicalism, the Coming Generation*, he finds evangelicalism succumbing to the pressures of modernity in ways that threaten its identity.

One way is in its use of the Bible: "The coming generation [of evangelicals] . . . is less demanding in its expectations of the Bible" (p. 30), and current debates reveal a "theological tradition in disarray" (p. 32). So significant is the changing character of evangelical orthodoxy that Hunter finds "reasonable grounds for pessimism" (p. 203), regarding the future of American evangelicalism.

Hunter's pessimism is matched by the optimism of another observer. In his article "The Rise of Evangelical Hermeneutical Pluralism," Douglas Jacobsen welcomes a perceived shift from hermeneutical monism to hermeneutical pluralism: "The crucial hermeneutical question that separates evangelical monists and pluralists is this: Does the Bible have one and only one meaning that resides in the text, or is it possible for the Bible to be interpreted validly and responsibly in different ways by different people? In simple terms, monists opt for the former of these alternatives; pluralists for the latter" (p. 326). Jacobsen does not hide where his sympathies lie: whereas monism is culturally arrogant and inevitably idolatrous, pluralism is humbling and responsible.

In another essay, Jacobsen traces the development of what he calls responsible hermeneutics. In "From Truth to Authority to Responsibility," he finds twentieth-century evangelical hermeneutics shifting from the rubric of truth (the fundamentalist era, 1915–1945) to authority (classic evangelicalism, 1945–1975) to responsibility (postclassic evangelicalism, 1975–    ). Jacobsen's framework is open to question, but particularly helpful is his analysis of the relationship of hermeneutical thinking to the decline of evangelical cultural hegemony.

Another call to responsible hermeneutics is made by Roger Lundin, Anthony C. Thiselton, and Clarence Walhout in their collaborative effort *The Responsibility of Hermeneutics*. The authors challenge us to see the connection between ethics and interpretation: "Hermeneutics is not simply a cognitive process whereby we determine the 'correct meaning' of a passage or text. . . . [Q]uestions of ethics and responsible interpretation are as germane to hermeneutics as questions of validity and correctness" (p. x).

Whether one agrees with Hunter's pessimistic assessment or Jacobsen's optimistic assessment of contemporary developments, this much is certain: the discussions will continue. For evangelical scholars do not explore these matters in spite of their commitment to inerrancy; rather, their high view of Scripture constrains them to pursue the difficult questions. The issues may change and the focus may shift, but the fundamental challenge remains the same: "If evangelical Bible scholars are to flourish, they must be wise as serpents with respect to the world of thought, as innocent as doves with respect to the gospel."[12]

12. Noll, *Between Faith and Criticism*, p. 197.

# Sources Cited

Abraham, William J. *The Divine Inspiration of Holy Scripture*. New York: Oxford University Press, 1981.

————. *Divine Revelation and the Limits of Historical Criticism*. New York: Oxford University Press, 1982.

Barr, David, and Piediscalzi, Nicholas, eds. *The Bible in American Education: From Sourcebook to Textbook*. The Bible in American Culture, vol. 5. Philadelphia: Fortress, 1982.

Boer, Harry R. *Above the Battle? The Bible and Its Critics*. Grand Rapids: Eerdmans, 1977.

Boice, James M., ed. *The Foundation of Biblical Authority*. Grand Rapids: Zondervan, 1978.

Brown, Raymond E. *The Critical Meaning of the Bible*. New York: Paulist, 1981.

Brown, Robert McAfee. *Unexpected News: Reading the Bible with Third World Eyes*. Philadelphia: Westminster, 1984.

Carson, D. A., and Woodbridge, John D., eds. *Hermeneutics, Authority, and Canon*. Grand Rapids: Zondervan, 1986.

————, eds. *Scripture, and Truth*. Grand Rapids: Zondervan, 1983.

Cone, James H. *Black Theology and Black Power*. New York: Seabury, 1969.

————. *A Black Theology of Liberation*. Philadelphia: Lippencott, 1970.

————. *For My People: Black Theology and the Black Church*. Maryknoll, N.Y.: Orbis, 1984.

Conyers, A. J. *How to Read the Bible*. Downers Grove, Ill.: InterVarsity, 1986.

Davis, Stephen T. *The Debate About the Bible: Inerrancy Versus Infallibility*. Philadelphia: Westminster, 1977.

Fee, Gordon D., and Stuart, Douglas. *How to Read the Bible for All Its Worth: A Guide to Understanding the Bible*. Grand Rapids: Zondervan, 1982.

Fiorenza, Elizabeth Schüssler. *Bread, Not Stone: The Challenge of Feminist Biblical Interpretation*. Boston: Beacon, 1984.

Frerichs, Ernest S., ed. *The Bible and Bibles in America*. The Bible in American Culture, vol. 1. Atlanta: Scholars, 1988.

Gadamer, Hans-Georg. *Truth and Method*. Translated by Garrett Barden and John Cumming. New York: Seabury, 1975.

Geisler, Norman, ed. *Biblical Errancy: An Analysis of Its Philosophical Roots*. Grand Rapids: Zondervan, 1981.

————, ed. *Inerrancy*. Grand Rapids: Zondervan, 1980.

Grant, Robert, and Tracy, David. *A Short History of the Interpretation of the Bible*. 2d ed., rev. and enl. Philadelphia: Fortress, 1984.

Green, Joel B. *How to Read Prophecy*. Downers Grove, Ill.: InterVarsity, 1984.

Gundry, Robert H. *Matthew: A Commentary on His Literary and Theological Art*. Grand Rapids: Eerdmans, 1982.

Gunn, Giles, ed. *The Bible and American Arts and Letters.* The Bible in American Culture, vol. 3. Philadelphia: Fortress, 1983.

Hagen, Kenneth; Harrington, Daniel; Osborne, Grant; and Burgess, Joseph. *The Bible in the Churches: How Different Christians Interpret the Scriptures.* New York: Paulist, 1985.

Hannah, John D., ed., *Inerrancy and the Church.* Chicago: Moody, 1984.

Hatch, Nathan O., and Noll, Mark A., eds. *The Bible in America: Essays in Cultural History.* New York: Oxford University Press, 1982.

Henry, Carl. F. H. *God, Revelation, and Authority.* 6 vols. Waco, Tex.: Word, 1976–83.

———. "The Interpretation of the Scriptures: Are We Doomed to Hermeneutical Nihilism?" *Review and Expositor* 71 (1974): 197–215.

Hirsch, E. D., Jr. *Validity in Interpretation.* New Haven: Yale University Press, 1967.

Hunter, James Davison. *Evangelicalism, the Coming Generation.* Chicago: University of Chicago Press, 1987.

Jacobsen, Douglas. "From Truth to Authority to Responsibility: The Shifting Focus of Evangelical Hermeneutics, 1915–1986." *TSF Bulletin* 10, no. 4 (March–April 1987): 8–15; no. 5 (May–June 1987): 10–14.

———. "The Rise of Evangelical Hermeneutical Pluralism." *Christian Scholar's Review* 16 (1987): 325–35.

Johnson, James Turner, ed. *The Bible in American Law, Politics, and Political Rhetoric.* The Bible in American Culture, vol. 4. Philadelphia: Fortress, 1984.

Kline, Meredith G. *The Structure of Biblical Authority.* Grand Rapids: Eerdmans, 1972.

Lewis, Gordon, and Demarest, Bruce, eds. *Challenges to Inerrancy: A Theological Response.* Chicago: Moody, 1984.

Lindsell, Harold, *The Battle for the Bible.* Grand Rapids: Zondervan, 1976.

———. *The Bible in the Balance.* Grand Rapids: Zondervan, 1979.

Longman, Tremper, III. *How to Read the Psalms.* Downers Grove, Ill.: Inter-Varsity, 1988.

Lundin, Roger; Thiselton, Anthony C.; and Walhout, Clarence. *The Responsibility of Hermeneutics.* Grand Rapids: Eerdmans, 1985.

McKim, Donald K., ed. *The Authoritative Word: Essays on the Nature of Scripture.* Grand Rapids: Eerdmans, 1983.

———, ed. *A Guide to Contemporary Hermeneutics: Major Trends in Biblical Interpretation.* Grand Rapids: Eerdmans, 1986.

———. "Hearkening to the Voices: What Women Theologians Are Saying." *Reformed Journal* 35, no. 1 (January 1985): 7–10.

Marsden, George M. *Fundamentalism and American Culture: The Shaping of Twentieth Century Evangelicalism, 1870–1925.* New York: Oxford University Press, 1980.

————. *Reforming Fundamentalism: Fuller Seminary and the New Evangelical-ism.* Grand Rapids: Eerdmans, 1987.

Michaels, J. Ramsey. *Servant and Son: Jesus in Parable and Gospel.* Atlanta: John Knox, 1981.

Nicole, Roger R., and Michaels, J. Ramsey, eds. *Inerrancy and Common Sense.* Grand Rapids: Baker, 1980.

Noll, Mark A. *Between Faith and Criticism: Evangelicals, Scholarship, and the Bible in America.* San Francisco: Harper and Row, 1986.

Packer, J. I. *Beyond the Battle for the Bible.* Westchester, Ill.: Cornerstone, 1980.

Payne, J. Barton. "Hermeneutics as a Cloak for the Denial of Scripture." *Bulletin of the Evangelical Theological Society* 3 (1960): 93–100.

Phy, Allene Stuart, ed. *The Bible and Popular Culture in America.* The Bible in American Culture, vol. 2. Philadelphia: Fortress, 1985.

Radmacher, Earl D., and Preus, Robert D., eds. *Hermeneutics, Inerrancy, and the Bible.* Grand Rapids: Zondervan, 1984.

Roberts, J. Deotis. *Liberation and Reconciliation: A Black Theology.* Philadelphia: Westminster, 1971.

Rogers, Jack B., and McKim, Donald K. *The Authority and Interpretation of the Bible: An Historical Approach.* San Francisco: Harper and Row, 1979.

Russell, Letty M., ed. *Feminist Interpretation of the Bible.* Philadelphia: Westminster, 1985.

Sandeen, Ernest R., ed. *The Bible and Social Reform.* The Bible in American Culture, vol. 6. Philadelphia: Fortress, 1982.

————. *The Origins of Fundamentalism: Toward a Historical Interpretation.* Philadelphia: Fortress, 1968.

Scott, J. Julius, Jr. "Some Problems in Hermeneutics for Contemporary Evangelicals." *Journal of the Evangelical Theological Society* 22 (1979): 67–77.

Segundo, Juan Luis. *Liberation of Theology.* Translated by John Drury. Maryknoll, N.Y.: Orbis, 1976.

Thiselton, Anthony C. *The Two Horizons: New Testament Hermeneutics and Philosophical Description, with Special Reference to Heidegger, Bultmann, Gadamer, and Wittgenstein.* Grand Rapids: Eerdmans, 1980.

Turner, David L. "Evangelicals, Redaction Criticism, and Inerrancy: The Debate Continues." *Grace Theological Journal* 5 (1984): 37–45.

————. "Evangelicals, Redaction Criticism, and the Current Inerrancy Crisis." *Grace Theological Journal* 4 (1983): 263–88.

Woodbridge, John D. *Biblical Authority: A Critique of the Rogers/McKim Proposal.* Grand Rapids: Zondervan, 1982.

# Index of Scripture

# Index of Persons

Abraham, William J., 256
Abrams, Meyer H., 138n, 146n
Albright, William F., 119, 127, 128n
Alexander the Great, 121
Alexander, J. A., 40, 92n
Allis, Oswald T., 81, 90n, 117, 137, 156
Allrik, H. L., 159n
Alster, Bendt, 125
Alt, Albrecht, 134
Alter, Robert, 120, 135, 139n, 140n, 145, 148
Ambrose, 126
Anderson, A. A., 92n, 93n
Archer, Gleason L., Jr., 134–35, 152n
Aristotle, 225n, 228
Ashley, Clinton M., 197n
Asimov, Isaac, 138
Athanasius, 168
Augustine, 126, 256

Balmer, Randall H., 73n, 256
Baltzer, Klaus, 125
Barr, James, 48–49, 64, 103
Barr, David, 254n
Barth, Karl, 16, 17, 18, 19, 21, 170, 187, 188
Bartsch, Hans Werner, 249n
Bateson, Mary C., 133
Battles, Ford Lewis, 197n
Bavinck, Herman, 19, 41
Beegle, Dewey, 62

Begg, C. T., 160n
Berlin, Adele, 120, 143n, 144n
Birkeland, Harris, 118
Blomberg, C., 152n
Bock, Darrell, 81–82
Boer, Harry R., 255
Boice, James M., 256n
Boyd, Jesse, III, 158n
Briggs, Charles A., 69, 92n
Briggs, Emilie G., 92n
Bromiley, G. W., 51n, 173n, 256
Brown, Raymond E., 97n, 259
Brown, Robert McAfee, 260
Bruce, F. F., 112
Brunner, Emil, 19
Bultmann, Rudolf, 17, 62, 69, 114–15, 187, 190, 223, 249n
Burgess, Joseph, 254
Burkard, Gunter, 127
Bush, Frederic W., 134

Cadbury, H. J., 203
Calvin, John, 35, 47–48, 58, 60n, 61, 73–74, 181, 197n, 256
Carson, D. A., 19n, 21n, 22n, 33n, 34n, 152n, 187n, 191, 256
Cave, C. H., 219n
Cave, F. H., 219n
Celsus, 104n
Childs, Brevard, 119
Clement, 177

# Index of Subjects

274